FACULTY REQUEST

PHILOSOPHICAL MYTHS OF THE FALL

—————————— • ꟼMꟼ • ——————————

PRINCETON MONOGRAPHS

IN PHILOSOPHY

Harry Frankfurt, Editor

————————— • ¶MP • —————————

The Princeton Monographs in Philosophy series
offers short historical and systematic studies
on a wide variety of philosophical topics

Justice Is Conflict by STUART HAMPSHIRE

Liberty Worth the Name by GIDEON YAFFE

Self-Deception Unmasked by ALFRED R. MELE

Public Goods, Private Goods by RAYMOND GEUSS

Welfare and Rational Care by STEPHEN DARWALL

A Defense of Hume on Miracles by ROBERT J. FOGELIN

Kierkegaard's Concept of Despair by MICHAEL THEUNISSEN

Physicalism, or Something Near Enough by JAEWONG KIM

Philosophical Myths of the Fall by STEPHEN MULHALL

PHILOSOPHICAL
MYTHS
OF THE FALL

Stephen Mulhall

PRINCETON UNIVERSITY PRESS

PRINCETON AND OXFORD

LIBRARY OF CONGRESS CATALOGING-IN-PUBLICATION DATA
Mulhall, Stephen, 1962–
Philosophical myths of the fall / Stephen Mulhall.
p.   cm.   — (Princeton monographs in philosophy)
Includes bibliographical references and index.
ISBN 0-691-12220-2 (alk. paper)
1. Fall of man. 2. Philosophical anthropology.
3. Nietzsche, Friedrich Wilhelm, 1844–1900—Contributions in
philosophical anthropology. 4. Wittgenstein, Ludwig, 1889–1951—
Contributions in philosophy and anthropology. 5. Heidegger, Martin,
1889–1976—Contributions in philosophical anthropology.
I. Title. II. Series.

BD450.M774 2005
128′.092′2—dc22   2004054931

British Library Cataloging-in-Publication Data is available

This book has been composed in Janson Text and Centaur display

Printed on acid-free paper. ∞

pup.princeton.edu

Printed in the United States of America

1   3   5   7   9   10   8   6   4   2

Contents

Acknowledgments
vii

Introduction
1

CHAPTER 1
The Madman and the Masters: Nietzsche
16

CHAPTER 2
The Dying Man and the Dazed Animal: Heidegger
46

CHAPTER 3
The Child and the Scapegoat: Wittgenstein
85

Conclusion
118

Index
125

Acknowledgments

I would like to thank Paul Cortois, and the other members of the Institute of Philosophy and the Faculty of Theology at the Catholic University of Leuven, who kindly invited me to give a series of lectures there, as part of a larger project on religion in which they are collaborating with the Religious Studies department at Antwerp University, and thereby encouraged me to try out early versions of each of these chapters before an exceptionally knowledgeable and accommodating audience. I would particularly like to thank Martin Stone, who not only made my week in Leuven outside the lecture hall a matter of real social and intellectual pleasure, but also acted as respondent to one of my lectures; and thanks are also due to William Desmond and Rudi Visker, my other respondents, with whom I also managed to combine stimulating conversation with good Belgian beer. Thanks, as always, go to Alison, Eleanor, and Matthew, for allowing me to spend the time needed to transform the text of my Leuven lectures into this book, and for distracting me from that text whenever I emerged from my study.

A version of chapter 1 appeared in *Tijdschrift voor Filosofie 66/1* (March 2004). Portions of chapters 2 and 3 traverse ground that I crossed earlier in parts of my *Inheritance and Originality* (Oxford University Press: Oxford, 2001), as well as in *Heidegger*

and Being and Time (Routledge: London, 1996); but juxtapos-
ing my interpretations of Heidegger and Wittgenstein with a
reading of Nietzsche for the first time allowed me to see ways
of modifying, refining, and going on from all three thinkers in
ways that I could not otherwise have managed.

PHILOSOPHICAL MYTHS OF THE FALL

Introduction

Now the serpent was more subtil than any beast of the field which the Lord God had made. And he said unto the woman, Yea, hath God said, Ye shall not eat of every tree of the garden?

And the woman said unto the serpent, We may eat of the fruit of the trees of the garden: but of the fruit of the tree which is in the midst of the garden, God hath said, Ye shall not eat of it, neither shall ye touch it, lest ye die.

And the serpent said unto the woman, Ye shall not surely die: For God doth know that in the day ye eat thereof, then your eyes shall be opened and ye shall be as gods, knowing good and evil.

And when the woman saw that the tree was good for food, and that it was pleasant to the eyes, and a tree to be desired to make one wise, she took of the fruit thereof, and did eat, and gave also unto her husband with her; and he did eat.

And the eyes of them both were opened, and they knew that they were naked; and they sewed fig-leaves together and made themselves aprons.

And they heard the voice of the Lord God walking in the garden in the cool of the day; and Adam and his wife hid themselves from the presence of the Lord God amongst the trees of the garden. And the Lord God called unto Adam and said unto him, Where art thou?

And he said, I heard thy voice in the garden, and I was afraid, because I was naked; and I hid myself.

And he said, Who told thee that thou wast naked? Hast thou eaten of the tree, whereof I commanded thee that thou shouldst not eat?

And the man said, the woman whom thou gavest to be with me, she gave me of the tree, and I did eat. And the Lord God said unto the woman, What is this that thou hast done? And the woman said, The serpent beguiled me, and I did eat.

And the Lord God said unto the serpent, Because thou hast done this, thou art cursed above all cattle, and above every beast of the field; upon thy belly shalt thou go, and dust thou shalt eat all the days of thy life; and I will put enmity between thee and the woman, and between thy seed and her seed; it shall bruise thy head, and thou shalt bruise his heel.

Unto the woman he said, I will greatly multiply thy sorrow and thy conception; in sorrow thou shalt bring forth children; and thy desire shall be to thy husband, and he shall rule over thee.

And unto Adam he said, Because thou has hearkened unto the voice of thy wife, and hast eaten of the tree, of which I commanded thee, saying, Thou shalt not eat of it: cursed is the ground for thy sake; in sorrow shalt thou eat of it all the days of thy life; thorns also and thistles shall it bring forth to thee; and thou shalt eat the herb of the field; in the sweat of thy face thou shalt eat bread, till thou return unto the ground; for out of it wast thou taken: for dust thou art and unto dust shalt thou return.

And Adam called his wife's name Eve; because she was the mother of all living.

Unto Adam also and to his wife did the Lord God
make coats of skin, and clothed them. And the Lord
God said, Behold, the man is become as one of us, to
know good and evil; and now, lest he put forth his hand,
and take also of the tree of life, and eat, and live for
ever: therefore the Lord God sent him forth from the
garden of Eden, to till the ground from whence he was
taken. So he drove out the man; and he placed at the
east of the garden of Eden cherubim, and a flaming
sword which turned every way, to keep the way of the
tree of life.

—Genesis 3

IN *AFTER VIRTUE*, ALASDAIR MACINTYRE suggests that the advent of the Enlightenment disrupted the existing structure of moral reasoning in a distinctive and deeply damaging way.[1] Hitherto, moral principles had functioned as a means of ensuring that human beings fulfilled their telos; they effected a transformation from raw, uncultivated human modes of being to ones in and through which human creatures lived well or flourished, realizing the full potential of their distinctive nature. Since the Enlightenment systematically rejected any teleological forms of understanding of the natural world (for a variety of reasons ranging from the apparently definitive overturning of Aristotelian modes of natural science by those based on more mathematical and mechanical models of the material realm, to the long-established association of such teleological forms of understanding with conservative—even reactionary—moral, political, and religious traditions), it could not make sense of human beings, and hence of morality, in such terms. But then

[1] Duckworth: London, 1981.

it faced the task of trying to find an alternative justification for the basic moral principles it had inherited—principles that deliberately and systematically went against the grain of untutored human nature.

According to MacIntyre's view, invoking the demands of reason was doomed to failure, since rationality in morals (as elsewhere) acquires substance only insofar as it operates within the context of a particular framework of moral concepts and moral understanding—what he calls a tradition; and of course, a fundamental aspect of the autonomy that Enlightenment thinkers sought (both for individual moral and political beings, and for specific spheres of human culture) was precisely freedom from the dead hand of tradition (understood as embodying claims to authority lacking any genuinely rational basis). Hence, once the failure of this project of finding a tradition-free rational grounding for morality became evident, the unfolding history of the West in the aftermath of the Enlightenment became one in which, as the common culture gradually watered down the demanding content of moral principles (bringing morality more into line with human nature as experience presents it, on the grounds that moral principles which demand that we subject that nature to radically transformative cultivation are merely arbitrary impositions from the superstitious past), philosophers gradually came to suspect that morality as a cultural structure was simply an exercise in coercive power (whether by specific cultures, or specific classes, or specific kinds of individual). The only alternative that MacIntyre can see to this Nietzschean vision of a vanishing dimension of evaluation in everyday human life, is a return to Aristotelian—more precisely, to Thomist—thinking, in which the idea of a human telos not only is capable of being made intelligible in the face of everything that the Enlightenment claimed to know, but also can make more sense of the difficulties and confusions confronting other intellectual traditions which lack that concept than they can make of the difficulties with which Thomism it-self must deal.[2]

To worry overmuch about the objective scholarly validity of every claim MacIntyre makes about the central figures of the Enlightenment period and its aftermath would risk missing the main point of his enterprise. For its real starting point lies in the present—in MacIntyre's sense that we currently view the claims of morality upon us as incomprehensibly demanding. And just as he argues that the individual human self can make sense of her present position, and hence of herself, only through the unity conferred by a narrative showing how she came to occupy it, so MacIntyre's book as a whole attempts to make sense of our collective moral condition by recounting it as the latest episode in the historical narrative of our culture. And since it is also central to his argument that there can be no perspective-independent account of moral phenomena, we must expect his account of our moral condition to be oriented by his own (first Aristotelian, and later Thomist) moral con-cepts and resources. In other words, the master narrative of *After Virtue* asks primarily for ethical evaluation—it offers a myth of our origins that must be tested against our current experience, in the name of a morally intelligible future.

But MacIntyre's own thought also has a narrative structure, that we must—according to his own lights—take into account. It is, I think, undeniable that in the first phase or episode of his recent work, post-Enlightenment thinking is presented as conflating its rejection of certain religious conceptions of the human telos with a rejection of the very concept of a human telos, and thereby as eliminating the option of an Aristotelian

---

[2] For a more detailed elaboration, and critical evaluation, of MacIntyre's deliberately simplified and dramatic portrait of our present cultural situation, see chaps. 2 and 6 and the conclusion of Mulhall and Swift, *Liberals and Communitarians*, 2nd ed. (Blackwell: Oxford, 1996).

conception of morality that is indebted neither to the Enlightenment nor to its religious enemies. But in the books succeeding *After Virtue* (beginning with *Whose Justice? Which Rationality?*), MacIntyre shifts his moral allegiance from Aristotle to Aquinas. In so doing, he not only suggests that the post-Enlightenment liberal tradition that he earlier accused of lacking room for any concept of human flourishing might be better viewed as having, rather, an inadequate conception of it (how, after all, could a tradition with liberalism's weight of historical and social reality ever really have lacked what he himself presented as essential to any coherent moral perspective?); he also implies that the Enlightenment's primary mistake was in fact its rejection of the distinctively Christian inflection of that concept.

Even if we prefer MacIntyre's earlier analysis to his later, we could plausibly argue that, if the Enlightenment is best understood as founded on a certain kind of resistance to the very concept of a human telos, such resistance without doubt originated—and found its most passionate expression—in a resistance to the specifically religious idea of the human telos as involving a relation to God, and of those who fail to fulfil that telos as existing in a state of original sin. The Christian doctrine of original sin is, of course, the subject of multiple interpretations, disputations, and reformulations across two millennia of theological and liturgical conversation and controversy; but at its core is the conception that human nature as such is tragically flawed, perverse in its very structure or constitution. Human beings are not only naturally capable of acting—even perhaps disposed to act—sinfully, but are always already turned against themselves, against the true and against the good, by virtue of their very condition as human. Hence, that sinful orientation will distort and ultimately invalidate any efforts they might make by themselves to alter that orientation; the only possible solution lies in their attaining a certain kind of orientation to the divine. But it is not just that without drawing on transcendental sources they cannot overcome their perversity; it is also that whether or not such resources are available to draw upon is not up to them—it is not within their power to ensure that they get the help they need, for that too is ultimately in the hands of the divine, an aspect of grace.

Such a doctrine patently violates a variety of interrelated and central Enlightenment precepts. It is fundamentally offensive to any conception of morality that places human autonomy at its heart; for it entails that our very ability to orient ourselves toward the good is dependent upon transcendental spiritual sources, and asserts the direct opposite of the liberal understanding of human beings as the self-originating sources of moral value (as Rawls puts his Kantian conception of the matter). For the Christian, we are, if anything, the self-originating source of sin; hence, our only hope of regaining any contact with goodness is by dying to ourselves. It is also offensive to reason—as is evident in the way the Genesis story of the Fall not only posits Adam's moral responsibility for the deed that constitutes his acquisition of the central precondition for moral responsibility, but also presents what appear to be the constitutive conditions for any recognizably human existence (reproduction, cultivation of the earth, death, even self-consciousness or self-awareness) as modifications—more specifically, as self-inflicted and penal deformations—of our truly human nature.

Perhaps, however, the central source of offence in this doctrine emerges most clearly if we note a distinction drawn by Wittgenstein:

> People are religious to the extent that they believe themselves to be not so much *imperfect* as *sick*.
>
> Anyone who is halfway decent will think himself utterly imperfect, but the religious person thinks himself wretched.[3]

---

[3] L. Wittgenstein, *Culture and Value*, trans. P. Winch (Blackwell: Oxford, 1980), 51.

This distinction bears some elucidation. There are, for example, a variety of ways in which Enlightenment modes of thought might accept a conception of human beings as naturally imperfect. To begin with, and despite a certain accelerating post-Enlightenment tendency to align our moral codes with what we judge a being of our nature might reasonably be expected to achieve, there is nothing terribly challenging to nonreligious forms of thought in the perception that an entirely raw or uncultivated human nature might be morally problematic. Aristotle, for example, provides a well-worked out conception of individual human beings as possessed of potential that they are not capable of realizing except under the right circumstances—with the input of properly educated elders and the culture they maintain—and in the absence of which they will certainly behave in immoral and otherwise damaging ways. But even in the absence of such nonreligious teleological structures of thinking, there can be little to object to from a naturalistic point of view in the idea that the human individual requires the attention and efforts of other human beings if he is to achieve what his natural capacities (and, in particular, his natural capacity to acquire capacities) allow. This, one might say, is simply an aspect of what is distinctive about the species *homo sapiens*; its plasticity, its developmental trajectory, its relations to other members of its species, are simply facts about the specific nature of humans.

Nor need there be anything provocative in the thought that individual human beings, as well as human collectivities, might deliberately and persistently perform immoral actions. Any being capable of doing good must be capable of doing evil; and the apparent benefits to the agent of, say, selfish behaviour (or more generally, behaviour harmful to other humans, as well as other nonhuman beings and indeed the natural world) are evident. One might further come to believe that the fundamental causes of immoral behaviour lie outside the mind and will of those who enact them—say, in the structure of society (in its political, economic, or familial aspects) or that of the natural world (in its zoological or genetic aspects). Even this need not do any fundamental violence to the Enlightenment conception of human self-sufficiency, since such extra-individual structural influences are themselves humanly comprehensible (identifiable and analysable by such thinkers as Marx, Freud, or Darwin); are in many cases the result of human action; and are, anyway, always in principle open to alteration, or at least amelioration, by collective human action. In short, even if the source of our problems lies beyond the individual wrongdoer, it does not lie beyond the human race as such; and so its resolution also lies within human hands.

In a certain sense, the doctrine of original sin also locates the cause of our problems in human hands (or at least in the first human pair's deeds), but it does so in such a way that the solution to that problem remains necessarily beyond our unaided grasp, and thereby prevents us from thinking of our natural state as merely imperfect in any of the senses outlined above. To put matters slightly differently: in order for us to conceive of divine assistance as essential to our reorientation or redemption, we must see ourselves as standing in need of a particularly thoroughgoing kind of redemption, and hence as presently existing in a particularly thoroughgoing kind of unredeemed state—as enslaved, but enslaved by ourselves (not only not autonomous, but autonomously nonautonomous); as having freely relinquished our freedom and so as having ourselves placed its recovery beyond our own reach.

It is not, perhaps, beyond halfway decent people to see how the public record of what human hands have done (to other humans, to other living beings, and to the planet) in the last century, not to mention more private memories of our own willingness to besmirch what we value despite (even because of) our valuing of it, might come to suggest or even force such a conception of ourselves upon us. But insofar as we do take issue with ourselves in these terms, we cannot think of such perverseness as simply a species of imperfection; or if one wishes

to view our recovery from it as a version of perfectionist thinking, then one must say that it is a recovery from a state in which
we go wrong not in some or other particulars but in everything
we do, and hence that nothing we initiate can right that wrong
unless it is rooted in a moment of passivity, one in which we
suffer the supplementation of an essential lack.

Moreover, it is not just the solution to our problem that is
beyond us; the same will be true of our sense that we have such
a problem to resolve in the first place. For if this conception of
ourselves as always already errant before any particular errancy,
as basically oriented away from the truth, is something we regard as (at least part of) the truth about ourselves, then we cannot coherently think of it as something that we could have arrived at from our own resources, but rather as attainable only
through a relation with a wholly external source of our redemption from that state of untruth—for the Christian, from He
who claimed to *be* (not merely to have or to convey) "the Way,
the Truth, and the Life." This means that, on the one hand,
any such perception of human beings will necessarily be offensive (both morally and rationally) to those who lack the relationship with the divine through which it might be revealed. In
the absence of that relationship, such a self-understanding will
simply make no sense to them, and those who claim to be attempting to live out that relationship should therefore expect
the self-understanding it demands to seem absurd to others.
But it also implies that the framework of thought within which
this perception of ourselves as sick or wretched makes sense is
also one within which it is internally related to a perception of
ourselves as capable of being cured, as somehow redeemable
even from such a deeply unredeemed state. One might say: to
accept such a self-understanding just *is* to relate oneself to the
divine, and thus to accept that, for all one's wretchedness, one
is redeemable. The conceptual structure of the Christian doctrine of original sin thus exemplifies with particular clarity—
even, one might say, with a kind of perverse extremity—the

MacIntyrean triad of unfulfilled human state, fulfilled human state, and transformative source.

What I want to suggest as a way of orienting the reader for the main business of this book, is that we might think of the three philosophers to whom I shall shortly turn as wanting to preserve a recognizable descendent of the Christian conception of human nature as always already averting us from the relation to truth, comprehension, and clarity that is nevertheless our birthright—hence, as structurally perverse or errant and yet redeemable from that fallen state—but as refusing to accept that such redemption is attainable only from a transcendental or divine source. In other words, these philosophers want to keep a conception of human beings as in need of redemption (rather than, say, improvement or self-realization) and as capable of it, but to relocate the source of that redemption within (or at least on the borders of) the world of human experience. They will neither attenuate their sense of the constitutive depths to which our difficulties must be traced to accord with a more generally secularized conception of the self and its world, nor accept that acknowledging the depth of such difficulties requires the invocation of a divine source to which the self must relate itself and its world if it is to be redeemed from them.

The religious reader will say that to dispense with such a relation to divinity threatens to deprive the interpretative schema—call it the myth—of redemption of its very intelligibility, since the divine is not simply the source of our redemption but also the source of our awareness that we stand in need of it; and she will further say that, as a consequence, the philosopher of redemption will find himself relocating the divinity that he is attempting to banish (perhaps even substituting himself in its place, and thereby instantiating one more version of the hubristic human desire to be God that, on the religious version of the myth, led to our need for redemption in the first place). The secular reader will say that to dispense with such a relation to divinity entails that one reject what is anyway a morally and rationally incomprehensible conception of the human condition. The philosophers I have in mind will say that since any adequate conception of the human condition leads us inexorably to a conception of ourselves as structurally perverse, and yet we cannot take seriously the idea of a divine source of transformation or rebirth, we must learn to live with a conception of ourselves as essentially enigmatic to ourselves. We stand incomprehensibly in need of redemption, and we are incomprehensibly able to achieve it, through a certain kind of intellectual practice that is also a spiritual practice, and that not only risks but aims to confront and internalize an idea of itself and its practitioners as ineliminably beyond our understanding—a practice of enduring and embodying the human being's constitutive resistance to its own grasp.

This last formulation may go some way toward accounting for the fact that the three philosophers I propose as committed to this conception of the human come either from the mainstream of post-Kantian German philosophy, or from the apparently inassimilable Austro-German fringes of post-Kantian Anglo-American philosophy. For one way of articulating the common (even if deeply misleading) picture of the divide between (the misleadingly named) analytic and continental modes or dimensions of modern Western philosophy is by specifying the other intellectual disciplines which that mode of philosophizing regards as cognate or other to it; and if analytical philosophers tend to look to the natural sciences, continental philosophers tend to look not only to the humanities and to art, but also to religion. Furthermore, the two (so-called) traditions have a very different attitude to contradiction. Analytical philosophers tend to view the unearthing of a contradiction as demonstrating the untenability of a line of thought or a conception of the world; continental philosophers are more inclined to consider the possibility that the phenomena under consideration are inherently contradictory—that reality (or at least some portion of it, and most commonly the human portion) is capable of maintaining itself in contradiction to itself, that to do so is in fact the distinctively human way to exist.

The conjunction of these two distinguishing marks of the continental side of the philosophical mind is perhaps most starkly evident in Sartre's early work, according to which the distinctively human mode of being—being for-itself—is what it is not and is not what it is (is essentially not coincident with or identical to itself); and the most fundamental aspect of the for-itself's internal negating of itself is the apparently ineradicable but essentially contradictory human desire to be God (since to be God would mean, incoherently, being both for-itself and in-itself, and thus to desire such an incoherent state is for the human, incoherently, to desire not to be human). What interests me about Nietzsche, Heidegger, and Wittgenstein is that they can be read as in a certain sense exemplifying Sartre's claim—in that, whilst each more or less explicitly aims either to criticize or at least to detach himself from Christian theological horizons, all three in fact engender a conception of the human condition that constantly inclines them to reiterate elements of a distinctively Christian structure of thought. Hence, the basic question to which the following chapters are an attempt to provide, if not an answer, then at least a clearer, more specific articulation of what is at issue in the asking of such a question, is: can one say what the Christian has to say about the human condition as fallen, and yet mean it otherwise?

The argument in the chapters to come is not cumulative, although it is progressive in at least two senses of that term. My reading of Heidegger does not depend upon my reading of Nietzsche, any more than my reading of Wittgenstein is dependent upon its predecessors; it is not necessary for the reader to accept the conclusions of the earlier chapters in order to find acceptable the claims of later ones. In that sense, each chapter can stand alone, although the chapters on Nietzsche and Wittgenstein are likely to be more accessible to those with little prior acquaintance with the texts under discussion than is the chapter on Heidegger (which is compelled to begin a little further on in the journey through his thought in order to reach the points of interest for this investigation without expanding to the length of a small book). Rather, a different facet or aspect of the doctrine of original sin turns out to be dominant in the inflection of it that I claim to find in each philosopher. In Nietzsche, the central issue is the idea of our fallenness as punishment (more specifically, as self-punishment); in Heidegger, it is the idea of fallenness as embodiedness (more specifically, as mortality and animality); in Wittgenstein, it is the idea of fallenness as transgression (more specifically, as the refusal of limits and the perversions of desire). So, one sense in which my argument is progressive is that each chapter aims to contribute one specific detail to a larger portrait of a certain dimension of the philosophical tradition, as informed by a response to a single doctrine that is itself formed by the internal relations between each such element.

Nevertheless, certain themes or issues do recur across the three chapters and thus provide a more straightforward sense in which my argument is progressive, insofar as their recurrence suggests a certain convergence in the work of these philosophers upon the most suggestive or pertinent dimensions of the doctrine of original sin for their specific cultural moments. Leaving aside the theme that I have already mentioned (that of the human as constitutively enigmatic to itself), three other such recurrences seem of particular interest. They are as follows: the idea of God as nothing (as no thing, a non-entity—hence, the implication that to conceive of him otherwise, as something in particular, is to fall into superstition or idolatry, whether one does so in affirming or denying His existence); the idea of a certain kind of linguistic confusion, an opacity in our life with words, as a marker of our perverseness; and the idea of an unending oscillation between experiencing our condition as a limit and as a limitation—call this the thought that properly distinguishing the necessary from the contingent is a spiritual as well as a logical matter.

The chapters to come develop such thoughts as I have about these interlocking themes with as much precision as I can muster; so I do not propose to anticipate them here. However, as a way of picking up at least one of those themes, and linking it to a methodological point that may not be obvious to all, I want to conclude these introductory remarks by pointing out that my reading of what the doctrine of original sin involves will be as controversial within the Christian community as my readings of Nietzsche, Heidegger, and Wittgenstein will doubtless be to those concerned to inherit their thinking. I want, therefore, to highlight a primary source for my particular way of grasping this doctrine by paraphrasing some remarks made by one of Kierkegaard's pseudonyms in his consideration of the Genesis story that this introduction begins by citing. For Vigilius Haufniensis, the doctrine of original sin essentially tells us that sin entered into the world by sin; this is not an attempted explanation of individual sinful acts, but rather an expression of the enigmatic fact that no individual sinful act can be explained—that sinful acts presuppose sinfulness, and sinfulness presupposes sinful acts. Some will take this as proof that the Genesis narrative cannot help us to understand the human mode of being; others might take it as proof that in this tale we find as helpful an expression as we might wish for our sense (perhaps intermittent, but surely always recurring) of a constitutive paradox at the heart of the very value on which the Enlightenment stakes its claim to our continued attention: that of human autonomy or freedom. For Haufniensis, the first Adam embodies the irreducible mystery of the way in which human beings endlessly discover themselves to have alienated themselves from what is most properly theirs, to have disowned their existence.

I

The Madman and the Masters: Nietzsche

1. ORIENTATION

As a way of orienting ourselves within this chapter's concern with Nietzsche but also within the broader concerns of the book as a whole, I would like to cite two closely linked passages from two rather different sources in the writing of Stanley Cavell. The first is taken from an early essay on one of Kierkegaard's less well-known works, *On Authority and Revelation* (perhaps better known by its subtitle, *The Book on Adler*); the second comes from the fourth part of Cavell's magnum opus, entitled *The Claim of Reason*, from a point at which his concern with questions of privacy, self-expression, and self-knowledge allow him to return to Kierkegaard and to link that return with a return to Nietzsche, who is a much-underestimated presence in this concluding portion of the book.

> Nothing an outsider can say about religion has the rooted violence of things the religious have themselves had it at heart to say: no brilliant attack by an outsider against (say) obscurantism will seem to go far enough to a brilliant insider faced with the real obscurity of God; and attacks against religious institutions in the name of reason will

not go far enough in a man who is attacking them in the name of faith.[1]

You may battle against the Christian's self-understanding from within Christianity, as Kierkegaard declares, or from beyond Christianity, as Nietzsche declares. In both cases, you are embattled because you find the *words* of the Christian to be the right words. It is the way he means them that is empty or enfeebling. Christianity appears in Nietzsche not so much as the reverse of the truth but as the truth in foul disguise. In particular, the problem seems to be that human action is everywhere disguised as human suffering: this is what acceptance of the Will to Power is to overcome.[2]

I find that these quotations suggest two interlinked questions, one for Nietzsche and one for the Christian, from which I propose to begin this inquiry. The question for Nietzsche is this: When we read his many-faceted critiques of Judaeo-Christian morality and culture, should we think of him as speaking from within or from without Christianity? For if, as Cavell suggests, the Christian's words are, from Nietzsche's point of view, the right words—if the critical task he sets himself is not to eliminate the Christian vocabulary but rather to recover it for a more human, a less life-denying, use—then he cannot simply abandon them. But how can he retain them and still succeed in speaking from beyond Christianity—from a perspective that can genuinely claim to have overcome the Christian inheritance?

---

[1] Stanley Cavell, "Kierkegaard's *On Authority and Revelation*," in *Must We Mean What We Say?* (Cambridge University Press: Cambridge, 1969), 174.

[2] Stanley Cavell, *The Claim of Reason* (Oxford University Press: Oxford, 1979), 352.

The question for the Christian is this: Is there a perspective available to the defender of Christianity from which Nietzsche's words of criticism, however radical and devastating in intent, can in fact be seen as the truth in foul disguise? After all, if Cavell is right in suggesting that Nietzsche can only achieve his purposes by retaining the Christian vocabulary, then what he has it in mind to say with those words—his attempts to mean them otherwise than the Christian—might well appear to the Christian as an enfeebling use of the right words, as going less far than one can go within Christianity. In other words, is there a way of understanding Christianity that would allow the Christian to think of Nietzsche's critique as insufficiently radical and insufficiently violent—as failing to see the truly radical violence that the Christian's words are capable of doing to the purportedly Christian culture and institutions (what Kierkegaard calls the domain of Christendom) in which they are uneasily domesticated?

2. Pronouncing the Death of God

In order to begin collecting the material for an answer to these questions, I want to examine in some detail one of the most well-known (perhaps, by now, rather too well-known) facets of Nietzsche's critique of Christianity—his claim that God is dead and, in particular, the way in which that claim is articulated in his parable of the madman, as recounted in *The Gay Science*:

> *The madman.*—Haven't you heard of that madman who in the bright morning lit a lantern and ran around the marketplace crying incessantly "I'm looking for God! I'm looking for God!" Since many of those who did not believe in God were standing around together just then, he caused great laughter. Has he been lost, then? asked one. Did he lose his way like a child? asked another. Or is he hiding?

Is he afraid of us? Has he gone to sea? Emigrated?—Thus they shouted and laughed, one interrupting the other. The madman jumped into their midst and pierced them with his eyes. "Where is God?" he cried; "I'll tell you! *We have killed him*—you and I! We are all his murderers. But how did we do this? How were we able to drink up the sea? Who gave us the sponge to wipe away the entire horizon? What were we doing when we unchained this earth from its sun? Where is it moving to now? Where are we moving to? Away from all suns? Are we not continually falling? And backwards, sideways, forwards, in all directions? Is there still an up and a down? Aren't we straying as though through an infinite nothing? Isn't empty space breathing at us? Hasn't it got colder? Isn't night and more night coming again and again? Don't lanterns have to be lit in the morning? Do we still hear nothing of the noise of the grave-diggers who are burying God? Do we still smell nothing of the divine decomposition?—Gods, too, decompose! God is dead! God remains dead! And we have killed him! How can we console ourselves, the murderers of all murderers! The holiest and the mightiest thing the world has ever possessed has bled to death under our knives: who will wipe this blood from us? With what water could we clean ourselves? What festivals of atonement, what holy games will we have to invent for ourselves? Is the magnitude of this deed not too great for us? Do we not ourselves have to become gods merely to appear worthy of it? There was never a greater deed—and whoever is born after us will on account of this deed belong to a higher history than all history up to now!" Here the madman fell silent and looked again at his listeners; they too were silent and looked at him disconcertedly. Finally he threw his lantern on the ground and it broke into pieces and went out. "I come too early," he then said; "my time is not yet. This tremendous event is still on its way, wandering; it has not yet reached the ears of men. Lightning and thunder need time; the light of the stars needs time; deeds need time, even after they are done, in order to be seen and heard. This deed is still more remote to them than the remotest stars—*and yet they have done it themselves!*" It is still re-counted how on the same day the madman forced his way into several churches and there started singing his *requiem aeternam deo.* Led out and called to account, he is said al-ways to have replied nothing but, "What then are these churches now if not the tombs and sepulchres of God?"[3]

The first thing to note about this passage is that the claim that God is dead is not made by Nietzsche in propria persona, but is, rather, put into the mouth of a madman; the ironic possibili-ties here are obvious and multiple, but they suffice at the very least to raise the question of how far Nietzsche himself thinks that one might succeed in meaning what the claim appears to say and still remain recognizable as a potential interlocutor (as, say, a writer for whom the acquisition of a readership remains something for which he can coherently hope). The second thing worth noting is that Nietzsche's madman addresses his claim to two audiences: to the atheists in the marketplace, and to the theists who call him to account from within the churches he visits. It seems fair to say that critical commentary has tended to concentrate on the first audience rather than the second. Perhaps this is because most such commentators would regard themselves as members of that first audience, and hence as most directly addressed in that stretch of the text; perhaps it is be-cause of the undeniably striking fact that Nietzsche's madman appears to think that it is the atheists rather than the theists who stand most (or, at least, first) in need of the news that God is dead, when one might rather think that making such a claim

---

[3] Friedrich Nietzsche, *The Gay Science*, ed. B. Williams, trans. J. Nauckhoff (Cambridge University Press: Cambridge, 2002), section 125.

to an atheist could not, logically speaking, be meant to convey a piece of information (if anyone knows this, surely the atheist does). But this preponderance of attention directed at the inhabitants of the marketplace has by now, in my experience, reached the point at which it can become hard to remain open to the presence in this parable of the inhabitants of the churches—hard to hold onto the knowledge that its final two sentences actually exist. My reading of the parable is an attempt to work out the consequences of assuming that Nietzsche is equally concerned with both audiences, and that his aim is to reinterpret the self-understanding of both of them.

2.1. The Atheists: Blood, Light, Falling

To think of God as dead is not to think of him as simply nonexistent; if God is now dead, then, to be sure, he no longer exists, but he was previously alive—hence, his corpse may still exist and be the subject of a search. But the marketplace atheists mock the madman's claim to be seeking God by the light of his lantern in the sunny town square; how can anyone think that God might be found in our daylight world? All right-thinking people have long known not only that there is no God but that there never was; belief in His existence was a childish superstition, a cognitive error revealed as such by advances in our understanding of the world, and human maturity requires that we learn to live in the clear, invigorating light of that knowledge. This is why the atheists variously compare God to a lost child, a sailor, and an emigrant in their mockery of the madman; these comparisons betray their underlying assumption that God is an entity of some kind (even if a supernatural one), and hence one whose removal from our list of what there is in (or within and without) the universe leaves the rest of that universe entirely unchanged.

But the madman finds this conception of God as an (illusory) entity to be far more childish than the religious faith it claims to have outgrown. His contention is that our perception of God as nonexistent does not amount to the transcendence of an illusion; it is not a discovery but a deed, and a bloody, terrifying one at that, for which we must take responsibility. We are God's murderers. His presence was real, part of the living tissue of our culture, our responses, our most intimate self-understanding. His destruction is therefore a radical act of violence, not only against Him but also against ourselves. Hence, the madman compares the death of God to the wiping away of our horizon, to the swallowing up of an ocean, to a loss of spatial orientation; such comparisons assume that God is not so much an entity as a medium or a system of coordinates, and thus that a belief in God is best understood not as the addition of one supernatural item to the supposed furniture of the universe, but rather as an atmosphere or framework that orients us in everything we say, think, and do.

Furthermore, God's corpse is as yet unburied; the stench of His putrefying culture still lingers in the madman's nostrils—in, for example, the instinct (perhaps already decaying, if the atheists' contempt for the madman is any indication) of compassion for the weak and the vulnerable that continues to direct our moral responses even after we discard what we think of as its theistic underpinnings. For the madman, as long as we continue to take our bearings—however roughly—from the values of Judaeo-Christian morality, we maintain the life of Christianity against the decomposition of the grave. Hence, the madman declares that he has come too soon, that his search for God's genuinely lifeless corpse is premature; the news he brings is not news but a prophecy. For the realization of what we have really done is yet to dawn on us; and only when it does can a higher human history truly unfold.

Beyond the madman's implicit critique of the marketplace atheists' superstitious conception of God, and therefore of their self-deluding conception of themselves as deniers of God, his rhetoric activates three other thematic or allusive registers that help to fill out our understanding of the significance of his pronouncement of God's death. The first of these turns on his deployment of the image of blood—blood as welling from God's corpse, as coating not only the knives with which we killed Him but also the hands with which we clutched those knives, and hence as needing to be cleansed from us; but with what water (a question that recalls us to his earlier talk of the sea, and of our taking a sponge to wipe away the entire horizon)? In certain moods, I find that these turns of phrase bring passages and themes from Shakespeare's *Macbeth* irresistibly to mind—as, for example, when Lady Macbeth declares: "Out, damned spot! Out, I say! . . . Yet who would have thought the old man to have had so much blood in him? . . . What, will these hands ne'er be clean? . . . Here's the smell of the blood still: all the perfumes of Arabia will not sweeten this little hand . . . Wash your hands, put on your nightgown; look not so pale, I tell you yet again, Banquo's buried; he cannot come out on's grave" (5.3. 37–71). Or again, when Macbeth asks: "Will all great Neptune's ocean wash this blood clean from my hand? No, this my hand will rather the multitudinous seas incarnadine, making the green one red." (2.2.60). If we were to take seriously the thought that Nietzsche's words might be intended to activate such an allusion, what would follow?[4]

First, Shakespeare's play presents a murder committed by someone who is both prompted to it and punished for it by

[4] William Desmond's essay "Sticky Evil: *Macbeth* and the Karma of the Equivocal" in D. Middleton, ed., *God, Literature and Process Thought* (Ashgate: London, 2002) links Nietzsche and *Macbeth* in a number of interesting ways, some of which intersect with the issues I go on to raise. For those with an interest in Cavell, it is worth pointing out that his recent essay "Macbeth Appalled" forges links between this play and a number of themes at work in the passage from *The Claim of Reason* that I quoted earlier; cf. the updated edition of *Disowning Knowledge* (Cambridge University Press: Cambridge, 2003).

witches, so that superstition appears as at once facilitating murderous deeds and ensuring that deeds so prompted turn upon
the doer, as well as offering human beings a way of sloughing off
ultimate responsibility for what they do. These are all aspects of
the madman's understanding of the superstition-filled relation
between God's murder and the marketplace atheists who committed it. Second, Duncan's murder turns out to be the beginning of a sequence of deaths (those of Banquo, Macduff's wife
and children, Lady Macbeth herself, and so on), just as the
death of God is understood by Nietzsche to herald the death
(however long drawn-out) of other aspects of Western culture—not only of Judaeo-Christian morality, but also of certain
closely related conceptions of science and philosophy. We will
look more closely into this matter later in this chapter.

But the link with *Macbeth* also takes us beyond points we have
already established about the madman's purposes. For example,
that link also suggests that we consider the murder of God as
the killing of a king; the play repeatedly links the political disor-
der of Macbeth's treasonous deed with a disordering or disorientation of the cosmos, and it thus follows that we should think
of life after God's murder as requiring that we establish a new,
decentred mode of inhabitation of the natural world, one
founded on a conception of nature as lacking any inherent, extrahuman structure of meaning, and hence requiring a conception of ourselves (understood as simply part of nature) as embodying only the significance we can confer on ourselves
(perhaps through festivals of atonement, perhaps through holy
games). The task God's death sets us is thus in part one of overcoming any conception of the natural world as dark, cold, and
disorienting, since it can appear to us as such only by contrast
with our previous conception of it as embodying an intrinsic
order and significance, and so that appearance indicates a lin-
gering nostalgia for a living God, which will hinder rather than
help the beginning of our higher history.

Macbeth's vicissitudes and fate suggest further layers of significance in the madman's conception of our responsibility for God's death. For whilst he begins by aiming to transpose himself (he imagines himself in another's place, and hence imagines the murder of that other purely as a means of achieving this displacement), he ends by losing himself. To be sure, Macbeth ultimately ascends the throne; but he always appears, in others' eyes as well as his own, not so much as the king but rather as the king's murderer—as the illegitimate usurper of authority, rather than its wielder. And under this self-description he no longer recognizes himself as continuous with the person who originally chose to implement this murderous plan, since the act of murder was meant only to be a temporary stopping-place on the journey to the throne, not a deed that would permanently mark and alter the identity of its doer to the point of preventing him from becoming—from really inhabiting the role of—king. The means to his chosen end thus obliterate the end, and render him incomprehensible to himself; since the deed has not achieved the goal that motivated it, and indeed now appears incapable of doing so (in part because the witches' prophecy always contained the undoing of Macbeth's intentions, in part because committing a murder necessarily makes a man a murderer, and hence could never have simply made Macbeth king in Duncan's place), the doing of it lacks any sense, even to him. Transposed to the parable of the madman, this structure of thought suggests that those who want to live in a world without God must accept that they can do so only if they can accept and even welcome a conception of themselves as God's murderers. The applicability of that self-description is not an essentially transitory fact, a simple condition that prepares the way for inhabiting a world in which God is simply absent; rather, it travels with us into that higher history, and its continued applicability to us grounds our claim to be living in that new dispensation of human culture. The challenge is for us to accept this self-description without thinking that it deprives our self-understanding of any substance.

But, of course, that is the fate that awaits Macbeth—more precisely, this murderer is driven mad (and then driven to his death) by his deed. And this raises the question of whether we should imagine Macbeth as representing not marketplace atheism but the madman himself. If so, we would have to regard the madman as God's murderer, and the atheists he accuses of the deed as at best accessories after the fact; after all, if God has been murdered but only the madman knows this, then who else could have done the bloody deed? Or perhaps, given his parting charge that "they have done it themselves," the madman instead intends the atheists to enact (or reenact) it on his behalf, their receipt of his prophecy then being the means of its fulfilment.

Either way, the sense in which the madman can or should be thought of as Nietzsche's proxy here becomes a pressing issue; for insofar as we are prepared to regard his utterances as Nietzsche's way of getting a hearing for his own thoughts, his way of admitting his authorship of them without exactly authorising them—as if so that we might confront them, and thus our responsibility for evaluating them, in the absence of first-person authority—then we might ask whether the madman is imagining or prophesying his own murder, even digging his own grave. Does Nietzsche expect his words not only to be dismissed as the ravings of a lunatic, but also to cause his own persecution unto death—to put him in the position of the sacrificial scapegoat upon whose corpse the human future might be constructed? After all, his madman does at least ask whether we do not ourselves have to become gods merely to appear worthy of our deicidal deed; but claiming divinity is the charge under which Christ is condemned to death by the Sanhedrin, and the death Christ suffers is understood by Christians not only as that of a scapegoat, but as the indispensable foundation for a fully human future.

We shall return to the issue of scapegoating more than once in the pages to come; but now, I would like to turn to the second of the three rhetorical registers I mentioned earlier—that of light, which I suggest is internally related in Nietzsche's thinking here to that of Enlightenment, and more specifically to the question: what is true Enlightenment? For the atheists, bright morning—the dawn of human maturity from the black night of religious superstition—is given by the light of the sun, and the clear perception it affords; to bring a lantern is insanely superfluous. But in the light of the madman's lantern, the sun takes on a rather different significance, particularly when we bring the images of light and enlightenment in section 125 of *The Gay Science* into conjunction with their inflections in section 108 of that work, which constitutes the beginning of the book that contains the madman's tale:

> *New battles.*—After Buddha was dead, they still showed his shadow in a cave for centuries—a tremendous, gruesome shadow. God is dead; but given the way people are, there may still for millennia be caves in which they show his shadow. And we—we must still defeat his shadow as well!

This conjunction of passages suggests the following ways of understanding the image of the sun as Enlightenment in section 125. First, the sun is Plato's sun: it may suggest a conception of goodness not underwritten by a conception of god (or at least not by the Christian conception of God), but it remains for Nietzsche a privileging of Being over Becoming, and so a valuing of stasis over change as well as a commitment to the idea that the true meaning of experience lies hidden behind its superficial flux; as an extrahuman, invisible condition for the possibility of human vision, it constitutes a way of systematically denigrating the everyday, despite its repeated claims to be doing otherwise. The problem with bright mornings is that they make for long and deep shadows. Second, the sun is God's Son: His death at our hands unchains the planet from its star, thereby prefiguring and fulfilling the vision of Copernicus, and making it—and us—truly wanderers, strays, errants; but this is precisely the disoriented, groping status that the marketplace atheists refuse to acknowledge as their own. And does not the brightness of the morning underwrite their refusal? But if, third, the sun is Copernicus's sun, it must be understood as a star whose light needs time to reach us. Hence, our present, illuminated state can prove only the past reality of their sun; its light might outlive, and so conceal, the death of its Platonic-Christian source. For Nietzsche's madman, then, true Enlightenment remains to be achieved. The bright morning of Enlightenment atheism is in fact dead light, and we men and women of knowledge will remain unknown to ourselves for as long as we continue trying to draw sustenance from it.

The third rhetorical register I mentioned earlier connects with the image of the earth as wandering unchained from its sun; it concerns the madman's inherently ambivalent sense of us as falling. For "falling" suggests uncontrolled movement, but in a definite spatial direction; whereas the madman talks, rather, of our falling as continuous, as moving us in all directions and none, as amounting to a complete loss of any sense of direction, and in particular any sense of higher and lower—and he thinks of this straying or erring as brought about by our dispossessing ourselves of that which is most holy. If the death of God precisely deprives us of a framework within which to locate and track ourselves, why characterize its loss in terms which presuppose its retention? Nietzsche's choice of imagery here prevents us from regarding the condition he describes simply as a state of disorientation; it suggests instead the very specific kind of disorientation that Christianity calls "the Fall"—a conception of human beings as originally sinful. Is not the madman's pronouncement of God's death verging dangerously closely here (and not here alone) upon a resurrection of Christian words, a way of meaning them that is not sufficiently unchained or dislocated from their origin to achieve the kind of human future that could be called genuinely higher?

2.2. The Theists: Easter Saturday

It may seem obvious that the madman's address to the theists, when he forces his way into their churches and sings his requiem to God, constitutes a straightforward act of blasphemy—the turning of a liturgical form of appeal to God into an insult. But in fact, every element of the madman's proclamation to the atheists (what one might think of as the prose version of his song) can be seen as internal to orthodox Christian belief; more precisely, it amounts to a call (to believers as well as unbelievers) to remember that Good Friday and Easter Sunday are conjoined by Holy Saturday—that the cross and the resurrection are held together by the grave.

It might be worth spelling out this point in a little more detail, by recalling the central elements of the Christian creed and the corresponding elements of the madman's discourse. According to their creed, Christians believe that Christ was crucified (the blood from His crown of thorns mingles with that from His nailed hands and feet); He died and was buried (the lance pierces His side to bring forth blood and water, ointment against decomposition is applied to the body, and it is placed in the grave); He descended into hell (the utter absence of God, echoing His cry of Godforsakenness on the cross); He rose from the dead (the breath of the cold, empty tomb on the disciples' faces indicating that the Risen Son is bright morning); and this Good News is to be preached until He comes again (by prophets seeking a God whose time is both already gone and yet to come). And underlying each element of this litany concerning God's death is the idea that we killed Him, that His death was at our hands, that we are His murderers. One might well wonder: What atonement is possible for us after such a deed? And how could it possibly presage a higher human history? And yet both are promised or prophesied to us.

In other words, the three interrelated core ideas of the madman's proclamation—the idea of God's present absence, understood as the result of His death, which is understood in turn as the result of our killing Him—are also central to the Christian proclamation of Good News. Once Jesus is understood as Christ, as fully human and fully God, then the unrestrictedness of His Incarnation requires that He not only be born but that He die; the meaning of His death (its salvific significance) turns upon His willingness to take upon Himself without resistance or complaint the worst that human beings can do to one another, and hence the worst that they can inflict upon their relationship to God, which requires that He suffer murderous victimization; and the hiatus between the Resurrection and the Second Coming presupposes at the very least that the Christian church conceive of itself as relating to God as absent from the world (as well as accepting, if only from Christ's enduring of it Himself, that human beings can be forced to understand themselves as utterly, but not unremittingly, Godforsaken). Of course, this idea of Godforsakenness and Godlessness as internal to the life of Christ and thus as internal to the life of God can be accommodated only in a Trinitarian context, which allows for the idea of Father against Son within Spirit; but then, without such a sense of internal differentiation-within-wholeness in the divine, the very idea of Incarnation would make no sense either.

It follows, then, that the idea of the death of God is absolutely integral to—although, of course, not absolutely exhaustive of—Christianity. Hence, carrying out funeral rites for God is both an essential moment of any liturgical acknowledgement of Easter, and the most apt expression of the Church's present experience of God (as absent, because He is between Resurrection and Second Coming and because He is capable of appearing to forsake utterly even those He loves). So, to say, as the madman does, that Christian churches should be God's tomb and sepulchre is not to blaspheme against Christianity, but rather to recall believers to an aspect of their faith that is absolutely essential, but often either underplayed or repressed altogether. Seen from this angle, the madman's attack on faith could as easily be made in the name of faith as in the cause of its overcoming; to use once more a central Kierkegaardian distinction, it confronts Christendom in the name of Christianity.

If, then, we are to make good this version of the possibility I sketched in at the outset of this chapter—that of finding Nietzsche's way of appropriating the words of Christianity to be less distant from orthodox ways of meaning those words than one might imagine—we must acknowledge that such orthodoxy is not always as current, or as dominating, in the Church's present self-understanding as it might be. In fact, one might argue that the recovery of this aspect of Christian faith by theologians over the course of the twentieth century—a project whose main stages might be associated with the work of Barth, Moltmann, and Jungel[5]—was itself in large part a response to Nietzsche's critique of Christianity, and to its impact on thinkers such as Heidegger and Sartre. But the fact remains that this project must nevertheless be understood as a recovery, or perhaps more precisely as a redistribution, of emphasis; even if it took the madman's critique actually to generate those versions of contemporary Christian theology that can accommodate the central elements of his reinterpretation of the self-interpretation of nineteenth-century Christianity, the (theo)logical space for such internal recountings was always already present in the core doctrines of the Christian faith.

---

[5] For a detailed and immensely thought-provoking account of this project and its implications, see Alan E. Lewis, *Between Cross and Resurrection: A Theology of Holy Saturday* (Eerdmans: Grand Rapids, Mich., 2001).

3. THE GENEALOGY OF HUMANITY

A few years after imagining a madman prematurely in search of God's corpse, Nietzsche published what one might think of as a prophetic autopsy of that divine body—an attempt to disarticulate or decompose the cadaver whose stench had yet to carry to other men's nostrils. In *On the Genealogy of Morality*, entirely in accordance with the madman's rejection of marketplace atheism's superstitious conception of God as an entity, and hence of faith in God as fundamentally a belief in the existence of an entity, from which certain moral principles can be established, Nietzsche critically considers Christian religion and morality primarily as a form of life—one in which a certain set of values orients everything one thinks, says, and does. The question he poses in that book is: what is the value—not the truth-value, but rather the real meaning or significance—of these values? The answer that emerges conjures the smell of hypocrisy.

For Nietzsche, the truth of Christianity lies in its veneration of the cross. For it is central to the self-understanding of Christian morality that it commit its followers to a life of altruism and self-sacrifice, in which the self becomes as nothing in order that the well-being of others (particularly the weak and vulnerable) become our exclusive concern. Furthermore, such selflessness is seen as the immutable essence of anything deserving the name of a moral system or code; the image of these values being delivered to us on tablets of stone precisely captures our sense of them as making timeless and absolutely authoritative claims upon us, as manifesting something about what it is to be moral that is ultimately a given, beyond question.

By arguing, in contrast to this, that such morality is possessed of a genealogy, Nietzsche puts in question every aspect of this self-understanding. If morality has a genealogy, then it has a history; it exists—like any other intraworldly phenomenon—in time, and hence not only had a point of origin (before which it did not exist at all) but also was subject to development and alteration. More specifically, that development displays a fissiparous form; like the genealogy of an individual, morality turns out to have branched in various directions, to have grafted itself onto other cultural strands, and thus to be internally differentiated—to have what one might call a family resemblance structure. And insofar as these variations and graftings are responsive to morality's historical contexts, its identity over time is fundamentally constituted by contingencies—by the vicissitudes of time, by forces and factors that might have been otherwise, and without which it might have been otherwise. Most importantly, if morality has a history, and hence a point of origin, then it might also have an end; other historical developments might spell not only its further alteration and fission, but also its destruction or overcoming.

As well as putting in question the idea that morality has an immutable, authoritative essence and the related idea that it is something to which we are fated beyond question, Nietzsche also assumes that the way to understand its significance is to grasp its purpose or function. This is not in itself an attack on Christian morality's self-image—its defenders might talk of it as serving God's purposes for the human race, or as a way of maintaining social harmony; the critical edge in Nietzsche's perspective here turns instead on his willingness to allow that the function of any morality might serve to drive a wedge between the meaning that morality appears to have (the self-understanding it presents to its defenders and opponents alike) and its true or underlying significance. It is his deployment of this distinction, as well as his emphasis upon the historicality and contingency of the phenomenon under analysis, that most closely connects Nietzsche's genealogical method with the various hermeneutics of suspicion practised by Darwin with respect to animal species, Marx with respect to economic and social systems, and Freud with respect to the structure of subjectivity.

Nietzsche's sense of the contingency of our familiar moral system allows him to take seriously the thought that not only might there be other possible ways of evaluating the phenomena of life, but that at least one of those alternative moral systems had a genuine historical reality (traces of which are to be found in etymological studies, as well as in our inherited conceptions of the ancient world). This is what he calls "master morality"—a system which contrasts good with bad rather than with evil, and which understands as good precisely that which is condemned as evil by its more familiar alternative. Master morality celebrates as good those "noble" souls who can spontaneously and courageously impose their will on the world, achieving their goals and directly translating their desires into effective and satisfying action; and it condemns as bad those persons who lack the greatness of soul needed to achieve such remakings of the world in their own image—the timid, the feeble, the weak, those who defer to the wants and needs of others. What we think of as true morality is a mirror image of these valuations; it transposes their positive and negative poles, and it gives primary emphasis not to the celebration of what it deems good, but to the condemnation of what it deems evil.

This doubled opposition within the moral domain between master morality and its counterpart is explained by Nietzsche not as a sheer accident, but as the result of a historical development. More specifically, Christian morality is a belated and secondary cultural phenomenon; its origin lies in a certain responsiveness, indeed a very powerful negative reaction, to the historically prior value system of master morality. And what in turn explains the reactive ressentiment of Christian morality is that it is designed to serve the specific function of protecting and advancing the interests of those in society who suffer most from the hitherto-unquestioned prevalence of master morality—the feeble, the timid, and the weak (those Nietzsche thinks of as nature's slaves). Life for them in a society governed by the values of master morality is not just one in which they are as a matter of fact pushed around by nature's masters, but in which their culture praises these natural nobles for so doing and condemns them for being the kind of people who allow it to happen. If, however, society's modes of evaluating human action and personality could be inverted, so that the kinds of behaviour that at once characterize and benefit nature's nobles could be condemned, and the kinds of behaviour that come naturally to the slavish, and that redound to their advantage, could be celebrated; then the lives of the slaves would not only become worth living, but would be reconceived by one and all as the pinnacle of human fulfilment.

Already, then, the overt meaning of slave morality—its espousal of selflessness—stands revealed by Nietzsche as in the service of self-interest. Christian altruism is not just a moral code that comes naturally to the naturally weak and feeble; its function is to serve their own interests against those of others, as a weapon in the war between nobles and slaves. Indeed, insofar as it inculcates a system that punishes the naturally noble for giving expression to their greatness of soul and invites us to take pleasure in the infliction of that suffering, it encourages and rewards an essentially sadistic aspect of our personalities. At the same time, however, it caters to our masochistic impulses, in that it encourages us not only to condemn and repress any behavioural manifestation of such noble impulses of self-expression and self-imposition that might arise in us, but also to root out even their internal (purely mental or imaginative) expression—to scour and scarify our souls as well as our lives. In other words, the inherent cruelty of slave morality turns inward as well as outward. And of course, in condemning any expression of the human capacity to impose one's will upon the world, as well as any desire to enhance that capacity, slave morality amounts (in Nietzsche's eyes) to a condemnation of the basic principle or impulse of life—what might be called the will to power; it therefore constitutes a denial of life, a refusal of the vital core of our own existence and that of existence as such.

For Nietzsche, then, the true meaning of Christ's cross is not only contrary to, but radically subversive of, its overt significance; Christian morality's apparent commitment to self-sacrifice is in fact an expression of a fundamentally self-interested, sadomasochistic denial of life. Little wonder, then, that the corpse of the Christian God reeks of hypocrisy; for Nietzsche, Christianity is a whited sepulchre, but what matters most is that it is essentially sepulchral, centred on the tomb of a stigmatized human body. To affirm it is to affirm death against life; and this recounting of the morality of self-denial is aimed not at demonstrating the falsity of its claims but rather at rendering them definitively repellent.

However, to understand the full complexity of Nietzsche's diagnosis here, we need to recall that his autopsy of the divine comprises in part a disarticulation of it—an acknowledgement of the internal complexity of its skeleton, the sheer variety of its constituent elements and the particularity of their development over time. To take one example: Nietzsche argues that the internalization of sadomasochistic cruelty that is effected through the Christian conception of conscience, and institutionalized in the practice of confession, is the historical seed of a broader cultural asceticism that he labels "the will to truth." This stance or attitude has its religious and moral inflections, in which extremes of self-imposed suffering are licensed by the invocation of an underlying internal reality that must be sought out despite the punishment that the search inflicts on the seeker; but the same ascetic conception of truth-seeking also finds expression in science (insofar as the scientist conceives of himself as a monk of knowledge, making himself as nothing in order that reality reveal itself to him as such, and conceives of reality as having an essence or rational order that lies behind and hence devalues the flux of appearances—a reality of Being rather than Becoming), and in philosophy (with its Socratic commitments to the intelligibility of the real, to the search for rational order—whether written into the world or imposed upon it, to the idea that our moral status is immune to contingency, and so on). From this perspective, the body of Christianity has rather more limbs and members, and hence is articulated rather more intensively and extensively, than one might imagine; consequently, its full decomposition will constitute a pervasive transformation of Western culture. Fully acknowledging the death of God will involve far more than endorsing atheism, and far more even than an overcoming of nonreligious versions of the Christian moral values of altruism and self-sacrifice; it will mean scouring science and philosophy of its inherent asceticism.

Another important disarticulation is the one Nietzsche attempts to effect upon the concept of conscience itself. From within slave morality, the possession of a conscience is internal to one's status as a human being; but Nietzsche claims that the Christian conception of what it is to possess a conscience is a specific, complex inflection of a structure of subjectivity that might be and has been inflected otherwise. He sees the origin of conscience in the human animal's capacity to see itself as indebted—that is, as legitimately subject to the claims of creditors as a result of its previous actions, and thus as capable of being held responsible in the present for what it did in the past. This is Nietzsche's basic conception of humans as those animals capable of making promises (and hence of keeping them, or failing to do so)—as binding themselves over time, and thus constituting themselves as one and the same subjectivity despite time's vicissitudes.

The idea of bad conscience emerges from this more basic idea of indebtedness when the individual comes to reinforce the creditors' external exaction of responsibility with an internal counterpart, one that is constituted by the subject's turning its instinctual cruelty on itself, and thereby establishing an inner, self-punishing voice. But Nietzsche sees a further element in the Christian notion of conscience—an absolutizing of our indebtedness, a searing and relentless sense of guilt, one that conjures and constitutes a sense of ourselves as not just guilty of specific transgressions but as fundamentally and structurally reprehensible and inadequate beyond or before any specifically reprehensible thoughts or deeds for which we might be responsible. On this reading, the distinguishing mark of the distinctively ascetic form of bad conscience is the despairing, masochistic, life-denying conception of human beings as originally sinful creatures.

The point of this disarticulation of the concept of conscience is thus to contest the Christian conception of human beings as necessarily, essentially guilty before God—as sinful simply by virtue of being human. For Nietzsche, that identification of humanity and sinfulness—the burden of the Christian conception of the Fall—is not only a contingent, but also a reactive and secondary episode in our development; it is not just that it could in principle be otherwise, but that in fact it was otherwise, before human beings turned away from an interpretation of themselves in the terms of master morality, and reconceived the necessary indebtedness of their subjectivity in terms of an absolute, self-annihilating guilt. This does not in itself show that Christian values are false, and nor did Nietzsche think that it does; but it certainly shows that Nietzsche's genealogy of Christianity embodies its own myth of the Fall. For Nietzsche, that profoundly determinative human perversion of the human is to be found in our acceptance of the Christian myth of the Fall; that is, our acceptance of the doctrine of human nature as Fallen is itself the moment of our true Fall, a falling away from celebrating natural nobility and life itself and a turning toward a reactive condemnation of nobility and life as evil. Our Fall does indeed lie in our catastrophic awakening to a knowledge of existence as evaluable in terms of good and evil, our eating of the fruit of that tree; but since that event is presented to us in Nietzsche's recounting of it as essentially historical, and hence contingent, it necessarily appears as dismantlable, alterable, capable of being overcome. This is Nietzsche's way of attempting to make the words of the book of Genesis mean otherwise.

But does he succeed in his attempt? Our doubts about this might be encouraged when we come to see that his counter-myth of our Fall from a paradisal state is ineradicably ambivalent about the value of the target of his genealogical critique. To begin with, if we accept Nietzsche's own conception of life as essentially will to power, and of this will as finding human expression in our ability to deploy and cultivate a capacity to remake the world in our own image, then the slave revolt in morality—its transformation of indebtedness beyond good bad conscience to guilt and original sin—cannot but appear as one of the most successful expressions of the will to power in human history. For human weaklings, lacking any direct physical and psychological resources to fight the nobles on their own terms and oppressed as much by the expression of that nobility in their system of valuation as by their courage and willpower—for such creatures so completely to revalue those values as to subject the naturally noble to punitive social critique, to the internalization of those self-critical values, and thereby in effect to enslave them to the purposes and interests of nature's slaves, is surely more than enough to identify these supposed weaklings as eagles in lamb's clothing.

Nietzsche's counter-myth thus appears to imply that the life-denying asceticism of Christianity must be regarded as itself an expression or affirmation of life; it posits a conception of life as will to power according to which life feeds on its own negation, enhancing itself not despite denials of it but most spectacularly and decisively through those denials. And this suggestion of something inherently perverse in Nietzsche's conception of life is reinforced by his genealogy of the Christian will to power in its deflected expressions as various forms of the will to truth.

For if the will to truth is itself an inflection of the Christian
ascetic impulse, and if Nietzsche's genealogy of that impulse
culminates in his discovery of the true meaning not only of
slave morality and asceticism but also of the will to truth, then
Nietzsche's own analysis is at once a radical unmasking of that
impulse and a further expression of it. Even the genealogical
method cannot shake off its indebtedness to the historical formations and reformations of the very life-denying, sadomasochistic impulse it aims to uproot; its subversive purpose is essentially a further step in the unfolding of the perverse form of
the will to power that is Christian asceticism. Hence, Nietzsche
finds himself in the perverse position of criticizing (as inherently perverse) the condition for the possibility of his own critique; and at the very least, this raises the question of whether
his conception of life as will to power is not just such that it
can find perverse, self-subverting forms of expression, but is in
reality incapable of finding any other form of expression. We
shall return to this.

Nietzsche's own understanding of what constitutes an affirmation of life, as well as the indebtedness of his own project
to the Christian asceticism it analyses, therefore gives him two
strong reasons to celebrate slave morality at least as strenuously
as he condemns it. But the entanglement of his own criticisms
in the value-system they aim to criticize in fact goes far deeper
than this; for the central elements of his genealogical counter-
myth run the risk of simply reiterating the Christian myth
they overtly deplore. For example, if Nietzsche is to maintain his claim that the true Fall is our world-historically significant but nevertheless dismantlable revaluation of ourselves as
fallen, then we must regard the slave revolt against master morality as an event in human history, and hence regard the reign
of master morality as itself a historical episode. This reading of
Nietzsche's tale is reinforced by his talk of etymological traces
of a human culture in which the familiar words of morality were
meant otherwise, and of his citation of ancient Greek literature

as exemplifying the form of life against which the Pauline revaluation of Judaism is a reaction. But it is hard to avoid a sense
that Nietzsche's descriptions of his nobles attain a mythic as
well as an archaeological register; their instinctive self-confi-
dence, their willingness directly to impose their will upon the
world, the joy they take in one another's natural nobility, and
their equally untroubled contempt for those who are not their
peers—these evoke a prelapsarian paradise in which the will to
power finds straightforward expression and achieves apparently
effortless dominance. By contrast, the vicissitudes of the will to
power after the slave revolt suggest an ineradicable perversity,
a sense of life as inherently tending toward its own denial, its
inner teleology always already awry, beyond hope of correction
even by the analyst who most clearly sees the pervasiveness of
its deflection from its own fulfilment.

For the mode of existence of the prelapsarian nobles to constitute a genuine, historically realizable alternative to Christian
asceticism, we would have to be able to recognize a form of life
untouched by the various expressions of slave morality's denials
of life as nevertheless human. But on Nietzsche's own account,
Western culture's institutional expressions of philosophical,
scientific, religious, and moral impulses are pervaded by asceticism; and it is hard to see how human life in society (hence, any
human life) would be possible without at least the internalization of the structures of the good bad conscience, and thus a
willingness to repress the direct external expression of instinctual cruelty by deflecting it back upon oneself. Indeed, it is hard
to see how anything resembling human subjectivity as such
would be recognizable without that capacity to introduce systematically a hiatus between an impulse and its external expression; for the concept of subjectivity seems internally related to
the idea of consciousness of oneself as possessed of an inner as
well as an outer life—a life or stream of thought and desire that
can continue to flow in the absence of its external manifestations. But Nietzsche's rhapsodies about the wholly spontaneous

instinctual life of the nobles have an inveterate tendency to suggest that for them there is no hiatus between impulse and expression—between conceiving a desire and acting to satisfy it; the distinction between an event in their interior lives and one in their exterior lives barely gets a grip. In other words, the very features of their mode of existence that most encourage Nietzsche's inclination to think of it as paradisal are just what give us grounds for doubting that it counts as a human form of life. Nietzsche's repeated resort to descriptions of them as blond beasts, and beasts of prey, inadvertently reinforces the suspicion that he is imagining a stage of human prehistory, a kind of animality, and thereby asking us—in just the way the author of the book of Genesis asks us—to think of the prelapsarian state as at once a fulfilment of human nature and a freedom from it.

The endlessly shifting, duplicitous status of the nobles is epitomized in the peculiar role Nietzsche assigns to the priests in his account of the slave revolt. For of course, there is a central opacity in that account, understood as the chronicle of a historical event. Whilst his analysis makes it crystal clear why such a revolt would be much to the slaves"benefit, and hence one they would want to bring about, it remains unclear how they *could* actuate it, when their pre-revolt state is one of physical weakness and cultural condemnation. Nietzsche's apparent answer to this question is to invoke the influence of a priestly caste; its members are sufficiently intelligent to see the usefulness of the slaves as a means of achieving power for themselves in and over society, and hence to lead or manipulate them into the revolt and into an acceptance of the structures of guilty conscience, confession, and ecclesiastical hierarchy, which will achieve that goal. But of course, on pain of endless regress, these priests must be understood not as a species of slave, but as a species of noble—a branch of the natural aristocracy who happen to see the slaves as a means of achieving power over their peers.

The problem with this apparently neat solution to Nietzsche's analytical problem is that this internal branching or self-differentiation of master morality requires that these priests be both recognizably noble and fundamentally distinct from other nobles. To begin with, they plainly possess in the highest degree a capacity to use thought to interpose between desires and action, and to find extremely indirect ways in which those desires might come to be satisfied; in short, they possess a complex interior life of just the kind that it is the natural glory of the nobles, as Nietzsche so often presents them in their unselfconscious, unmediated expression of self-aggrandizing impulses, to lack. And in acting on their plans to enhance their own capacity to impose themselves on the world, they create and defend a value system and a culture that give expression to a pervasive denial of life. In other words, in order to explain the emergence of the perversely life-denying expression of life that is slave morality, Nietzsche has to attribute the impulse that defines it to a branch of the family of natural aristocracy whose status is defined by the lack of that impulse. In short, in recounting his version of the human fall from paradise, Nietzsche has to impute fallenness to some of those who dwell in paradise—exactly the offence to reason with which the Christian myth of the Fall is repeatedly charged.

What I have argued thus far is that, precisely because a number of considerations deriving from his own self-understanding force Nietzsche to conceptualize our emancipation from the Christian myth of our need for redemption as a kind of redemption from it, central aspects of that myth perversely persist even in his ferociously radical attempts to free himself (and us) from it. And it is worth asking, in conclusion, whether these reiterations of the pivotal, and pivotally objectionable, elements of the myth that Nietzsche is attempting to displace with his own counter-myth are not themselves caused by a certain blindness on Nietzsche's part to another, generally discounted element of that model.

The *Genealogy*'s fundamental aim is to re-present our slavish self-interpretation in terms of original sin as not necessary—as the outcome of ultimately contingent historical happenstance rather than as a revelation of our immutable essence—and thereby to open the possibility of our existing otherwise, as redeemed from a sense of ourselves as requiring divine redemption. But the doctrine of original sin is always already self-subverting in exactly this sense. For the Christian perception of humanity as originally sinful is inseparable from its perception of humanity as not only redeemable but as redeemed. The shocking, incomprehensible idea that human nature is such that we are in the wrong before God beyond any specific wrongdoing for which we could be held accountable is itself conveyed (and is in fact only conveyable) to us by Christ, by God Incarnate in human form; and that same Incarnate deity embodies the possibility of our redemption from the structurally perverse state He reveals us to occupy. In other words, in showing us to be originally sinful, Christ simultaneously shows that our sinful nature can be overcome or reborn, and hence reveals our fallenness as contingent, as no longer necessary.

Once again, then, Nietzsche's apparently heterodox project of aiming to redeem us from our conception of ourselves as structurally perverse turns out to reproduce rather than transcend a paradoxical structure of Christian thought. It therefore returns us to the second question with which we began: does Nietzsche's genealogy of the human amount to anything more that the Christian truth in foul disguise? Now, however, we are in a position to sharpen the question by rephrasing it thus: does his genealogy of morality constitute a recounting of our fallenness and our redemption, which works essentially by transposing Nietzsche himself into the role occupied in the Christian tale by Christ, and hence achieve nothing more than a further exemplification of the perennial human desire to be god—to deny the human? This was, after all, an implication glanced at by Nietzsche's madman, when contemplating the magnitude of the deicidal deed for which he claims that we are responsible: "Do we not ourselves have to become gods merely to appear worthy of it?" If so, then Nietzsche's critique of Christianity's so-called libel against ordinary, embodied, historical human existence is in fact a further expression of that libel.

2

The Dying Man and the Dazed Animal: Heidegger

IT IS NO SECRET that the concepts and values of Christianity constitute a fundamental reference point for Heidegger's existential analytic of the human mode of being (what he calls "Dasein") throughout the pages of *Being and Time*.[1] He is well aware from the outset that, given that every exercise of Dasein's capacity to question is historically situated, his own concern with the meaning of Being ("that which determines entities as entities" [*BT*, 2: 25]) must necessarily find its orientation within the philosophical tradition of questioning about Being—even if it will progress only by putting the achievements and assumptions of that tradition into question. And he further asserts that the ways in which the tradition has conceptualized human existence have been pervasively inflected by Christian theology. For the biblical vision of humans as made in God's image has, in his view, ensured that philosophical conceptions of human beings take it for granted that we are creatures at once rational (possessors of the originally divine *logos*) and transcendent (reaching yearningly beyond our merely creaturely existence). Heidegger sees traces of this theological inheritance in philoso-

---

[1] Translated by J. McQuarrie and E. Robinson (Blackwell, Oxford: 1962); hereafter, *BT*. Citations of the text refer to section number followed by page number, citations of notes in the text locate division, chapter, and then note numbers.

phy's sense of our rationality and transcendence as a supplement to our animality, and hence in what philosophers have to say not only about that which distinguishes us from other animals (our soul, spirit, rationality) but also about that which links us to them (since our bodies will be understood as that which is essentially not soul, spirit, rationality).

More generally, Heidegger thinks that theology here encourages a conception of human beings as essentially compound—as forming a whole consisting of essentially distinct elements (body, soul, and spirit) combined together. The assumption is that each element can be studied separately—by biology, psychology, and anthropology respectively—and then the results simply added together to give us a complete vision of Dasein's essential nature. In subjecting this ontotheological philosophical tradition to questioning, Heidegger means above all to take issue with the underlying assumption that Dasein's Being is compositional or additive, as well as with the claims made about each element in the putative compound. But his own analyses do not so much reject as radically rethink the theological roots of the traditional conception of human being; Dasein's internal relation to the *logos* is not only embedded in the very name of Heidegger's philosophical method (phenomenology) but also appears (under the heading of "discourse") at the heart of his account of Dasein's Being, as does an idea of Dasein as transcendent. Accordingly, we must say that his fundamental ontology detaches itself no more from its theological than from its philosophical horizons.

And of course, there is a more proximate relation to Christian thought in the genesis and working-out of Heidegger's existential analytic of Dasein—one that lies in Heidegger's relationship to Kierkegaard. In three notes, Heidegger at once acknowledges his indebtedness to Kierkegaard's work and stresses its limitations: "The man who has gone furthest in analysing the concept of anxiety . . . is Søren Kierkegaard" (*BT*, div. 1, chap. 6, n. iv); "Søren Kierkegaard explicitly seized upon the problem of existence as an existentiell problem, and thought it through in a penetrating fashion. But the existential problematic was so alien to him that, as regards his ontology, he remained completely dominated by Hegel" (*BT*, div. 2, chap. 1, n. vi); "S. Kierkegaard is probably the one who has seen the *existentiell* phenomenon of the moment of vision with the most penetration; but this does not signify that he has been correspondingly successful in interpreting it existentially" (*BT*, div. 2. chap. 4, n. iii). The point of criticism here is clear: Kierkegaard is a penetrating analyst of certain specific, concrete modes of Dasein's Being (what Heidegger calls "existentiell states"), but leaves entirely unclear the underlying ontological bases for these states, that about Dasein's basic nature which makes them possible, and hence does not even begin any genuinely fundamental ontological analyses of Dasein (the distinctive purpose of Heidegger's existential analytic).

It is far from clear, however, that Heidegger's claims establish the distance he seeks from his Kierkegaardian sources of inspiration. After all, it is central to his own understanding of human inquiry that it can never be free of presuppositions; the idea of an Archimedean starting-point for questioning conducted by a being who is always necessarily situated, and hence always already oriented in relation to its questioning (which would anyway be entirely directionless in the absence of some provisional understanding of the subject matter of its questioning) is an empty fantasy. But if the Kierkegaardian analyses that contextualize and orient Heidegger's account at critical points in its development are, as Heidegger admits, themselves contextualized and oriented by "the purview of Christian theology" (*BT* div. 1, chap. 6, n. iv), then his own inquiries cannot simply leave behind or otherwise straightforwardly neutralize Kierkegaard's initiating orientation. They must, rather, acknowledge it by actively deconstructing it. Hence, Heidegger famously and extensively resorts to quasi-theological terminology (falling, guilt, conscience, and so on) whilst denying that what he means to say with it either is or presupposes any theological claim.

This is not an obvious contradiction, or a piece of self-serving disingenuousness; it is an unavoidable structure of his thinking. If the form of his existential analytic of Dasein is not to subvert its content, it must conform to the conditions which that analysis claims must hold for any mode of Dasein's questioning kind of Being; and (amongst other things) that means he must use the words of Christianity, at both general and specific levels, whilst meaning them otherwise. Our question is, can he—any more than Nietzsche—succeed in so doing? And this question is sharpened by the knowledge that one of the pivotal Kierkegaardian analyses by which Heidegger orients himself is that of anxiety—angst or dread. For in Kierkegaard's hands, that concept is explicitly worked out by reference to the Christian myth of the Fall, and hence to the doctrine of original sin. Can Heidegger benefit from the existentiell roots and fruits of this myth and doctrine without remaining too close for comfort to its theological horizon?

1. AUTHENTICITY AND FALLING

Of the three sources of tension or instability entrained by this specific theological indebtedness that I propose to examine in this chapter, the first is perhaps the most obvious. It concerns Heidegger's claim that Dasein's average everyday mode of existence—the state it typically occupies—is inauthentic, and his correlative conception of Dasein's Being as falling.

Heidegger's initial definition of Dasein's Being entails the thought that Dasein is always subject to evaluation as authentic or inauthentic; for when he claims that Dasein is the kind of Being for whom the Being—the essential nature—of beings is an issue, something that is at once comprehensible and questionable (that presents itself as meaningful, but in such a way as to provoke and reward further inquiry), that claim necessarily includes the issue of its own Being. He means by this that Dasein's existence is such that it constantly confronts the question of whether and how to continue that existence into the future; and the answer it gives is never ultimately determined by (although it may be importantly conditioned by) anything outside its own decision to project upon, and hence realize, one of the existential possibilities available to it.

Dasein has no essence that simply finds expression in its particular modes of existence, as an acorn fulfils its nature by becoming an oak tree; Dasein may have fundamental biological needs, and it may confront profound social and cultural demands, but the precise significance or meaning to attach to any of them remains a question that each Dasein confronts, and to which it necessarily gives a specific answer, in the choices it makes about how to live—choices that reveal and reinforce a commitment to certain values, and hence to certain conceptions of what constitutes a valuable form of human life, and thus to certain conceptions of what it is to be human. In other words, uniquely amongst beings, Dasein's existence precedes and determines its essence.

Thus, Dasein's existence manifests what Heidegger calls "mineness": it is the kind of thing for which Dasein can take responsibility, something it owns, an expression of its individuality; hence, its life can equally manifest a refusal of mineness, a disowning of responsibility, a loss or absence of individuality. Heidegger's view is that, for the most part, Dasein evades its responsibility for its existence, exhibiting what he calls inauthenticity; and since on his analysis Dasein's Being is Being-with—since its modes of self-relation necessarily go together with modes of relating to other Dasein—this inauthentic state is called "das man," existence in the "One" or the "they." In the "they," one's individuality is neutered or neutralized: one thinks, says, and does whatever one thinks, says, and does because that is what is done—that is what one does, what everyone is doing. One's opinions, preoccupations, and losses of interest, the films one sees and the books one reads, the achievements one values—these are all related to as beyond question, as not raising any issues of personal choice or judgement, as if something to which we are fated or determined.

For Heidegger, this impersonal, unquestioning relation to our own existence and that of other Dasein also finds expression in a peculiarly unquestioning relation to all the beings we encounter in our world. This mode of disclosing entities in their Being is what Heidegger calls "falling"; he specifies it in terms of idle talk, curiosity, and ambiguity. In this state, our understanding is uprooted from any attentiveness to entities as they are in themselves; instead it takes up, and is taken up by, what is typically said about them—how they are to be understood, how anyone and everyone understands them. Our interest in the entities themselves is deflected into an interest in what is said about them, and hence our desire to penetrate more deeply into their true nature is perverted into an endless search for novelty (whether new situations and experiences or new ways of talking about old ones) purely for novelty's sake, and a consequent inability to distinguish the insightful from the superficial—indeed an inability to find a grip for that distinction at all, a loss of any sense that discourse (human talk and thought, the *logos*) might be weighty or profound as opposed to free-floating and empty.

The idea of Dasein's fallenness thus captures the phenomenon of inauthenticity from the point of view of our engagements with entities in the world. It delineates our everyday state as one in which an Adamic ability to name the essence of things has degenerated into the sophistic nightmare of words engendering more words in an increasingly turbulent Babel within which the very idea of an external reality to which human speech might be responsive and responsible is rendered null and void. As Heidegger will elsewhere express it: for the most part, Dasein lives in untruth, in flight from its fundamental capacity to encounter beings in their Being, and hence in flight from itself.

Notoriously, however, Heidegger's text is profoundly ambivalent about the ontological status of our fallen absorption in the they, and thus about the very distinction that he uses to fence off Kierkegaard's analyses from the field of fundamental ontology—that between the merely ontic (in the case of Dasein, the domain of the existentiell) and the genuinely ontological (the domain of Dasein's existentialia). His initial discussion of the they in chapter 4 of division 1 suggests a simple regimentation of the analysis: the relevant ontological structure is Dasein's Being-with (which indicates that there is no such thing as a mode of Dasein's Being that is not a mode of relatedness to other Dasein), and the they is one—admittedly common and even dominant—concrete, existentiell inflection of Dasein's Being-with. And yet, at the end of that chapter, Heidegger describes the they "as an essential existentiale" (*BT*, 27: 168)—in other words, as an aspect of Dasein's ontological structure. The same ambivalence attends his discussion of fallenness in chapter 5. Once again, the relevant ontological structure seems clearly to be that of Being-in—Dasein's openness to its world as mattering or meaningful, in ways that its thoughts and actions must accommodate but can also alter; then "fallenness" would appear as one (admittedly typical or even all-but-unavoidable) specific ontic variant of Dasein's Being-in. And yet, in the very next chapter, Heidegger tells us that "the fundamental ontological characteristics of [Dasein] are existentiality, facticity, and Being-fallen" (*BT*, 41: 235); in effect, our fallenness is internal to our Being.

This ambivalence matters not so much because it confronts us with an unclarity that asks to be removed, but because fallen existence in the they is inauthentic; so if Heidegger's analysis built these markers of inauthenticity into Dasein's ontological structure, there could no longer be a particular concrete state of Dasein that did not manifest them, and hence authentic existence would be inconceivable. In the context of our concerns in this book, that would amount to a conception of Dasein as not just commonly or even inveterately in flight from its own authentic fulfilment, but as inherently perverse or fallen beyond any conceivable redemption—a conclusion that would make it hard to accept Heidegger's claim that "ontically, we have not decided whether man is 'drunk with sin' and in the *status corruptionis*, whether he walks in the *status integritatus*, or whether he finds himself in an intermediate stage, the *status gratiae*" (*BT*, 38: 224).

Interpretative charity alone would surely suggest that we correct Heidegger's ambivalence here in the direction of the stable solution that the basic structure of his analysis anyway allows—consigning the they and fallenness definitively to the realm of the ontic rather than the ontological. However, there are good grounds for believing that Heidegger's apparently isolated and excisable contradictory claims are in fact responsive to an important aspect of his conception of Dasein's situation—more specifically, of his conception of Dasein as always inhabiting a world (in his terms, Dasein's Being-in-the-world). For in the chapter preceding that concerned with the they, Heidegger unfolds the ontological structure of this worldliness in a way that commits him (at the very least) to the view that it is no accident inauthenticity should be the average everyday human state.

According to him, the underlying structure of Dasein's world is a widely ramifying web of socially defined concepts, roles, functions, and functional interrelations, in the absence of which human beings could not grasp and question objects as they are, whether as the matrix for their practical activities or for the purposes of more "pure" cognitive inquiry. So when Heidegger points out that Dasein's Being is also Being-with, he underlines the fact that human beings, no less than objects, are part of that same web. The primary terms in which they understand themselves are given by their socially defined and culturally inherited roles, whose nature is in turn given prior to and independently of their own individuality, and that typically will not be significantly marked by their temporary inhabitation of them. In other words, we relate to ourselves as practitioners—as followers of the rules, customs, and habits definitive of proper practice in any given field of endeavour. Such practices are necessarily interpersonal, and so importantly impersonal.

It must be possible for others to occupy exactly the same role, to engage in exactly the same practice, if only because society and culture could not otherwise be reproduced. Accordingly, Dasein always begins by understanding itself in terms that have no essential connection with its identity as an individual, that do not pick out any particular individual even if they do require particular kinds of skill or aptitude. They specify not what you or I must do in order to occupy them, but rather what one must do—what must be done. The role-occupant thus specified is an idealization or construct, an abstract or average human being rather than anyone in particular; it is, in effect, akin to the they-self.

Little wonder, then, that Heidegger presents the they as a "primordial phenomenon [belonging] to Dasein's positive constitution" (*BT*, 27: 167), thereby expressing an unwillingness simply to regard it as ontic—which might be thought to imply that it is merely one amongst a range of concrete possibilities any one of which we might occupy. That would certainly be misleading since, given our worldliness, inauthenticity must at the very least be our default position, and authenticity an achievement—a state we attain by wrenching ourselves away from inauthenticity, rather than one that we will always find ourselves already occupying. As Heidegger puts it: "If Dasein discovers the world in its own way and brings it close, if it discloses to itself its own authentic Being, then this discovery of the 'world' and this disclosure of Dasein are always accomplished as a clearing away of concealment and obscurities, as a breaking up of the disguises with which Dasein bars its own way" (*BT*, 27: 167). And yet it seems at least as misleading, for reasons already rehearsed, to say that the they is "an essential existentiale" of Dasein (*BT*, 27: 168); for that would seem to prevent us from viewing authenticity as a conceivable achievement, however belated—and hence would block the very idea of it as "an existentiell modification of the 'they' " (*BT*, 27: 168).

Even this account of Heidegger's thinking does not, then, justify his strongest claims about the depth of our fallenness, although it may explain their presence. It also suggests a certain instability at the heart of his analysis. For it implies that our inauthenticity is neither straightforwardly factual (a sheer contingency—a simple fact that might as easily have been otherwise) nor straightforwardly necessary; and something about any given Dasein's state that is more than a fact but less than a necessity is neither ontic nor ontological. Hence, this dimension of evaluation to which Heidegger tells us Dasein's Being is necessarily subject fundamentally unsettles the distinction between ontic and ontological matters around which the whole of his philosophical project is meant to pivot.

However, the deepest problem posed by the question of Dasein's fallenness concerns the way in which his investigations here (as elsewhere) run up against obstacles and obscurities that not only block the way to a clear understanding of Dasein's Being, but appear to emerge from the depths of that Being. Heidegger is insistent throughout his analysis that Dasein is essentially the Being for whom the Being of beings is an issue; and Dasein's capacity for authenticity is simply an aspect of this distinctive nature—an implication of the fact that Dasein's own Being must therefore be an issue for it. Hence, Heidegger is committed to the thought that clarity about its own Being and an authentic realization of that questioning comprehension constitute the fulfilment of Dasein's distinctive kind of (relation to beings in their) Being. Yet he is also committed to the thought that Dasein systematically lives out its life inauthentically, in flight from what is most proper to it, most its own. And our exploration of fallenness suggests that the cause of this pervasive perversion of our Being lies in us. For if what persistently entangles and absorbs us in the worlds we inhabit is something inherent in our worldliness, then the very structures that make it possible for Dasein to comprehend and question the Being of beings are also what hinder it from exercising that capacity. Dasein's nature is such that it bars its own way to what belongs most properly to that nature.

Heidegger's analyses endlessly return to this self-subverting aspect of Dasein and display its pervasiveness, but without ever exactly accounting for it; in effect, they elaborate upon his opening claim that in Dasein's ways of comporting itself towards entities "there lies *a priori* an enigma" (*BT*, 1: 23). But if Heidegger's conception of Dasein's enigmatic turning away from itself, its self-inflicted blindness to its defining capacity to own its own life, is that it is more than an error and less than a fate, then he is reiterating with remarkable faithfulness the Christian perception of human beings as at once irremediably lost and open to redemption.

2. Mortality and Wholeness

This suggestion is, of course, one that Heidegger would resist; he constantly claims that his existential analytic of Dasein is scrupulously neutral with respect to theological matters—neither presupposing nor criticizing them. And yet, the way in which he elaborates upon his conception of Dasein's authenticity in division 2 of *Being and Time*, by arguing that Dasein's existence can become at once genuinely individual and genuinely whole only by relating in a particular way to death, appears to mount an implicit critique of Kierkegaardian understandings of the human need for God.

Kierkegaard's philosophical pseudonym, Johannes Climacus, shares the Heideggerian view that human beings continuously confront the question of how they should live, and so must locate some standard or value by reference to which they might make that choice. And insofar as it is intended to govern every such choice, it confers significance on the whole life that these moments make up; the life that grows from a series of choices made by reference to the same standard will necessarily manifest an underlying unity. Climacus thus understands that question of how to live as a question about what gives meaning to one's life as a whole; and he goes on to argue that only a religious answer to that question will do.

Suppose we start by aiming at a specific goal or achievement to give our life meaning—the pursuit of power or wealth, the development of a talent. Since such goals have significance only insofar as the person concerned desires them, what is giving meaning to her life is in reality her wants and dispositions. But such dispositions can alter, and even if they do not, they might have been otherwise; so staking my life on a desire I merely happen to have would amount to staking it on a sheer accident, and thereby to depriving it of any genuine meaning. And anyway, since I always have more than one desire, when I do act in accordance with one as opposed to another of my desires, I am in effect choosing between them; so the true foundation of my existence is not whatever desires I happen to have but my capacity to choose between them.

Can we avoid our difficulty, as well as self-deception, by explicitly grounding our lives on our capacity to choose—by, for example, relating to our sexual impulses by choosing an unconditional commitment to marriage, or choosing to view a talent as a vocation? We can thereby choose not to permit changes in our desires or in the circumstances of their implementation to alter the shape of our lives; we simply will to maintain their unity and integrity regardless of fluctuations in the intensity of our wants, and so create a self for ourselves. Even if this insulates us from the impact of shifting contingencies, however, it presupposes that the human will can be the source of life's meaning; but that capacity is still a part of the person's life, and so a part of that which has to be given meaning as a whole, and no part can give meaning to the whole of which it is a part. With respect to it, as with any of a person's desires and dispositions, we can still ask: What justifies the choice of the capacity to choose as the basis of one's life? What confers meaning on it?

This way of stating the difficulty plainly suggests that the question existence sets us is not answerable in terms of anything within it; life cannot determine its own significance in terms of (some element of) itself. Meaning can only be given to one's life as a whole by relating it to something outside it; for it is only to something outside it that my life can be related *as a whole*. Only such a standard could give a genuinely unconditional answer to the question of the meaning of one's life. Only by relating oneself to such an absolute Good, and thus relativizing the importance of finite (and so conditional) goods, can we properly answer the question existence poses. And such an absolute Good is, for Climacus, just another name for God; we can relate properly to each moment of our existence only by relating our lives as a whole to God.

Against this background, the striking thing about Heidegger's analysis of authenticity in division 2 is how much of it he accepts. We might, for example, want to question Climacus's insistent conjoining of authenticity and wholeness, and his valuing of the absolute or unconditional over the contingent. Even if our life as such can be at stake in our choices, why must we choose in such a way as to make that life into a single, integrated whole? And if the choice of a life of multiplicity would actually manifest an integrating commitment to a single standard of choice (i.e., diversity), does that not make the idea of wholeness an empty, and so unconstraining, condition on our thinking here? As for Climacus's idea of the Absolute, the key issue here may not so much be why we should prefer it over the contingent, but rather how we might give it any content at all.

But Heidegger does not take up any of these possible lines of criticism. On the contrary: he restarts his existential analytic of Dasein at the beginning of division 2 by invoking the idea of wholeness or completeness as both an individual and a methodological goal, and criticizing his earlier analysis for failing to achieve that goal. In part, this is because he has hitherto focussed on Dasein in its average everyday modes of existence, and hence omitted (in effect left unanalysed) its less familiar, more exceptional authentic modes. But most importantly, he has overlooked an aspect of Dasein's Being that resists the ideal of completeness to which he continues to aspire. For if Dasein is confronted with the task of realizing some or other possibility of its Being for as long as it exists, then it can never achieve wholeness, for it will always be ahead of itself, necessarily relating itself to something that it is not yet. And yet, of course, Dasein does have an end; it understands itself as relating to its own future completion, even though when its span of existence completes itself, it will no longer be there—it will be dead.

It appears, then, that every Dasein must acknowledge its own necessary relation to an end and yet be incapable, for as long as it exists, of bringing that existence into its own grasp as a whole by actually relating to it as having an end, as being (at least in principle) capable of completeness. And if this task appears impossible from the viewpoint of any actually existing Dasein, how can it be achieved within an ontological account of Dasein's kind of existence? How can any individual produce a genuinely complete existential analytic of its own kind of Being if it cannot even bring its own Being into view as a whole?

Heidegger's solution to the problem is not to follow Kierkegaard's Climacus in saying that we must invoke a reference point lying wholly outside Dasein's existence. But neither does it involve invoking something lying wholly inside that existence—such as one's will or capacity for choice. Rather, it involves relating from within that existence to one of its limits or conditions—that of death. In effect, Heidegger says that Dasein cannot understand its Being as a whole by grasping its own death (since when its death becomes actual, it is no longer there to grasp it or anything else); and it cannot do so by grasping the death of other Dasein (since that would not permit it to grasp the mineness of that death, and hence the mineness of death as such—its always being the death of someone in particular). Hence, we must understand death in the way we understand the being whose end death is—we must grasp it existentially. We must, in other words, regard it not as an actuality but as a possibility—a possibility that we relate to, or fail to, not when we actually die but in our life.

In these terms, death distinguishes itself as our ownmost, non-relational, not-to-be-outstripped possibility. It is that possibility in which what is at issue is nothing less than Dasein's Being-in-the-world; it impends at every moment of our existence; its realization at some point or other is certain, and hence inescapable; and in relating to it, all our relations to any other Dasein are undone—no one can die my death for me.

And what that analysis reveals is that no one can live my life for me. For Dasein to live out its life in relation to its mortality (so understood) is for it to acknowledge that there is no moment of its existence in which its Being is not at issue—that its Being matters to it, and that what matters is not just its individual moments but the totality of those moments: its life as a whole. Its life is its own to live, or to disown; it makes a claim that cannot be sloughed off onto Others. And insofar as our kind of life is fated to be utterly nullified by death, we must acknowledge its utter non-necessity: the non-necessity of our birth, of the actual course of our life, of its continuation from one moment to the next. Being-toward-death is thus a matter of living in a way that does not treat the merely possible or actual or conditionally necessary as a matter of fate or destiny beyond any question or alteration—the stance that the they exemplifies and inculcates. It means stripping out false necessities—becoming properly attuned to the real modalities of finite human existence.

In effect, then, understanding ourselves as essentially Being-toward-death counters our typical inauthentic flight from our individuality, our fallen absorption in the world; it offers us a way of grasping our existence as a *finite* whole, and hence offers Heidegger's existential analytic as a way of representing Dasein's Being as such a whole, without our having to relate that existence to anything wholly external to, and hence other than, Dasein—any Kierkegaardian notion of an absolute Good, a non-finite Other. On Heidegger's understanding of human mortality, a proper grasp of human existence as essentially conditioned does not require any notion of a transcendental Deity, and hence of the absolutely unconditioned, as its horizon; rather, insofar as any such horizon is necessary, it is given by (our relating to) one exemplary instance or aspect of our conditionedness—death. Since a condition or limit of our existence is not a part of that existence—not an element or component of it in the way our desires or will might be—it avoids the Kierkegaardian critique aimed at positions that invoke such parts to give meaning to the whole, and thereby reveals the non-necessity of Climacus's transition from that which lies within our existence to that which lies without. We are, in short, not fated to faith.

Such a reading of Heidegger's analysis of human mortality is cogent; but it conceals certain difficulties that must be disclosed in the context of this book's concerns.[2] First, it depends upon an incomplete reading of Kierkegaard's Climacus, and in particular of his invocation of an absolute grounding for any adequate answer to the question of the meaning of Dasein's existence. For if we look more closely at what Climacus takes to be

---

[2] These are difficulties that I was forced to pass over in my necessarily summary treatment of this issue in *Heidegger and* Being and Time.

involved in our relating absolutely to an absolute Good, he does not propose to clarify the matter by giving us a specification of the substance of the absolutely Good, as if it were another (transcendental or supernatural) kind of entity in contrast to such natural kinds as money or power or talents—a move that would indeed raise the troubling question of how we can give any sense to the idea of a supernatural or transcendental being, when our grasp of what it is for something to be, to exist, is wholly given by and in our worldly relations to worldly beings. Rather, he defines it solely by contrast with its nonreligious counterparts.

They amount to various modes of relating absolutely to what is relatively good—that is, to treating some particular contingent, changeable thing (such as money, power, or talents) as always to be preferred whenever their pursuit comes into conflict with other goods. Relating absolutely to the absolutely good, by contrast, means relating relatively to such relative goods—that is, treating no such good as absolutely valuable in the above sense, but rather regarding them all as possessed of real but finite or relative value, as never amounting to something for which anything and everything else should be sacrificed. It is not that we relate relatively to such goods and in addition relate absolutely to something else—the absolutely Good, or God. It is, rather, that relating absolutely to the absolute *just means* relating relatively to every existing source of value; insofar as one treats every worldly value as non-absolute, then to precisely that extent one is relating to God as the only absolute value.

In short, to live out a relation to God understood as the absolutely Good just is to live out a certain kind of intraworldly existence; the substance of this vision of existence is given entirely in terms of a certain kind of worldly form of life. Accordingly, on this reading, Climacus's conception of the religious form of life is not vulnerable to the charge that it invokes a notion of the infinite or the transcendent that lacks content, or that treats human conditionedness or finitude as a limitation that deprives us of participation in another, better mode of existence that would somehow lack the defining limits of any recognizably human form of life. The Kierkegaardian point would instead be that to regard any interworldly goods as absolute would be to misunderstand their worldly, and hence essentially contingent, nature, and so to misrelate oneself to the world, and thereby to misrelate oneself to oneself (understood as a worldly being). In this respect, Heidegger's talk of authenticity as a matter of properly attuning oneself to the finitude or contingency of existence, and Climacus's talk of relating absolutely to the Absolute, are in fact different ways of saying exactly the same thing.

Recalling Nietzsche's madman and his rejection as superstitious of the idea of God as any kind of entity, one might say that the burden of Climacus's conception of relating absolutely to the absolute is not to reinforce but to reject any conception of God as some kind of thing, a substance or a something. His point is, in effect, that God is best understood as no thing at all—as nothing; and this merely underlines the uncanny intimacy between Heidegger's conception of authenticity as a matter of relating oneself to death understood as an aspect of nullity or negation, and the Kierkegaardian conception of religious authenticity. The connection would be even more obvious if we recall the fact—to which Nietzsche is also sensitive—that the key symbol specific to Christianity, and hence to the version of the absolute that Kierkegaard's Climacus ultimately aims to elucidate, is that of Christ crucified. For this not only connects Climacus's notion of a refusal to absolutize the relatively valuable to a more familiar religious notion of self-sacrifice; it also suggests that we must think of this self-sacrifice not only as itself a kind of dying to or nullification of the self, but as pivoting on a certain reconception of the meaning of death. In short, to live a Christian life is to realize a radical reconception of one's relation to death, and hence of one's mortality. The more one presses the real terms of Heidegger's implicit dialogue with Kierkegaard at this pivotal point, then, the more questionable becomes the assumption that Heidegger's words transcend, or at least distance themselves from, the orbit of Christian discourse.

There is one further difficulty that requires some exploration—this time not on Kierkegaard's side of the dialogue but on Heidegger's. For it is important to see how far the phenomenon of death puts in question the powers and reach of his existential analytic of death, even when he executes the shift into genuinely existential discourse specified above. On one level, that shift appears to dissolve the problem that death poses to any practitioner of the phenomenological method. This method amounts to a specific deployment of Dasein's distinctive capacity to comprehend the phenomena it encounters, and hence to disclose them as they really are. But if death is not something that any Dasein does or could directly experience or properly open itself to, how could there be any phenomenological understanding of death in its mineness?

Analysing death existentially—that is, not as an actual event but as a possibility to which we relate ourselves from within our existence—may seem to solve the problem; but in fact it does not, or at least not without a substantial revaluation of the principles of the philosophical method being deployed. For death cannot in fact coherently be thought of as an existential possibility. Any such possibility is one that might be made actual by the Dasein whose possibility it is; we might actually produce the meal we intend to cook, or play the game for which we are training. But we cannot conceivably actualize our own death in our own life; it is not just the possibility of our own nonexistence, of our own absolute impossibility—it is an impossible possibility, an existential impossibility, a contradiction even when expressed in existential terms. An impossibility is not an unusual kind of possibility, and hence not in fact analysable in existential terms at all.

Heidegger's analysis can only succeed, therefore, if we appreciate that it works not only by shifting into existential terms, but by shifting from the ontic to the ontological level. Being-toward-death is an existential structure of Dasein's Being, not a relation within its realized existence toward a particular existential possibility; we relate to it essentially indirectly, in and through the relations we establish to any and every genuine existential possibility of our Being. In effect, for Heidegger, death is essentially a phenomenon of life; it shows up only in and through life, in and through that which it threatens to render impossible. Phenomenologically, life is death's representative, the proxy through which death's resistance to Dasein's grasp is at once acknowledged and overcome—or rather, overcome only in and through its acknowledgement as unrepresentable in itself.

So, just as any individual Dasein can achieve authenticity only by acknowledging its own internal relation to nullity or negation as the necessarily ungraspable condition for its capacity to disclose things (including itself) as they really are, so Heidegger's existential analytic of Dasein can achieve completion or wholeness only by acknowledging its internal relation to that which is beyond phenomenological representation—to nothingness, that which does not appear as such and is not an object of a possible discursive act (it is neither a phenomenon nor of the *logos*). It is not a representable something, and not an unrepresentable something either; hence, it can be represented only as beyond representation, as the beyond of the horizon of the representable, its self-concealing and self-disrupting condition. And phenomenological philosophy can only acknowledge it by allowing "nothing" first to conceal itself and then to disrupt its concealment, to constitute itself as that upon which the existential analysis is shipwrecked. Only in this way can an existential analytic of Dasein achieve the kind of completeness that its condition allows—by presenting itself as essentially incomplete, beyond completion, as completed and completable only by that which is beyond it.

But if we give death its full status as the simultaneous condition of the possibility of Dasein and the condition of its impossibility, and appreciate the degree to which the rest of division 2 further unfolds the matter of Dasein's (and hence, *Being and Time*'s) self-disrupting relation to its own negation or nothingness (in its account of guilt, conscience, and so on), then we might perhaps see an even stronger case for reading Heidegger's analysis as transposing Kierkegaard's into an only apparently different register. For Kierkegaard, our relation to God is internal to who we are and revelatory of our essential incompleteness; it is only in relation to Him that we come to see that we are constitutively enigmatic to ourselves and hence enigmatic as such—brought into and maintained in existence by our intimate relation to what is wholly Other to us, beyond our comprehension and yet endlessly met with at our every attempt to demarcate and live within our own limits or conditions.

For both Kierkegaard and Heidegger, then, it is a mark of the adequacy of any account of human nature that it find itself confronting and acknowledging a constitutive resistance to its desire for a complete and total account of its object; if any such account claims self-sufficiency it is either mistaken about itself or has failed properly to grasp its subject matter. From this perspective, the myth of the Fall—insofar as it presents the origin of human existence as essentially enigmatic and perverse, and the essential aspects of human nature (our fatedness to freedom, our unavoidable and yet self-annihilating desire for knowledge of good and evil, our essential autonomy and dependence on creation) as beyond coherent representation—bears the distinguishing marks of truth.

3. Humanity as Animality

One standard criticism of that Christian myth is that, in apparently conceiving of the familiar facets of embodiment (desire, labour, survival and reproduction, death) as manifestations of the Fall, of our falling away from our paradisal selves, it constitutes a libel against the body. It has also long been a commonplace of criticism about Heidegger's *Being and Time* that its existential analytic of Dasein overlooks or represses, let us say closes its eyes to, the embodiedness of human existence. We are repeatedly told that, in the whole of *Being and Time* "one cannot find . . . six lines on the problem of the body"—that, even at those places in Heidegger's analysis where one might expect to find a more detailed confrontation with the issue, it is avoided. And more recently, this putative omission has been linked with another popular criticism of Heidegger's work—its tendency to overlook, repress, or directly deny any essential connection between human existence and the modes of being of nonhuman animals. Against this background, Heidegger's supposed avoidance of human embodiedness appears as a compulsive or anxious aversion from that which most obviously indicates the undeniable animality of human being. So, can we conclude that this is another respect in which Heidegger's work has failed to distinguish itself sufficiently from its theological horizons?

In the end, this may turn out to be the correct conclusion, but not for the reasons just adduced. For its proponents tend to have rather too simple a conception of Heidegger's account of the relations between humanity, embodiment, and animality, and rather too simple a conception of those relations themselves. They do not sufficiently consider the possibility that Heidegger's own position is both complex and resistant to any straightforward comprehension, and that this is because Dasein's relation to its embodiment and to animality are complex and resistant to any straightforward comprehension. The truth of the matter, as Heidegger sees it, is that there is neither a simple discontinuity nor a simple continuity between humanity and animality; there is, rather, an essentially enigmatic, uncannily intimate distance between the two—and of a kind that is (I suggest) more satisfactorily encapsulated in the Christian myth of the Fall than in its secular alternatives.

Certainly, the charge that Heidegger flatly avoids embodiment in *Being and Time* can quickly be countered. For example, his analysis of Dasein's existence in space makes a point of discussing Dasein's "bodily nature" with reference to the human hand—utilizing the examples of tools and gloves to show that the left and right of bodily orientation are constitutive of Dasein's worldliness (*BT*, 23: 143ff); do such discussions repress the human body? More generally, can an existential analytic of Dasein's worldliness that articulates itself around a distinction between the readiness-to-hand and the presence-at-hand of objects, so that reference to their handiness or unhandiness for humans pervades the text, really be said to repress Dasein's embodiedness? One may, of course, feel (with Derrida) that Heidegger's pervasive inclination to treat the hand as the human body's sign and signature is open to question; but then the original objection to Heidegger's analysis simply cannot be maintained.

Moreover, the dearth of explicit references to the body in *Being and Time* surely reflects the fact that Heidegger is suspicious of any ready-to-hand concept of the human body for just the reasons he is suspicious of any ready-to-hand concepts of the human soul, spirit, subject, or consciousness—precisely because they will encapsulate theologically-rooted conceptions of both sides of a putatively dual or doubled human nature. Heidegger's term "Dasein" is carefully designed to avert his analysis from such biological and philosophical ideas of the body as much as from psychological, anthropological, and philosophical ideas of the soul or spirit. His existential analytic is, rather, intended radically to put those ideas in question, and with them the idea that the human body (any more than the human soul or spirit) is one distinguishable element in an essentially compositional human essence. In this sense, his account of Dasein's kind of Being can be read as both explicitly refusing the assumption that it must contain a specific moment or phase devoted to an account of human embodiment, and as implicitly providing such an account in every phase of its elaboration. We cannot find six sentences devoted to the problem of the human body because, in a sense, every sentence devoted to Dasein is devoted to it.

And yet, there are reasons to doubt whether Heidegger lives up to the standards he sets himself in this respect. Take, for example, another aspect of his treatment of death—surely a central point at which any analysis of the human mode of being runs up against its embodiment and hence its animality. At its outset, he distinguishes sharply between "dying," "perishing," and "demise":

> The ending of that which lives we have called "perishing." Dasein too "has" its death, of the kind appropriate to anything that lives; and it has it, not in ontical isolation, but as codetermined by its primordial kind of Being. In so far as this is the case, Dasein too can end without authentically dying, though on the other hand, *qua* Dasein, it does not simply perish. We designate this intermediate phenomenon as its *"demise."* Let the term *"dying"* stand for that *way of Being* in which Dasein *is towards* its death. Accordingly we must say that Dasein never perishes. Dasein can, however, only demise as long as it is dying. (*BT*, 49: 291)

If Dasein never perishes, and yet perishing is the end of that which lives, does it not follow that for Heidegger Dasein does not live, is not alive or animate? Yet he also wants to say that Dasein has the kind of death that is appropriate to anything that lives; and a little earlier he says that Dasein "may be considered purely as life," and that so considered, "from the viewpoint of biology and physiology, Dasein moves into that domain of Being which we know as the world of animals and plants" (*BT*, 49: 290). A little later, however, such investigations into Dasein's relation to death are redescribed as looking into "demising"—an intermediate phenomenon that is neither perishing nor dying—which implies that Dasein can never be said properly or fully to have moved into the world of animals and plants, that it is always and essentially removed from the world of the animate and hence of animality.

Heidegger's ambivalence here is very close to the surface; but is it a weakness in his analysis or, rather, an insufficiently worked-out response to some essential instability or ambivalence in the phenomena under discussion—to the way our embodiment at once relates us to and removes us from the animal realm? We certainly need not assume that Heidegger is unaware of the problem. After all, he explicitly acknowledges an inclination to defer the issue, as if sensing a deep difficulty in his attempt to deal with it implicitly throughout his existential analytic of Dasein—as when he says that "[t]his 'bodily nature' hides a whole problematic of its own, though we shall not treat it here" (*BT*, 23: 143). This deferred treatment is to be found in his 1929–30 lectures on *The Fundamental Concepts of Metaphysics: World, Finitude, Solitude*.[3]

These lectures restate and elucidate Heidegger's understanding of Dasein's kinship with the animal realm in the form of three interlinked theses:

> The stone is *worldless*; the animal is *poor in world*; man is *world-forming*. (FCM, 42: 177)

[3] Translated by W. McNeill and N. Walker (Indiana University Press: Bloomington, 1995); hereafter, *FCM*.

The notion of impoverished worldliness appears to imply that animals have at least a diminished capacity to grasp beings as beings. But Heidegger denies this, declaring, for example, that "[w]hen we say that the lizard is lying on the rock, we ought to cross out the word 'rock' in order to indicate that whatever the lizard is lying on is certainly given *in some way* for the lizard, and yet is not known to the lizard *as* a rock" (*FCM*, 47: 198). He further specifies this mode of givenness as captivation ("Benommenheit"), claiming that animals relate to themselves and their environment as if fascinated, dazzled, dazed, benumbed. The instincts that drive them also ring them or fence them in: objects forcibly impinge upon them solely as disinhibitors of drives (as food or mate, predator or prey), and so as not only withholding other objects (until circumstances allow those other objects to disinhibit other drives in the ring) but also as withholding themselves *qua* objects.

These formulations certainly do not look promising—as recent critics have emphasized. In his Carus Lectures, published as *Dependent Rational Animals*,[4] Alasdair MacIntyre has suggested that, whilst Heidegger's discussion of nonhuman animals is an improvement upon most parallel discussions in the analytical philosophical literature in its breadth of reference (bees, moths, freshwater crabs, lizards, sea urchins, woodworms, and woodpeckers appear alongside the more familiar dog and squirrel), it is nevertheless doubly flawed. First, it aims to characterize nonhuman animals *as such*, and hence assumes that differences between nonhuman species are of (almost) no importance. On MacIntyre's view, this is "because . . . he insists [that] we can *only* understand nonhuman animals by contrast with our own human condition, and what all nonhuman animals share is a lack of what human beings have: a relationship to beings in which not only are beings disclosed, but the difference between beings and being is disclosed. That relationship

---

[4] Duckworth: London, 1999; hereafter, *DRA*.

depends upon the ability of human beings to apprehend what they apprehend "*as such and such*" (DRA, 45).

However, whilst the thesis that nonhuman animals lack the as-structure (and hence the possibility of language) is compelling in the case of moths, crabs, and lizards, it is much less compelling when we consider dogs, chimpanzees, gorillas, and dolphins. Their behaviour, MacIntyre claims, seems to manifest an ability not only to respond to but actively to explore features of their environment, to devote perceptual attention to them from a number of angles, to recognize what is familiar, to treat one and the same object first as something to be played with and then as something to be eaten, perhaps even to recognize and grieve for what is absent. Of course, they cannot grasp the world as a whole, or stand back from their immediate environment—in particular, they cannot put the present in a temporal context; but they are not merely captive to their single, encircling environment. Hence, by failing to discriminate within the realm of nonhuman animality, Heidegger fails to see that certain of such species display elementary analogues of the as-structure that he presents as exclusive to human beings.

For MacIntyre, Heidegger's monolithic vision of nonhuman animals also occludes the fact that distinctively human behaviour is founded upon animal powers and capacities shared with members of other species. "[O]ur whole initial bodily comportment towards the world is originally an animal comportment, and . . . when, through having become language users, we under the guidance of parents and others restructure that comportment, elaborate and in new ways correct our beliefs and redirect our activities, we never make ourselves independent of our animal nature and inheritance" (*DRA*, 49). Certain aspects of our bodily condition (defecation, sleeping, eating) remain constants in our lives; and the genuinely distinctive human capacities to reflect upon, evaluate, and modify our reasons for action presuppose that we have reasons for action prior to any reflection—the kinds of reasons also manifest (in MacIntyre's view) in the behaviour of dolphins and chimpanzees. At its most general, then, for MacIntyre, what results from the (in his view, primarily linguistic) reconstitution of our comportment to the world is a transformation of our animality rather than a transcendence of it.

In short, Heidegger's analysis errs in assuming that human beings are animals and then something else in addition—the very error Heidegger claims to reject.

> We have, on this view, a first animal nature and *in addition* a second distinctively human nature. The force of the "and" is to suggest that this second nature can, at least in the most important respects, only be accounted for in its own terms. Its relation to our given biological nature is thought of as external and contingent in a way and to a degree that permits a single sharp line to be drawn between human beings and members of all nonhuman species. And that line is the line between those who possess language and those who do not. (*DRA*, 50)

For MacIntyre, by contrast, an exclusive attention to the genuinely significant differences between language-possessing and non-language-possessing animals obscures the significance of the continuity and resemblances between some aspects of the intelligent activities of nonhuman animals and the language-informed practical rationality of human beings. What he proposes instead is that we think of the relationship of human beings to other intelligent species in terms of a scale or spectrum rather than a single dividing line between "them" and "us."

It is striking how far MacIntyre's criticisms of Heidegger (mounted from a broadly analytical perspective, with a specifically Thomist ethical conclusion in mind) overlap with criticisms developed several years earlier by a commentator of a far more "continental" bent. David Farrell Krell's book *Daimon*

Life[5] ranges widely over Heidegger's various engagements with what Krell calls "life-philosophy," and includes a chapter of highly critical commentary (much influenced by Derrida) on Heidegger's 1929–30 lectures. From the outset, Krell is suspicious of Heidegger's avowed desire to inquire into "the essence of the animality of the animal and the essence of the humanity of man" (*FCM*, 43: 179); he sees any such inquiry as presupposing an essential separation between inquires into essence and merely empirical—say, zoological—inquiries, an essential separation between the dumb animal and the questioning human being, and a refusal to acknowledge any significant distinctions within the realm of nonhuman animals. Krell further notes that, although Heidegger explicitly rejects all talk of higher and lower animals, "he defines the poverty of the animal world in terms of deprivation without for the moment wondering whether all talk of deprivation does not reinstate all the hierarchies he would have wanted to dismantle."[6]

Krell is, however, more interested in the way in which Heidegger's own language, in its struggles to elucidate the animal's essentially nonhuman mode of being, betrays its own purpose by attributing characteristics to the animal that Heidegger wants to reserve exclusively to human beings. He points out, for example, that Heidegger's talk of animals as benumbed or bedazzled by their environment deploys a term ("Benommenheit") that is regularly employed in *Being and Time* to characterize modes of Dasein's being—primarily to characterize its average everydayness, but once even to characterize its route to authentic everydayness[7]). In a similar way, whilst wishing urgently to deny that animals have any inherent relation to "the nothing" or "the nullity" that is so central to *Being and Time*'s

[5] Indiana University Press: Bloomington, 1992.

[6] Ibid, 115.

[7] Cf. *BT*, 26:149, for an example of the former use, and *BT*, 68:394 for an example of the latter use. Krell lists these and other occurrences of the term in *Being and Time* in the introduction to *Daimon Life*.

analysis of authentic human existence, Heidegger's talk of the animal's encircling ring as disinhibiting drives, and of those drives as themselves tending toward the elimination or eradication of the objects that disinhibit them, cannot avoid relating the animal to negation. For Krell, however, these multiple indications of a certain continuity or even identity between animal and human modes of existence remain self-subversions; Heidegger's explicit or official concern is to affirm an essential discontinuity, whatever contraindications his own thinking may suggest. Krell therefore finds it at once unsurprising and deeply shocking that Heidegger is driven to the following kinds of formulation of the difference between animal and human behaviour. "We designate the being-with-itself that is specific to animals, which possesses nothing of the selfhood that the human being has, inasmuch as the human being comports himself towards himself as a person, and we define the containment of the animal in itself, in which its every form of behaviour is possible, as *benumbment*" (*FCM*, 58: 238–9).

In *Being and Time*, Heidegger restricted himself to the term "Dasein" to characterize human modes of being precisely in order to avoid the ontotheological inheritance written into such terms of the philosophical tradition as "selfhood" and "personhood." His resort to them now suggests that his desire sharply to distinguish human from animal modes of being merely continues the metaphysical and moral prejudices of that tradition, and hence of the culture it informs. Krell therefore concludes that Heidegger's best efforts to uncover a positive or fruitful reading of the blatant anthropocentricity of his contention that the animal is poor in world (deprived of a vigour and vitality, the capacity to encounter beings as beings, possessed by humans) inevitably fail, leaving us with a highly traditional picture of Dasein as distinguished from merely animal existence by its supplementary possession of *logos*.

Must we accept the shared assumption of these suspicious readings of Heidegger's lectures? Must we read them (with

MacIntyre) as simply intended to enforce a deep distinction between the human and the animal, where there is in reality a deep continuity? And when such an interpretation is confronted with the various ways in which Heidegger's words seem to recoil from or even subvert any such distinction, must we read those effects (with Krell) as simply beyond, rather than beholden to, their author's control—as not at all expressive of his understanding of his topic? Heidegger does, after all, advise us to read the phrase "world-poverty" under erasure—as if placing animals at once within and without the reach of the term "world," and as if animals place the limits of its reach in question. And he repeatedly, pivotally puts his own formulations in question like this.

In sections 49 and 50, for example, he questions his very ability to form his theses, arguing that far from presupposing a human capacity for self-transposition into three different domains of otherness, they instead show that this capacity is in fact elicited only by the animal realm (since the otherness of stones neither invites nor resists the transpositions of a self, and the otherness of other humans is always already internal to Dasein, whose kind of Being is Being-with). More precisely, Heidegger claims that animality is "essentially a potentiality for granting transposedness, connected in turn with the necessary refusal of any going along with" (*FCM*, 50: 211). In other words, animals neither simply lack access to objects in their own right (as do stones) nor do they simply possess a humanly accessible mode of access to objects (as do other Dasein); their singularity in our experience lies in their having a mode of access to and dealing with the world from which we are excluded. Animal dealings with objects are accessible to humans, but only as resistant to human accessibility; hence, to grasp animality is to grasp it as a mode of being from which human beings are fenced out, that they can grasp only as beyond them. The analogy with Heidegger's treatment of death is striking.

How, then, does this underlying sense of humans as excluded from animal worldliness become the official thesis that animals are excluded from human modes of being? If humans are fenced out from animality, why declare that animals are fenced out from humanity? An answer to this question begins to emerge as Heidegger reinforces his sense of animals as both within and without human modes of accessibility by considering not only lizards, crabs, and squirrels, but also dogs and cats. He thereby emphasizes the subdivision of animality in our experience into domesticated and wild forms—the fact that animals both resist and permit domestication. The wildness of wild (undomesticated and undomesticatable) animals signifies the excluding, repulsive self-sufficiency of all animal existence, the sheer alterity with which they confront our grasp; but domestic animals signify that animality is also internalizable within the human mode of being, even if never exactly assimilable to it.

> We do not describe them as [domestic animals] simply because they turn up in the house but because they belong to the house, i.e., they serve the house in a certain sense. . . . We keep domestic pets in the house with us, they *"live" with us*. But we do not live with them if living means: being in an animal kind of way. Yet we *are with* them nonetheless. But this being-with is not an *existing-with*, because a dog does not exist but merely lives. Through this being with animals we enable them to move within our world. . . . [The dog] eats with us—and yet, it does not really "eat." Nevertheless, it is with us! (*FCM*, 50: 210)

Domestic animals belong to our domiciles, we dwell with them; their lives are not only conducted alongside ours but intertwined with ours; they move not only through our world but within it. These expressions of our kinship with pets invoke ways in which an animal's encircling ring can intersect with, or be encompassed by, the human world; then there opens up the possibility of disrupting and expanding both ring and world, a vision of animal being as becoming more fully itself within a human world that is itself enriched thereby. Hence the thought that for us to be fenced out of the animal's encircling ring is for the animal to be fenced within it. Talk of the animal's refusingly responsive poverty in world might then express a sense that the otherness of animality answers to something deep within our world, that animal and human beings can acknowledge their intimate otherness, and that its denial constricts both the encircling ring of their being and the horizon of our world.

A further part of the answer to our question emerges in section 63, when Heidegger continues his self-interrogation, preempting his critics by accusing himself of characterizing animal world-poverty in terms which imply that they do have world. His response is to recall two key features of his broader project. First, his primary concern is to characterize properly the worldliness of human being; hence his characterization of animals as world-poor, whilst identifying one essential determination of animality as such, is itself determined by his decision to regard the animal in comparison with humanity. Let us assume that this is not a simple admission of anthropocentrism, but rather a hint that his second thesis might say as much about the being advancing it as about the beings it characterizes; then we might revise our grasp of the third of Heidegger's theses, that man is world-forming.

Unlike the formulations of *Being and Time*, which talk of Dasein as worldly or as Being-in-the-world, this thesis implies a more active human contribution to shaping the world—and perhaps more faintly invokes the idea of a plurality of such worlds (as if the human world can always be formed otherwise—perhaps so as to constrict, or to redraw more expansively, the encircling ring of an animal). This invocation is more explicit in the final pages of the lectures, when Heidegger glosses the idea of world-forming as projection, which is a "*turning towards that is a removal*" (*FCM*, 76: 363)—carrying us out of ourselves, removing us into whatever has been projected, in such a way that we simultaneously turn toward ourselves. Heidegger glosses this reflexive removal as a "raising away into the possible . . . in its possibly being made possible," as binding us "not to what is possible, nor to what is actual, but to *making-possible*" (*FCM*, 76: 363)—thus recalling projection as *Being and Time* understands it. But "reflexive removal" also implicitly transposes his earlier idea of human self-transposition, bringing out its psychoanalytic resonance; it thus implies that world-forming can be a defensive operation, the externalization of rejected elements of ourselves. Perhaps, then, projecting a world in which animality is fenced in upon itself is a projection of an aspect of ourselves from which we feel—or wish to feel—fenced out. Perhaps the thesis that animals are world-poor is a projection of our own rejected animality, a defence against the animal capacity to address and even to cohabit with the inhabitants of human worlds because of what that implies about the never-entirely-transcended animality of those who form them.

Can Heidegger really be asking us to treat his own core theses as questionable in such ways? But it is essential to his understanding of human inquiries that they are situated, and hence expressive of an attitude or stance—call it a mood—through which the questioner already finds himself oriented with respect to his topic. And Heidegger draws our attention to the formative context of his own questioning, when, as part of his second response to self-criticism in section 63, he recalls that his lectures begin by claiming that contemporary human society discloses its world through the fundamental mood or attunement of boredom (to an analysis of which more than half of the lectures are devoted before animality even becomes an issue). But then, any authentic questioning must be receptive to that mood (cf. *FCM*, 37: 160); hence "we constantly already question concerning the essence of world [and thus the essence of animality] from out of this attunement" (*FCM*, 63: 272).

And if the Dasein whose questioning these lectures record is in the grip of boredom, then the theses it advances in response must be advanced out of boredom—must be informed and pervaded by it. How, then, does Heidegger understand that mood?

Beneath or within such experiences as being marooned for hours at a railway station, or the self-induced emptiness of yet another pleasant dinner with friends, Heidegger detects the more profound possibility of encountering the world as a whole in such terms; fundamental boredom is "Dasein's being delivered over to beings' telling refusal of themselves as a whole" (*FCM*, 31: 139), a discovery of beings in general as indifferent to us, and hence of us as indifferent to them. Such boredom induces a kind of suspension among beings, an inhabitation of limbo or of death in life (perhaps even a Holy Saturday moment, between departure from and return to life). And it indicates that Dasein's existence is not only a matter of having a world of possibilities from which to choose, but also of having a desire or drive to realize one or another of those possibilities, to be drawn or gripped by the possible worlds they hold out.

Heidegger's analysis concludes by emphasizing that the emptiness of Dasein uncovered by beings' self-refusal is not exactly nothingness but "emptiness as lack, deprivation, *need*" (*FCM*, 38: 162). Fundamental boredom is not therefore overcome by, but is instead given expression in identifying specific social, political, or aesthetic needs and trying to meet their demands; for what we lack is a neediness essential to our Dasein as a whole. Fundamental boredom is "the absence of any essential oppressiveness" or mysterious demand, and of "the inner terror that every such mystery carries with it, and that gives Dasein its greatness" (*FCM*, 38: 163–64). This deprivation can be met, our entrancement by our needy deprivation of need can be disrupted, only through a moment of vision which discloses "*that Dasein as such is demanded of man, that it is given to him—to be there*" (*FCM*, 38: 165); and it is just such a disclosure that genuine questioning within the attunement of boredom must seek. "[T]o question concerning *this fundamental attunement* . . . means . . . to liberate the humanity in man, to liberate the humanity of man, i.e., the *essence* of man, *to let the Dasein in him become essential*" (*FCM*, 38: 166).

Do Heidegger's theses envision Dasein's inhabitation of a world as an oppressive demand? The second thesis claims that animals exhibit a responsive refusal to humanity; their seductive self-withdrawals thus exemplify the world's revealing refusal to go along with the essentially situated and attuned comprehension of human beings. But it further claims that animals suffer deprivation in that they are entranced or benumbed by the world, enslaved by one drive-disinhibitor after another. It thus transposes to animality as such the predicates Heidegger has just attributed to humans in the grip of boredom—covering over the oppressive absence of a genuinely demanding world in which they can take an interest by an endless round of bustling attempts to manufacture and satisfy specific needs (the turbulent Babel of fallenness). This may seem simply to cast boredom as tending to reduce the human to the animal, as if Heidegger's analysis reiterates a simple opposition between genuine or authentic humanity and fallen animality. But if this transposition is also—as Heidegger himself tells us—a further expression of our boredom, of the way that mood discloses our world to us, then it will instead seem to indicate our refusal of interest in animals as they are in themselves, and (if understood as a defensive projection) an implicit awareness that our suspension in boredom (and thus, the possibility of our disrupting that needy deprivation of need) is somehow internally related to our animality.

Hence, when Heidegger says that letting the Dasein in human beings become essential is a matter of liberating the humanity in man (as if *from* his animality), this need not imply a simple opposition between humanity and animality; it might, rather, envisage the realization of Dasein in human beings as a disruption of their animality *from within*. Dasein's existence is always a transcendence of animality, a disruption of it—but a disruption from within, because the situatedness (what Heidegger calls the "thrownness") from which Dasein's distinctive projection always emerges is a modification of desire or need, and hence of Dasein's embodiedness or animality. Realizing Dasein's mooded comprehension of its world thus neither negates nor reiterates animality; it is a demand made upon a particular species of it, a radicalization of animality as such. This is why Heidegger characterizes man's *enraptured* transition toward authentically human questioning as "being seized by terror" (*FCM*, 76: 366). For, whereas fear is attuned to danger and horror of the monstrous, terror is a response to violence, to that which might violate one's flesh and blood; and to let Dasein be is to do the most intimate, uncanny violence to one's animality, but thereby to answer the most originary demand that our particular inflection of embodiedness (our form of subjection to desire) makes upon us.

For Heidegger, then, humanity and animality are neither simply continuous nor simply discontinuous with each other; rather, discontinuity is the mode of their continuity. In elaborating his thesis that animals are poor in world, Heidegger not only finds himself claiming that we grasp the being of nonhuman animals as essentially resistant to our grasp; he also finds himself inclined to resist that resistance by grasping animal being in the terms he requires to understand Dasein in its pervasive but not inevitable fallenness into boredom. But if animals are essentially bored, then human states of boredom are both essentially different from animality (not being ontological qualifications of the human mode of being), and yet essentially expressions of it (being states in which the human takes on, and hence shows itself to be essentially capable of taking on, an aspect of what it understands to be sheer animality). Thus his thesis delineates a conception of animality (both nonhuman animality, and the animality of the human) as both within and without (beyond or before) humanity's grasp, and hence as essentially enigmatic.

The root of this discontinuous continuity is that within humanity which makes us subject to boredom, namely our subjection to embodiment, need, and desire. But the human mode of that subjection is distinctive, in that our thrownness is always already projective, and thus leaves us subject to the call of individuality—the need or desire to find the world, hence ourselves, and hence the project of realizing ourselves in a questioning comprehension of that world, to be worthy of interest. We experience this call as oppressively demanding, in part because it is addressed to us in our usual state of self-alienating boredom, in part because answering that call amounts to being driven beyond the animal realm by our distinctive animal nature (insofar as accepting it appears to entail that our own animality, as well as animality as such, becomes essentially enigmatic to us). Hence, to conceive of nonhuman animals as if always already bored or poor in world is to use them to distract ourselves from our distractions. In truth, it expresses a loss of any interest in them as they are in themselves (i.e., as essentially, enigmatically resistant to our interest in them), and so gives expression to our boredom with the world; and it also expresses a refusal to interest ourselves in our own animality as it really is (i.e., as essentially, enigmatically resistant to our understanding), and thus gives expression to our boredom with ourselves.

So, for Heidegger, that which apparently distinguishes human from animal modes of being (our freedom, which presupposes a knowledge of good and evil, and makes individuality possible) is also what relates us to them (since such projectiveness is always thrown, and hence subject to need and desire). Human beings fulfil their nature as a species by suffering a radical reorientation of their creatureliness from within; their mode of animal existence confronts its own animality, and animality as such, as always already turned away from itself, as perverted for reasons and in ways that are beyond its ability to grasp. And the nonhuman animal becomes an externalised figure of that inner perversity, understood as essentially alien to humanity in order to deny the essential, and essentially enigmatic, animality of the human, which both threatens the loss of our humanity (in ever-diminishing rings of increasingly primitive responses to the world) and informs its achievement (through our allowing ourselves to become genuinely interested in the world, and thus in ourselves).

This conception of the enigmatically perverse animality of the human is plainly a concise recounting of the Christian myth of the Fall. Genesis presents the human animal's perverse drive beyond animality as conjured by a nonhuman animal (a snake), the external embodiment of its subjection to desire, in particular its subjection to the desire to be free (hence knowing good and evil, hence capable of genuinely individual existence); and through achieving such existence, it confronts animality (in itself and in its world) as essentially opposed to its needs, desires, and interests (the snake now ground, spitting and biting, beneath Eve's heel) for reasons that are beyond its grasp. Is Heidegger's deliberately questionable portrayal of animality as Dasein's enigmatically intimate other essentially different in these respects from Genesis's invocation of the snake as speaking to and for our self-subverting subjection to desire, and as victimized by that which it makes incarnate?

3

The Child and the Scapegoat: Wittgenstein

On my path to the present I emerged from infancy to boyhood, or rather boyhood came upon me and succeeded infancy. Infancy did not "depart," for it has nowhere to go. Yet I was no longer a baby incapable of speech but already a boy with power to talk. This I remember. But how I learnt to talk I discovered only later. It was not that grown-up people instructed me by presenting me with certain words in a certain order by formal teaching, as later I was to learn the letters of the alphabet. I myself acquired this power of speech with the intelligence which you gave me, my God. By groans and various sounds and various movements of parts of my body I would endeavour to express the intentions of my heart to persuade people to bow to my will. But I had not the power to express all that I wanted nor could I make my wishes understood by everybody. My grasp made use of memory: [when people gave a name to an object and when, following the sound, they moved their body towards that object, I would see and retain the fact that that object received from them this sound which they pronounced when they intended to draw attention to it. Moreover their intention was evident from the gestures which are, as it were, the natural vocabulary of all races, and are made with the face and the inclination of the eyes and the movements of other parts of the body,

and by the tone of voice which indicates whether the
mind's inward sentiments are to seek and possess or to
reject and avoid. Accordingly, as I heard words repeatedly used in their proper places in various sentences, I
gradually learnt to understand what objects they signi-
fied; and already I learnt to articulate my desires by
training my mouth to use these signs.] In this way I communicated the signs of my wishes to those around me,
and entered more deeply into the stormy society of
human life. I was dependent on the authority of my parents and the direction of adult people.

                                              —*Confessions* 1.8

THE *CONFESSIONS* is the spiritual autobiography of a fourth-
century Christian bishop, who, amongst many other claims to
fame and influence in the history of Western culture, is perhaps
best known as one of the most significant interpreters of the
Christian doctrine of original sin. And, as is also well known,
Wittgenstein chooses to begin his *Philosophical Investigations*
with a quotation from Augustine—and specifically from that
initial portion of Augustine's text which recounts his transition from infancy to speech, hence from biology to culture, and
so from original birthright to social inheritance.[1] (The passage
from the *Confessions* reproduced above gives the sequence
quoted by Wittgenstein in square brackets, together with its
immediate context—the whole in an English translation drawing on that employed in the Anscombe translation of the *Investigations* as well as that recently published by Henry Chadwick.)[2]
It is beyond question that Wittgenstein means to contest something (perhaps everything) in that passage concerning the nature of language, although it is far from uncontroversial exactly
what it is about Augustine's words about words to which he

---

[1] Translated by G.E.M. Anscombe (Blackwell: Oxford, 1953); hereafter, *PI*.
[2] Oxford University Press: Oxford, 1991.

objects, and contest it sufficiently strongly or fruitfully for that critique arguably to constitute the basic orientation of the *Investigations* as a whole. But in the context of this book, I raise a question that might otherwise seem impossible to take seriously. How far can Wittgenstein be read as contesting Augustine's account of our hereditary sinfulness as well as, even perhaps through his contestation of, his account of language? What I hope to show is that the tenability of such a reading—the possibility, if not the necessity, of so taking Wittgenstein's words—can be demonstrated without going beyond the first two sections of Wittgenstein's book, and hence without going beyond the immediate context of influence of that book's opening citation.

1. Augustine's Picture

Wittgenstein's own first words of response to Augustine's, making up the first paragraph of the first section of the *Investigations*, run as follows:

> These words, it seems to me, give us a particular picture of the essence of human language. It is this: the individual words in language name objects—sentences are combinations of such names.—In this picture we find the roots of the following idea: Every word has a meaning. This meaning is correlated with the word. It is the object for which the word stands. (*PI*, 1)

It is, perhaps, the final sentence of the quoted passage from the *Confessions* that justifies the first two sentences of this paragraph; for if Augustine were not taking it for granted that all words were names of objects, why would he implicitly equate the task of understanding words (as employed in the sentences they make up) with that of understanding which object they refer to or represent? But Wittgenstein immediately distinguishes Augustine's picture from an idea that he claims is rooted in that picture—an idea that is strongly reminiscent of his own, Tractarian conception of propositions as ultimately composed of simple names whose meaningfulness is determined by the simple object for which each name stands. To claim that an object named by a word is not merely its referent but its meaning is to go beyond anything contained in Augustine's picture (one not only could believe that "table" is the name of a particular piece of furniture without thinking that the object it refers to *is* its meaning, one should; for destroying the referent of a name does not make it meaningless). But the extremity of this kind of idea would only look tenable if its author's starting-point is something like the Augustinian picture.

Hence, Wittgenstein's image of rootedness: the picture is the soil from which the idea grows. This tells us that the idea is logically secondary to the picture, that it depends upon it for its existence and flourishing; and just as soil is not typically nutritious for only one (type of) plant, so a picture can nourish a range of more or less distantly related ideas. Since, however, soil is not a kind of plant, neither can pictures be thought of as just another kind of idea or set of ideas; and since Wittgenstein's example of an idea is a philosophical theory, we might restate this by saying that a picture is not a theory. His image of rootedness suggests, rather, that a picture is a pretheoretical framework or orientation, providing that without which a certain kind of theorizing would not be possible—an initial conceptualization of the area of investigation; a specific set of theory-building tools or resources; a conception of which problems are worth addressing, of what a good solution to them might be; and so on. As well as echoing Heidegger's guiding thought that there is no questioning without a situated and orienting grasp of what is in question, Wittgenstein's distinction suggests a limited analogy here with Kuhn's notion of a paradigm as informing normal phases of scientific work.

But for our purposes, the key implication of the idea of pictures as paradigms is that, if one's primary concern is with pictures rather than ideas, then one's terms of criticism cannot be those appropriate to ideas. Theories can be criticized with respect to the accuracy of their descriptions of data, the validity of their reasoning, the correctness of their predictions, and so on; but if Wittgenstein's concern is with the way such theories manifest their authors' commitment to Augustine's picture, such terms of criticism would be futile and inappropriate. Any such theory could be altered to accommodate an inaccurate observation, an invalid line of reasoning, or a falsified prediction without losing its rootedness in Augustine's picture. In fact, part of the point of Wittgenstein's image of "rootedness" is precisely to imply that any specific alterations in a theorist's work—in the content of her theory, in what she takes to be a serious problem and what a serious solution to it, in any decision she may take about jettisoning one theory in favour of another—will be implicitly shaped by the picture which governs her attitude to the phenomena under examination. Loosening the grip of a picture means effecting a shift in a person's sense of what matters to her intellectual project; it requires not that she respond to criticism, but that she be responsive to a reorientation of her interests. It asks, in short, for a kind of conversion.

Wittgenstein's second paragraph addresses itself to the business of effecting that conversion:

> Augustine does not speak of there being any difference between kinds of word. If you describe the learning of language in this way you are, I believe, thinking primarily of nouns like "table," "chair," "bread," and of people's names, and only secondarily of the names of certain actions and properties; and of the remaining kinds of word as something that will take care of itself. (*PI*, 1)

Wittgenstein has no objection to anyone saying that "table" is the name of a piece of furniture, or that "pain" is the name of a sensation, or that "five" is the name of a number. As he elsewhere acknowledges (*PI*, 10), such statements can (for instance) usefully remove certain misunderstandings about how words are used, to what they refer, and so on. His concern is, rather, with how the employment of such utterances can lead us to overlook or repress the differences between kinds of word.

Suppose we examine the applicability of Augustine's picture to three words that will be highlighted later in Wittgenstein's first section—"apple," "red," and "five." We might perfectly legitimately explain the meaning of "apple" by saying that it is the name of a type of fruit, and reinforce the explanation by pointing to the contents of the fruit bowl. If, however, we then go on to use the same form of explanation with respect to "red" and "five," it will be difficult to avoid assuming that the same ways of supplementing the explanation will also hold good. How, though, might we point to the referent of "red"? We can, of course, point to a red object—the very same apple, perhaps—but how do we point to its colour (as opposed, say, to its shape or the type of fruit it betokens)? Such pointing can seem very difficult to do, as if we need to isolate or dig just under the apple's skin with our pointing finger.

But there is a way of succeeding in this task, under the right circumstances—when, for example, we have a colour chart to hand; in short, we point to an object's colour by pointing to another object with the same colour. So someone in the grip of Augustine's picture can think of the colour patch aligned with the word "red" as its referent, that which the word designates or signifies. We might accept this, although it means accepting a significant disanalogy with the original case of "apple," where no such additional apparatus was felt necessary; but what about "five"? Pointing to the number instantiated by the group of five apples in my fruit bowl seems even more difficult than pointing to their colour; and even if we imagine a number table (analogous to the colour chart), aligning numerals with groups of strokes, it does not seem to supply us with numbers in just the way a colour chart supplies us with colours (are the strokes not just another system of numerals?).

Wittgenstein does not suggest that such questions cannot be answered; philosophers have done so by imagining a Platonic realm containing numbers of which numerals are the names, and have tried to grapple with the new problems that such a strategy throws up (the relation of this realm to the world we experience through the senses, our capacity to refer to and grasp such entities, and so on). But the moral of the tale is clear. As we find ourselves building more and more elaborate epicycles into our theory to cope with the apparent differences between kinds of word that our clutch of examples quickly brings to the surface, as every proposed solution generates further problems of its own, Wittgenstein invites us to consider stepping back from our guiding, pre-theoretical assumption that all words are names and hence must show the same kinds of links with objects and activities in the world.

Applying the Augustinian template for language across the board forces us to distort the everyday facts of language use in increasingly extreme ways, to elide or repress the very different kinds of ways in which words are used, rather than reflecting proper attention to those differences. If, however, we try to avoid such distortions by jettisoning more and more of the substance of that form of description—so that, for example, we preserve the "'x' names 'y'" paradigm but no longer require that ys be the kind of things we can point to—then our continued use of the paradigm across the board will eventually tell us nothing whatever about a word's kind of employment, its role in language and human life; it will be an empty form, to which we can regiment every such description only by evacuating them of content. It would be like saying that all tools serve to modify something (*PI*, 14); this works fairly well for hammers and saws, but to apply this template to rulers, glue, and nails would require intellectual gymnastics of a kind that distorts the facts about tool use and empties the descriptive form of the content it requires to be usefully applicable even to hammers and saws.

The problem with Augustine's picture is therefore not that it makes a substantial claim about language as a whole that turns out to be true only of some subset of language (applying happily to nouns and proper names, less happily to verbs and adjectives, and flatly inapplicable elsewhere). It is instead that it makes what appears to be a substantial claim about language as a whole that turns out to lack any substance whatever. If the Augustinian's claim that all words are names employs the word "name" in its ordinary sense, then it has a plain content, but it is also so self-evidently false that it makes little sense to imagine it being advanced by mistake (as if he might simply have failed to notice the obvious differences between proper names and other types of word); whereas if his words are read as advocating the introduction of a regimented form of description of word-meaning, then it fails to advance a substantive claim at all.

He can, of course, use his form of words in either of these two ways; but for Wittgenstein, the Augustinian's attraction to those words actually depends upon his wishing to use them both ways at once, to make a substantive claim that all words can be seen to satisfy—and this he cannot do, for "all words are names" cannot be both a proposal for adopting a certain form of description and a substantive descriptive claim at one and the same time. He has, then, become confused about the significance of his utterance, has lost control over his words; one might even say that he is talking nonsense. But it might be more accurate to say that he has suffered a hallucination of sense; he has maintained his conviction of saying something self-evidently true only because his utterance hovers between two very different possibilities of sense or meaning without ever actualizing either. Once the necessity of separating out those two possibilities is made clear to him, he will see that there is nothing here to be said—no claim of the kind he took himself to be making; and then his attraction to this form of words will wither away, his interests will undergo a reorientation. He will, in other words, have begun to turn away from the picture that fascinated him.

Suppose we think of the state of philosophical confusion in which Wittgenstein finds Augustine as exemplifying our tendency to become grammatically disoriented—to find ourselves speaking beyond or outside language games; Stanley Cavell— one of Wittgenstein's most exacting readers—calls it a condition of scepticism. Augustine's condition thereby illustrates Wittgenstein's conception of the form of any distinctively philosophical confusion; and his practice of reminding us of what we say when, of recalling us to the grammar or criteria of our words, is dedicated to overcoming that confusion. But this in turn raises some questions: How and why does he imagine that we can fall into such confusions in the first place? Why and how can otherwise competent speakers suffer such a loss of control when under the pressure to philosophize?

For Wittgenstein, the criteria of our words articulate what makes a given phenomenon count as an instance of any particular kind of thing; the marks or features by reference to which we judge something to be an apple, a cloud, a pain, a state of hope or expectation, are those without which it would not constitute a member of the relevant class or category—call this the essence of the relevant kind (Heidegger would call it the "Being of that being"). Accordingly, those things over which we lose control in our grammatical disorientation constitute the limits or conditions of the human capacity to know, think, or speak about the world and the various things that are in it; they are that without which there would be no human comprehension of the world.

But of course, as we have seen over and over again in this book, it is fatally easy to interpret limits as limitations, to experience conditions as constraints. Indeed, this is precisely how the sceptic often understands her own motives: she repudiates our ordinary reliance on criteria because she regards what we ordinarily count as knowledge as nothing of the kind—as failing to put us into contact with the world as it really is. But it would only make sense to think of the conditions of human knowledge as limitations if we could conceive of another cognitive perspective upon the world that did not require them. And philosophers from Kant onwards have variously striven to show that there is no such perspective—that the absence of the categories or concepts in terms of which we individuate objects would not clear the way for unmediated knowledge of the world, but would rather remove the possibility of anything that might count as knowledge. Thus, what begins as an honourable attempt to guarantee our invulnerability to the sceptic's charge that our words are essentially unanchored in the real, ends by ensuring that we become guilty as charged.

In other words, what the sceptic understands as a process of disillusionment in the name of true knowledge, Wittgenstein interprets as an inability or refusal to acknowledge the fact that human knowledge—the knowledge available to finite creatures, subjective agents in an objective world—is necessarily conditioned. But it is worth recalling that nothing is more human than the desire to deny the human, to interpret limits as limitations, and to repudiate the human condition of conditionedness (finitude) in the name of the unconditioned, the transcendent, the superhuman—the inhuman. On this understanding of criteria, the human desire to speak outside language games is an inflection of the prideful human craving to be God, and Wittgenstein's philosophical practice aims not so much to eradicate this apparently ineradicable hubris but instead to diagnose it and to track down the specific causes and inflections of its endlessly renewed realization in particular cases.

And what, in general terms, this tracking requires is a fully acknowledged relationship with a particular human other—call him the therapeutic philosopher—one whose words have the power to identify and make us ashamed of our present confused and disoriented state; one who, by exemplifying a further, attainable state of clarity and self-possession, can attract us to it whilst respecting our autonomy and individuality. The specific analogy with Augustine that this self-conception of Wittgenstein's generates should by now be clear. For the *Confessions* records its author's successive self-overcomings, his attainment of a spiritual state beyond both his initial paganism and the Manicheanism that succeeded it; and this confession of his past sinfulness to God is also a confession of praise to God for his help in this process of conversion, and an invitation to his readers to find their own way to that divine intercessor. But this simply reveals a further analogy behind the first: for in Christian thought more generally, our unending sequence of particular sinful acts reveals that human beings are possessed of a nature that disposes them to sin and prevents them from escaping their bondage by using their own resources. What they need to attain their true nature is a fully acknowledged relationship with a particular person—one through whose words divine grace is made accessible, one who exemplifies the further, unattained but attainable human state to which God wishes to attract every individual whilst respecting her freedom to deny its attraction and spurn His grace.

Little wonder, then, that many readers of Wittgenstein detect an air of spiritual fervour in his work—not because he makes particular, explicit moral or political exhortations, but because of the structure of the philosophical practice that engenders every word he speaks and that gives both the one who utters those words and the one to whom they are addressed (who may, of course, be one and the same person) a role in a very specific transposition or displacement of a very familiar kind of relationship. The question is: how much distance from its religious original does this transposition succeed in establishing for itself and for those inclined to inherit it? More specifically: even if it does constitute a phase in the perennial battle against the human denial of the human, does not its conception of the philosopher's role in that battle amount to a further expression of the very hubris that it aims to combat?

2. Perversions of the Ordinary

So far, we have examined Augustine's cited tale as an exemplification of philosophical confusion about words. But that tale patently and emphatically frames or contextualizes its assumed picture of words as names within a nested set of assumptions about what those names are employed to achieve in the world, and hence with a picture of those who so employ them, and of the culture they inhabit—the culture that Augustine acquires in acquiring language from the example of his elders. And Wittgenstein invites us to read him as being just as much interested in these aspects of Augustine's tale as in the picture of language in which it is embedded. After all, as he will tell us a little later in the *Investigations*, "[T]o imagine a language means to imagine a form of life" (*PI*, 19); from which it would seem to follow that any given failure responsibly to imagine the functionings of words will be in the service of (will be both cause and consequence of) a corresponding fantasy—a deformed imaginative inhabitation—of the lives we lead with them. This becomes clear in the third paragraph of the first section of the *Investigations*:

> Now think of the following use of language: I send someone shopping. I give him a slip marked "five red apples." He takes the slip to the shopkeeper, who opens the drawer marked "apples"; then he looks up the word "red" in a table and finds a colour sample opposite it; then he says

the series of cardinal numbers—I assume he knows then by heart—up to the word "five" and for each number he takes an apple of the same colour as the sample out of the drawer.—It is in these and similar ways that one operates with words.—But how does he know where and how he is to look up the word "red" and what he is to do with the word "five"? —Well, I assume that he *acts* as I have described. Explanations come to an end some-where.—But what is the meaning of the word "five"? — No such thing was in question here, only how the word "five" is used. (*PI*, 1)

It is usual to regard this fiction of a shopping trip as an everyday tale of buying and selling, designed to recall us to the differ-ences between kinds of word, differences that are self-evident in the context of their practical employment. This is not exactly wrong; but is Wittgenstein exactly right when he remarks that "it is in these and similar ways that one operates with words"? I do not recall ever attempting to buy apples by mutely pre-senting my shopping list to the shopkeeper. Nor have I ever gone shopping in a grocery store where the shopkeeper kept his fruit in drawers, employed a sample chart when selecting among them by colour, and counted aloud as he deposited each apple in my bag. Analogues to some of these "operations" might have gone on in other kinds of store—say, a DIY shop, when I am in search of particular nuts or screws, or paint of a specific colour—but to transfer and amalgamate familiar elements of other kinds of shopping trips into a trip to the grocer is not to construct a familiar tale of our commerce with apples. And for Wittgenstein to present such a surreal transposition as an unre-markable example of our life with words places our conception of everyday human transactions under intolerable strain. Surely nothing could be more extraordinary than this scene of suppos-edly ordinary life.

Why, then, present it in such a way? Well, one effect of its presentation is that Wittgenstein's interlocutor is driven to express dissatisfaction with it—although not with its ordinariness. She finds that the tale's unremitting emphasis on behaviour (both linguistic and non-linguistic) leaves entirely unaddressed the question of whether, and if so how, that behaviour can be thought of as manifesting understanding. She wants to know what it is behind that behaviour, within the agent's mind, that constitutes the understanding it appears to indicate; only something essentially interior will satisfy her. In other words, she seems to inhabit a sharply dualist conception of the relation between minds and bodies (just like Augustine, who presents his elders as moving their bodies toward objects, as if puppet-masters of themselves; and his child as training his mouth to form signs to give expression to his given desires, as if residing in his own infant body like a homunculus).

But suppose we could establish the existence of such interior states or processes of the kind for which the interlocutor yearns, and in the absence of which she feels that the issues of understanding and meaning have not been properly broached. Suppose, for example, we could show that the shopkeeper was able to use the word "red" to discriminate between apples because he could recall an earlier internal correlation between the word "red" and a mental image of red. This kind of discovery might well overcome the interlocutor's scepticism, but it would do so only by offering an internalized version of the public processes of correlation and comparison that the shopkeeper goes through in Wittgenstein's story; and this immediately suggests more than one moral.

First, if the public versions of such procedures were not enough to establish the presence of understanding, why should their inner counterparts? Unless one is inclined to fetishize their sheer interiority—as if the inner were a realm of magic beyond rational accounting—there appear to be no important differences between, say, a mental image of red and a sample of red on a colour chart. Accordingly, either the interlocutor's doubts apply to the internal as well as the external procedures and mechanisms, in which case we are no further forward; or our explanations can—as Wittgenstein claims—perfectly well come to an end in the public realm to which his tale restricts itself.

The second moral is this. If Wittgenstein's shopkeeper's way with words strikes us as surreal and oddly mechanical, to the point at which we want to question the nature and even the reality of his inner life, and yet his public behaviour amounts to an externalised replica of the way we picture the inner life of all ordinary, comprehending language users, then our picture of the inner must be as surreal, as oddly mechanical, as Wittgenstein's depiction of the outer. What his story shows is that the interlocutor's imaginings would have us zombies inside as well as out; her supposed solution to her sceptical problem is in fact a further, deeper expression of her scepticism. In other words, Wittgenstein's tale is not a depiction of ordinary life, but a realization of one of our fantasies of it; the drawers and tables of his grocer's shop reflect the architecture and furnishings of the mental theatre we attribute to ourselves, and the robotic, chanting shopkeeper is the homunculus who occupies its stage.

Hence, we confront a third moral of this tale. If we, as readers, happily accept Wittgenstein's invitation to regard this oddly mechanical tale as an episode from ordinary life and proceed to berate his interlocutor for failing to do likewise, then we are participating in the very confusions that we are so quick to condemn in others. This suggests more than the need for humility. It teaches us not to think of the interlocutory voices in Wittgenstein's texts as somehow essentially other than our own (or, indeed, his own). It also warns us that what Wittgenstein might mean by the "ordinary" is not necessarily obvious nor ordinary. In particular, it may not be intended to pick out a domain immune to philosophical distortion or colonization, even if it is also capable of providing the resources to overcome them. For if a fantasy of our life with words can inform and misdirect our philosophizing, then it is always already realized in those reaches of our cultural institutions, our individual exchanges, and our self-communings that go by the name of philosophy; and if realizable there, why not elsewhere in the form and the content of our social existence? Indeed, why not anywhere our fantasies of ourselves might engender and motivate substantial thoughts, words, and deeds—which means pretty much anywhere at all?

So much for the shopkeeper; but what about the shopper? I suggested earlier that we do not typically think of shopping lists as made for use as an alternative to speech, but rather as employed in conjunction with further words—for example, as an aide-memoire for conversational exchanges with shopkeepers. Are there, nevertheless, ways of imagining Wittgenstein's scene as ordinary or everyday in this respect? Suppose we recall that Augustine's story (which Wittgenstein's is, after all, supposed to counter) concerns a child learning to speak, and we then ask ourselves in what kind of uncontroversially ordinary circumstances we might expect to find someone wordlessly handing over to the shopkeeper a shopping list itself handed to him by another person. I believe that we might answer: when observing a child sent on an errand—someone being taught how to shop, and hence how to do things with words. So understood, what specific counters to the details of Augustine's tale might Wittgenstein's story manage to muster?

First, the juxtaposition brings out that there is rather more teaching than learning going on in Augustine.[3] Augustine's child is clearly working hard to learn the language of his elders—observing their utterances and movements, grasping the connection between sounds and objects with the help of facial

---

[3] Cf. Cavell, "Notes and Afterthoughts," in *Philosophical Passages* (Blackwell: Oxford, 1995), 169.

expressions and intonation, and then employing those connections for his own purposes. But this enormous expenditure of effort is called for because the child's elders appear to be making no effort to teach him. It is as if the child acquires language despite the indifference of his elders, as if he is forced to pick it up by stealth—to steal it rather than be gifted with it, inherit it. Wittgenstein's elders, on the other hand, are fully engaged in the task of handing on the inheritance of language, and their favoured form for this teaching or training is that of encouraging the child to play a part in their life with words.

Cavell offers some pertinent observations on this theme: "You *and* the child know that you are really playing—which does not mean that what you are doing isn't serious. Nothing is more serious business for a child than knowing it *will* be an adult—and *wanting* to be, i.e., *wanting to do the things we do*— and knowing that it can't really do them yet. What is wrong is to say what a child is doing as though the child were an adult, and not recognize that he is still a child playing, above all growing."[4] I think we can say that Augustine describes himself as a child who is already an adult, even if in miniature; he may expand, but growing larger is not always growth. It is as if he writes knowing that he cannot have grown into adulthood in the face of his elders' failure to acknowledge his desire to do so, in the absence of their responsive, welcoming recognition of him as a child, and so as someone who will be an adult, and who must therefore play at being an adult; and yet, since he *is* now an adult, telling his tale of unacknowledged childhood, he must always already have been one. Wittgenstein's child is growing toward language, and so toward adulthood; like Augustine's child, he has the desire for growth, but unlike him he also has its necessary condition—that of his elders' desire to reciprocate his desire, and their willingness to play.

[4] Cavell, *The Claim of Reason*, 176.

Second, the juxtaposition tells us that there is more subordi-
nation than emancipation in Augustine's tale. Augustine's child
will struggle to inherit a willingness to play with words, or
any sense that human life with language is playful rather than
sheer hard labour. And since his words are stolen, his right
to them unacknowledged by others, they will (for him) always
ultimately belong to his elders, be their private property; so
his way with them will inexorably, fearfully repeat their ways,
devoid of any sense that there is enough flexibility (enough
play) in human language and culture for him to find his own
way within it.

This may seem like a highly speculative extrapolation from
a very slender textual basis. But it is confirmed by the ways in
which Augustine continues the tale of his life into boyhood, in
the remainder of book 1 of the *Confessions*.[5] For there we find
him recalling that his continued impulses toward play rather
than study met with continued repression by his elders, through
the repeated meting out of punishment (*C*, 1:10); and his general authorial commentary on his schooldays shows the long-
term success of that repression. For, speaking as the adult who
developed from such instruction, he condemns his stubborn
childish preference for the playfulness of literature over the
rules of grammar (*C*, 1:13); and by more or less clearly associat-
ing literature (in both content and form) with self-indulgence,
the temptations of the flesh, and sinfulness, and grammar with
austerity, self-discipline, and an earthly image of divine authority (*C*, 1:16–19), he thereby dissociates playfulness from the essence of language in an essentially Manichean way. This gesture
sets the fundamental tone of Augustine's account, even though
he admits at one point that he learnt Latin quickly and easily
"from my nurses caressing me, from people laughing over
jokes, and from those who played games and were enjoying

[5] Hereafter, *C*.

them" (*C*, 1:14), even though his conversion is signalled by words seemingly overheard from a children's game (*C*, 9:12), and even though the mode of reading that emblematizes that conversion (enacted in book 13) revels in the allegorical play of the divine Word. We might think of this as indicating the incompleteness of Augustine's conversion—a conclusion entirely in keeping with his conception of conversion as always essentially incomplete, endlessly in need of repetition and renewal (as his account in book 10 of the self's essential unknowability to itself, the depths of its motivations so labyrinthine and unsurveyable that regression is always possible, would lead us to expect).

In short, Augustine's tale manifests the schizophrenia or hypocrisy he attributes to the elders whose teaching he has internalized—their capacity to pass over the essentially playful, self-indulgent, and sinful nature of their own activities when condemning that same nature in their young charges, their praise for poems about adultery modulating into condemnations of adulterous practices, their criticism of the mote of incorrect speech intimately juxtaposed with their endorsement of the beam of capital punishment. In this respect, the child who fathers the narrator of this tale is himself made in the image of his fathers, and grows to recount his own past in a manner that reiterates the worst of his culture rather than remaking it in the more humane image that his words elsewhere recognize and aim to attain. In Wittgenstein's child, human culture finds an independent life, an unpredictable future: he and his culture can grow and develop together; in Augustine's child, human culture is haunted by its past, and doomed to repeat it—its future is foreclosed.

Third, the juxtaposition brings out the fact that there is more sin than innocence in Augustine's portrait of desire. Augustine's child not only possesses the desire for language and the adulthood it emblematizes; he also plainly thinks of language *as such* as an instrument for the communication and satisfaction of desire, and depicts the adult world into which that language is woven as pervaded with desire—more precisely with a particular inflection of desire. It is a realm in which human beings struggle to possess what they want and reject what they do not want—in which their basic urge is to rearrange the world in the image of their own desires, in a manner reminiscent of Nietzsche's naturally noble exemplars of the will to power. One might say that Augustine here weaves together naming with mastery or domination over that which is named. It is as if somewhere in the background of his thinking, Augustine is assuming that Adam's divinely-granted authority to name every living thing (as recounted in Genesis) was meant solely and directly to prepare the ground for his consumption of those things (first the apple, and then—outside Eden—whatever he encountered in his sweat-soaked, anxious struggle for survival), rather than as a way in which he might register their independently-created essences and recognize the world they constitute as one naturally intended to accommodate his interests as well as to provide a fitting helpmeet.

Interestingly, Wittgenstein's tale does not exactly reject or avoid this Augustinian conjunction of language and desire, if taken at its most general level. Wittgenstein's child is, after all, playing at shopping; he acts as a messenger for one elder's linguistic expression of desire to another, he will (presumably) act as a messenger for the other's attempt to satisfy it—and the fruit he seeks links his tale with another, much earlier one that links apples with desire (the story with which we have been concerned throughout this book, a story from the book with which Augustine ends the *Confessions* by occupying himself). On the other hand, the very concreteness of Wittgenstein's tale militates against its reliance on desire being taken as a figure for the whole of the adult realm into which the child is being invited; the matter-of-factness of the adult exchange he facilitates, the downbeat sense it creates that the elder's investment in his desire for an apple allows for the possibility of the shopkeeper's inability to satisfy it, lacks the background sense (perhaps metaphysical, perhaps spiritual) of a world of unceasing, desirous struggle conjured up so effectively by Augustine—a world of original sinfulness delivered over to its own reproduction, as children imbibe their elders' enacted conception of words as instruments of self-satisfaction.

Of course, it is not just that Augustine's adult world is essentially sinful; in the immediate context of the quotation Wittgenstein chooses, he repeatedly portrays himself, even before properly entering that world, in similar terms.

> When I did not get my way, either because I was not understood or lest it be harmful to me, I used to be indignant with my seniors for their disobedience, and with free people who were not slaves to my interests; and I would revenge myself upon them by weeping. (C, 1:6)

> I have personally watched and studied a jealous baby. He could not yet speak and, pale with jealousy and bitterness, glared at his brother sharing his mother's milk. (C, 1:7)

> By groans and various sounds and various movements of parts of my body I would endeavour to express the intentions of my heart to persuade people to bow to my will. (C, 1:8)

Here, however, we need to recall that these claims about infant desire are based not on memory but on observation—the observations of an adult whose maturation was essentially conditioned by the condition of the stormy society into which he grew up, a society of sinfully desiring adults. If in order to grow up he had to insert himself into that system of self-interest and self-satisfaction, how could he interpret infant behaviour in any terms other than those in which he thereby learnt to interpret himself? But we should not forget that this is the kind of way in which philosophical fantasies of language and its users can find practical, concrete realization; when such fantasies inform our self-interpretations, they shape our actions and the thoughts and actions of those to whom our own actions are directed, and thereby come to reshape the reality they concern.

Wittgenstein's main purpose here appears to be that of trying to drive a wedge between two aspects of Augustine's picture—his sense of a fundamental connection between language and desire, and his Nietzschean vision of human beings as driven and mastered by the need to submit the world to their will. Wittgenstein offers no criticism of the former: indeed, since his tale variously implies that the inheritance of language is emblematic of human maturation, that this inheritance depends upon the child's willingness to desire it and to accept it as the medium for expressing his own desires, and that play is the primary mode of its acquisition, his narrative invites the conclusion that to acquire language is to participate in the play of human desire. But by implicitly dissociating himself from Augustine's vision of human beings as always already given over to the urge to remake the world in their image, he also implies that human desire is distinguishable from, say, need or fixation—that properly human growth should take us past an inability to accept the world's independence from our will, beyond a fixation on satisfying the relentlessly needy ego.

Having arrived at the claim that Wittgenstein's portrait of childhood can be read as contesting a Nietzschean strand of Augustine's tale, this might be a good point to ask a Nietzschean question about Wittgenstein's own philosophical practice—the practice called for by the specific deformations in our understanding of our life with words and in that life itself, which Augustine's picture exemplifies. In short, we must ask ourselves: what is the value of Wittgenstein's therapeutic procedures? We cannot simply dismiss this question by asserting that a practice of methodological neutrality must be morally neutral. After all, John Rawls's political liberalism aims to generate respect for as extensive a domain of neutrality as possible on the part of those deploying the state's coercive power between competing conceptions of the good, and does so by imposing a kind of methodological neutrality (through the veil of ignorance); but that patently does not make his vision of the just society morally and politically neutral—say, between liberalism and religious fundamentalism. The meaning or significance of methodological neutrality is never beyond ethical question.

Suppose we call Wittgenstein's philosophical practice a recovery of the ordinary: deploying other phrases of Wittgenstein's that I do not have the space fully to elaborate here, it asks us to work upon not just our intellects but our wills, with a view to coming to accept forms of life as given, to learning to leave everything as it is. The point of these admonitions can be derived from a clearer understanding of the philosophical impulse they are intended to counter; and for Wittgenstein, the key characteristic of that impulse is that it betrays and reinforces a false sense of necessity. The philosopher approaches the phenomena in the grip of a prior conviction that things must be a certain way, and is then forced to distort or deny the way things actually are or to posit an underlying realm of essence in which things really are the way she knows they must be; Wittgenstein calls this "subliming the ordinary," a phenomenon that Nietzsche might recognize as one form of the philosopher's preference for Being over Becoming, for a fantasy of the true world over the world of appearance. Hence, when Wittgenstein recommends that we look and see, and challenge ourselves simply to accept, how things actually are, when (as Heidegger might put it) he asks us to attune ourselves to the real modalities of our existence, this amounts to a self-denying ordinance directed against philosophical wilfulness and its desire to remake the everyday in its own image—whether in sceptical or Nietzschean expressions of the Augustinian impulse.

In this respect, Wittegenstein's later methodological neutral-ity echoes his early conception of ethics: the happy man of the *Tractatus Logico-Philosophicus* is not he who finds answers to the problems of life, but he who finds life unproblematic. He is the one for whom the solution to the problem of life is seen in the vanishing of the problem, in coming to see what happens simply as what happens, as opposed to something that opposes or resists our conception of what should or must happen. And underlying this Tractarian echo, there is a biblical one—as when Christ reminds us that the rain falls on the just and the unjust alike, or the prodigal son's brother is invited to accept that the rewards and love unstintingly lavished on his returning sibling are neither misplaced in themselves nor degrading of the rewards and love unremittingly directed at him.

These are all variations on the key spiritual idea of accepting the world's independence of our will, and hence acknowledging this aspect of our own finitude. One might express it as a con-ception of the self as dying to a conception of itself as being at the centre of the universe, and accepting thereby the utter non-necessity of things going well for it—at least as it judges flour-ishing. For if life is a gift to be accepted beyond wish, will, and craving, then we cannot think of anyone or anything, and thus of the world, as owing us a living. A Nietzschean nose might well detect more than a whiff of God's decomposing body in the vicinity.

3. THE WORLD IN AUGUSTINE'S IMAGE

I want to conclude my exploration by examining the second section of the *Investigations*, in which Wittgenstein elaborates his initial response to Augustine's picture of language a little further.

That philosophical concept of meaning has its place in a primitive idea of the way language functions. But one can also say that it is the idea of a language more primitive than ours.

Let us imagine a language for which the description given by Augustine is right. The language is meant to serve for communication between a builder A and an assistant B. A is building with building-stones: there are blocks, pillars, slabs, and beams. B has to pass the stones, and that in the order in which A needs them. For this purpose they use a language consisting of the words "block," "pillar," "slab," "beam." A calls them out;—B brings the stone which he has learnt to bring at such-and-such a call.—Conceive this as a complete primitive language. (*PI*, 2)

This passage raises a number of questions that are relevant to our purposes. First, given Nietzsche's presence in this book, as well as in Wittgenstein's and Augustine's previous stances, it is striking that—not only in section 2, but in every succeeding section of the *Investigations* in which Wittgenstein returns to and elaborates his tale of the builders (cf. *PI*, 8 and 16)—the distribution of the roles of builder and assistant never varies. A is always the builder and B is always his assistant; despite the fact that the language game in which they are participating does (and, for good Heideggerian as well as Wittgensteinian reasons, must as a matter of principle) allow for either participant to occupy either role, no swapping of roles in fact ever takes place. In effect, then, B is always the slave of A's desires; and the language with which their practice equips them both appears as A's way of mastering the world, of remaking it in the image of his own will through B's efforts, and hence of reducing B to a means to that end. Since this language game is Wittgenstein's best attempt to provide a context for which Augustine's description of language is actually right, it seems that we are invited here to acknowledge that an inflection of the master-slave

model of human social relations that Hegel made famous, but
to which Nietzsche (along with many others) gave his own inflection, is implicit in the conception of human society that Augustine's picture of words at once engenders and presupposes.

Second, one might feel inclined to ask whether Wittgenstein's aim of imagining a fit context for Augustine's vision
of language is realized (insofar as it is realized) only because
what he imagines is a primitive use of language, or the use of a
primitive language. In other words, is the legitimacy of talking
of what the builders are doing as the use of a language made
tolerable only because the concept of a language is here being
paired with and inflected by the concept of the primitive (a concept anyway likely to be called up in Augustine's thinking by
his focus on childhood)? And this in turn raises the question:
in what sense is the builder's language "primitive"?

Stanley Cavell has specified at least three main interpretative
possibilities that open up from this conjunction of concepts.[6]
First, one might imagine that the builders are primitive human
beings, a species of Neanderthal; unlike human children, these
builders evince no capacity or willingness to experiment with
combining their words, to project them into new contexts, to
play with them; they appear to be completely lacking in imagination, their future with their words foreclosed, and hence the
claim of their calls to be words uncertain. Second, one might
imagine that this system of communication is designed for a
modern building site, with huge amounts of noisy activity as a
permanent background. Here, the language is stripped back to
its essentials relative to the purposes at hand; the language may
be primitive, but its users are not. The question about this line
of imagination does not relate to the humanity of such builders,
but to the fact that Wittgenstein's tale does not explicitly allow
for any of the wider cultural and social contexts within which

---

[6] Cf. "Declining Decline," in *This New yet Unapproachable America* (University of Chicago Press: Chicago, 1989).

such a sophisticated deployment of words could alone make sense (since that would be a context in which these "words" would not be the whole language of the builder's society, as Wittgenstein appears to claim [*PI*, 6]).

But it is Cavell's third interpretative possibility that relates most directly to our concerns. This is the suggestion that the primitiveness of the builders is an allegory of the way people in modern culture in fact speak. Accepting for a moment that it is part of Wittgenstein's challenge to us as readers of his tale to fill in the unspecified wider context of the builders" lives, then we can imagine that their unvarnished, almost psychotically functional deployments of their words constitute a microcosm of their ways with words off the building site. The idea is not that their vocabulary might be restricted to these four words; it is that their orientation to their words for building exemplifies that of their culture as a whole to its words (an orientation not so distant from that of the characters in Wittgenstein's tale of the shopping trip). We might, in other words, take them as non-primitive human beings in the surroundings of a developed culture who nonetheless find themselves speaking primitively—in more or less simplified expressions of more or less uncultivated, fixated desires. Here, the culture as a whole must be thought of—as Heidegger insistently thinks of our fallen culture, and Augustine uninsistently assumes about his culture—as pervaded by debilitating noise and distraction, as a collectivity that is stupefying itself by the poverty of its practices and conceptions, stultifying the human imagination and depriving itself of a future.

Wittgenstein's parabolic projection of a context that fits Augustine's picture thus brings out a way of understanding that paradigm as representing not an empty or incoherent fantasy of our solid, self-sustaining ordinary life with words, but rather a depiction of the way we presently, ordinarily inhabit our language as tending toward, if not already reduced to, the primitive—as a form of life that is already staking a claim to the

Heideggerian predicates of idle talk. And his choice of Augustine as the starting-point of his own investigation further suggests that he takes this primitive depiction and realization of human culture to be exemplary—not just accidentally true of us then (when Augustine wrote) and now (when Wittgenstein cites that writing), but a persisting tendency in human imagination and life, both within and without philosophy, and hence presumably the result of forces that are fundamental to our nature and self-understanding, however hard they may be to identify and anatomize. Nevertheless, where Augustine thinks of this enigmatic perversity as one to which we are fated, as an aspect of our fallen condition, Wittgenstein's representation of Augustine's picture as primitive instead suggests that things need not be this way. The wager upon which his therapeutic philosophical practice is uninsistently founded is that we can inhabit our life of and with language otherwise.

Our investigations have suggested that Wittgenstein's agonistic relation to Augustine's ways of thinking about words and the human world they exemplify and reinforce might be summarized in the following way. Wittgenstein accepts Augustine's view that human maturation is a mimetic process structured around desire. It is not just that human children will grow into their humanity only insofar as they desire to do so, and so are not only able but also possessed by a desire to mimic their elders; it is also that they grow precisely by acquiring arrays of wants and interests that internally reproduce the desires to which their elders' modes of active engagement with the world give expression. Thus, the structure of desire-creation is not straightforwardly linear (a matter of subjects directly fixing upon objects immediately understood as desirable to them) or even reflexive (a matter of one subject desiring another's desire—desiring to be the object of another subject's desire), but rather triangular or mediated (we desire what another desires, according to the other's desire). Wittgenstein also accepts that everyday life tends to exemplify a particular inflection of that triangular mimetic structure: children inherit essentially self-interested desires, hence a conception of the world as to be remade in our image, and hence (given the assumption that there will never be enough desirable objects in the world to satisfy all who want to have them) a conception of others as our rivals in that task, beings who will deprive and in this respect victimize us unless we victimize them. But Wittgenstein rejects the thought that this inflection of the structure of human reproduction is necessary: it is rather primitive, rooted in a certain picture of words, speakers, and world from which we must achieve a certain kind of conversion.

This might seem to demonstrate that Wittgenstein's work does indeed aim to engage with Augustine's words at a spiritual or theological level—specifically by isolating and bringing out the extent to which his picture of language, being necessarily a picture of the human form of life, is also a depiction of the human condition as originally sinful. But it also seems to show that Wittgenstein intends (and intends his readers) to engage critically with this dimension of Augustine's thinking—to reject the idea that the condition Augustine depicts is one to which we are fated by virtue of our sheer humanity. In this respect, however, appearances may be deceptive. For the terms of the Wittgensteinian critique of Augustine as I have just laid them out are a virtual transcription of another reading of the doctrine of original sin—one that is primarily associated with the work of René Girard.[7]

According to Girard's famous and highly influential analysis, a triangular mimetic structure constitutes human selfhood and

---

[7] The best general, theologically-inflected account of Girard's work of which I am aware is James Alison's *The Joy of Being Wrong* (Crossroad Herder: New York, 1998).

leads to conflict in the ways sketched above, a conflict whose pressures are relieved only when someone (or some group) in society is scapegoated and cast out. But no such casting out can definitively resolve the conflict that provokes it. For each such exclusion generates ambivalence toward the victim, as at once the focus of extreme hatred and the foundation of social peace (hence the need for rites and ceremonies in his praise, of the kind that Nietzsche's madman invokes on behalf of his fellow-murderers); and most importantly, it provides only temporary relief, given the inevitability of rivalrous desire. Thus, after a period—sometimes perhaps quite long-lasting—of social harmony, more rivalry will develop and another scapegoating will take place.

What is required for a truly decisive response to the problem is a forceful intervention into these mechanisms of rivalry and victimization—one that allows us to see what is happening, which means seeing our own complicity in arbitrary violence and the possibility of reconstituting ourselves otherwise, via a non-rivalrous mode of desire and desire-creation. On Girard's reading, Christ provides the necessary intervention: He identifies with the guiltless victim to the point of becoming one, without ever victimizing others in imitation or recompense; and He exemplifies a mode of non-rivalrous desire—a desire for the satisfaction of the other's desire as if it were one's own—that can be replicated and incorporated by others without generating rivalry and victimization.

This model of sinfulness can genuinely be thought of as hereditary or original, since rivalrous desire is not a contingent habit of our present selves, but rather our endlessly reiterated mode of constituting ourselves and our children by inheriting and bequeathing a victimizing (and hence, as Nietzsche intuited, a self-victimizing) self. But the very same constitutive mechanism also provides the means of its overcoming—the possibility of a non-victimizing counter-mode of mimesis, the *imitatio Christi.* The scapegoat mechanism is thereby deployed so as to found a community not founded on scapegoating but on its refusal, even to the point of accepting the role of scapegoating without responding in kind. Hence, Christ shows that what is most deeply "me" is utterly illusory; in revealing the depth of our sinfulness, He also reveals the possibility of our turning away from it, of a conversion or rebirth of humanity and human culture.

But since the rivalrous mimesis of desire is so deeply rooted in us, then it is always possible even for those whose goal is determined by its reshaping to maintain or fall back into an interpretation of ourselves that blocks this conversion. And from the perspective represented by Girard, Augustine's reading of human infancy as always already wilfully sinful prior to its authorization by sinful parents and adults both exemplifies a certain falling-back, and yet (in the honesty and depth of its internal contradictions and self-indictments) also provides the resources needed to wrench ourselves away from that fall. We might also note that Girard's analysis would entail a certain rereading of the Genesis story of the Fall itself (which is, we should never forget, an Old Testament and hence pre-Christian tale); for that tale pictures Adam's and Eve's entry into the realm of desire as an appropriation of what is proper to God: and this pictures God as having proclaimed His identity over theirs by a prohibition, and thus as exemplifying the essentially unchristian sense that not only all humans but even their divine original are constituted by rivalry beyond all redemption. In these ways, Girard is committed to arguing that the idea of humans as originally sinful can as easily be detached from its internal relation to the idea of humans as open to redemption through Christ within the precincts of Christianity as without them, and hence might require a critique of Christendom in the name of Christ. Even Christians need to recall that we could not have attained the conception of ourselves as originally sinful without receiving it directly from Christ (it runs so counter to the ways of conceiving the world and ourselves that structure our selfhood); but then its reception and comprehension are made possible by the very relationship that promises an overcoming of our inheritance. One might say: from the Christian perspective, the first Adam appears and can be properly understood only in the light, or through the eyes, of the second Adam.

Thus, Wittgenstein's sense that things might be otherwise than Augustine appears to present them as being does not entail that he rejects the very idea of human beings as originally sinful, or at least not all available versions of it (whether avowedly Christian or not). And we have already seen a number of ways in which his philosophical practice appears importantly, internally, mimetic of certain related aspects of the Christian understanding of the world—in its conception of human hubris, of our denial of our finitude and its overcoming, and of the nature, limits, and goal of therapeutic philosophizing. So we are now in a position at least to pose a question that may have at first seemed inarticulable in relation to so discreet, even self-denying, a text as the *Philosophical Investigations*. Is Wittgenstein's implicit presentation of his philosophical practice as a species of radical cultural and spiritual critique to be read, from a theological point of view, as hubris or as acknowledgement? Does it depend upon transposing essentially divine attributes to the therapeutic philosopher, in a manner reminiscent of Nietzsche's deliberate blasphemies; or does it, rather, declare the therapeutic philosopher's unavoidable indebtedness to certain basic forms of the life of the mind in Western culture, whilst reserving the right to contest their sense of where redemption is to be found? How are we to respond to Wittgenstein's late remark that "Bach wrote on the title page of his *Orgelbuchlein*, 'To the glory of the Most High God, and that my neighbour may be benefited thereby.' That is what I would have liked to say about my work"?[8] Why exactly might Wittgenstein feel that, even allowing for differences of historical context, he would, or could, not mean what Bach said? And must we share his feeling? Whatever the right answer to these questions may be, it appears that Christianity is in possession of at least some of the right words for what Wittgenstein has it at heart to say.

[8] From a 1949 letter to Drury; cf. R. Rhees, ed., *Recollections of Wittgenstein* (Oxford University Press: Oxford, 1984).

Conclusion

I HAVE BEEN TRYING to show that the three philosophers examined in this book share a conception of human beings as standing in need of redemption, rather than—say—of instruction in avoiding specific cognitive or moral errors, or help in improving (even perfecting) their capacity to grasp and realize the truth and goodness of things. For if redemption is what we need, then our present state must be seen not as one of imperfection but as one of wretchedness—more specifically, one of perversity. These philosophers find that we are flawed in our very structure and constitution—not only naturally capable, or even disposed, to act in ways that go against our own best interests and deepest nature, but always already turned against ourselves by virtue of what makes us human.

For Nietzsche, this inherent perversity is to be found in the decisively Christian terms in which we have conceived and realized our distinctively human form of life from its outset (terms that condemn the underlying truth of that life), as well as in the underlying truth of that life (insofar as Christianity's inherent perversity constitutes the most enduringly successful expression of the will to power, and thereby an exemplary manifestation of its nature). For Heidegger, that which makes it possible for us to grasp and interrogate the true nature of all things and thereby to fulfil our distinctive nature, also ensures that we are systematically inclined not only to fail to realize this capacity but also positively to flee from it, even to do everything in our power to suppress the mere awareness that we might do otherwise. For Wittgenstein, talking is the distinctively human form of life; but the very linguistic inheritance that constitutes our humanity and that will ultimately make it possible for us to recover it, is also what bewitches and subverts it. For it ensures that otherwise competent speakers are inveterately prone to find that they have lost control of their words, reducing themselves to the making of empty sounds exactly when they are most convinced that they are articulating the ultimate truth about reality.

These variations on the theme of a structural or constitutive human perversity engender corresponding variations on the theme that human beings are importantly, even essentially, enigmatic or mysterious to themselves. How can the most powerful and determinative human expression of the will to realize and enhance one's capacity to impose oneself on the world be a radical condemnation of itself—a venomous rejection of its own essence that simultaneously fulfils and enhances it? How can the creature whose nature is most fully realized in actively pursuing its inquiries into the true nature of all things (including itself) be inherently inclined to do everything in its power to lose itself in uncomprehending boredom? And what drives the speaking animal endlessly to attempt to transcend the very conditions of speech, thought, and knowledge in the name of their ultimate grounding or purification? All three thinkers catch us aiming in different ways to deny our own humanity, and are more or less reluctantly brought to see this impulse as distinctively human—hence, to conceive of the human as essentially turned against itself in ways that can neither be denied nor fully accounted for, given the basic assumptions of their own thinking.

At the core of this enigmatic perversity are certain specific formations and deformations of desire. In Nietzsche, this dimension of our humanity takes a sadomasochistic form; in Heidegger, it primarily concerns the ways we manage to take and lose an interest in the world and its possibilities. In Wittgenstein, it has to do with both—with a dual oscillation between (on the one hand) the desire to master the world by naming and the desire to suffer its overcoming; and (on the other) our capacity to make our words genuinely expressive of our interest, and the capacity entirely to empty words of any such interest by dislocating them from genuine human responsiveness. Overall, however, all three thinkers converge upon a conception of humans as inherently subject to a perverse and enigmatic desire either for or to be God. For Nietzsche, this desire epitomizes our sadomasochistic tendency, appearing as the most extreme available way to punish other human beings and ourselves; for Heidegger, it is the most revealing existentiell trace of the internal relation between the human and the nothing; for Wittgenstein, it projects the fantasy of a perspective from which we are excluded by our linguistic conditionedness.

Taken together, these are the points underlying my claim in the introduction that these thinkers wish to retain or reconstruct an originally Christian conception of ourselves as in need of redemption from ourselves, whilst detaching that conception from its companion notion of an essentially divine source of redemption (and indeed, of our conception that we require it)—even, one might say, whilst reconceiving our subjection to that companion notion as itself part of what we require redemption from. The basic structural difficulty of such a critical stance is plain. For these thinkers not only continue to retain the general notion of redemption (as opposed to amelioration or perfectibility) in portraying us as needing to be redeemed from the Christian idea of our need to be redeemed; their more detailed delineation of that general notion, in terms of an enigmatic structural perversity of desire, uncannily reproduces the key articulations of the very Christian conception of fallen humanity from which we are supposedly to be redeemed. At the very least, this suggests that it will be far more challenging than many seem to think to construct successfully a conception of the human condition that genuinely transcends the Christian theological horizon within which Western culture has developed. But it might also give us reason to take seriously the possibility that any sufficiently rigorous attempt to give an account of the human mode of being will find itself recurring to (even reiterating) the core tenets of Christianity precisely because those tenets are genuinely responsive to something deep and determining in human nature.

Even if one is not inclined to draw quite so controversial a moral from these structural affinities, there is one further specific consequence of this kind of project of detachment and reconstruction that is worth noting. For its constraints are such that it is destined to leave us with a conception of the human condition that is substantially more bleak than the Christian conception from which it aims to turn away. By retaining the idea of human perversity as structural and rejecting any divine means of overcoming it, we are left with merely human sources of therapeutic or emancipatory help; and if these are indeed conceptualized as merely human, and hence as available to us only from within the condition of mysterious perversity to which they aim to respond, then they can hold out no hope of overcoming that condition. At best, they can provide us with an understanding of its inherent perversity, and a way or ways of attempting to bear up under its burden.

Thus, Nietzsche's scathing account of Christianity is rather stronger on its diagnosis of the nature and pervasiveness of the problem than on what it might look like to get beyond the institutional and individual formations within which this perversity is embodied. Heidegger also tends to depict genuinely individual humanity as surviving only on the margins of an ever-strengthening constellation of cultural inauthenticity; and he famously declared that only a god could save us. The Wittgenstein depicted in these pages offers no reason to believe that the sceptical impulse to deny our linguistic conditionedness and condemn ourselves to forms of speech that spin free of their objects as well as their source, will ever be eradicated (as opposed to being countered from case to case of its specific expression).

Naturally enough, then, there are moments when these thinkers threaten to fail to live up to their condemnation of the human desire toward God, and are tempted instead to transpose the attributes of Christ onto those occupying the merely human position of therapist in their own spiritual and intellectual practices. This is most explicit in Nietzsche's late attempt to characterize the stakes of his writing in terms of an opposition between Dionysus and the Crucified; but it is prepared for by his ambivalent awareness of the degree to which his own genealogical practice inherits and furthers the distinctively Christian will to truth, and thus as taking on Christ's role even in trying to subvert it. Heidegger's presentation of himself as exemplary of authentic philosophizing throughout *Being and Time* tends to underplay his own indebtedness to others in his achievement of that perspective, even perhaps to the point of implying that he is a self-originating source of philosophical insight into our lostness to ourselves, an uncaused cause of self-overcoming.[1]

Such outbreaks of hubris are not absent from Wittgenstein's personal life and academic career; but is it not possible to argue that he, alone of our three thinkers, seems to have been capable of keeping his philosophical strategies essentially free of them? Against this, his ideal of philosophical practice might be thought to posit an inhuman ideal of self-restraint and self-denial; for it advocates a mode of therapy whose strictly correct implementation would amount to the self's complete removal of its own interests and opinions from the scene of its philosophical exchanges with others, a ceding of the ground entirely to the words and thoughts of that other, a pure responsiveness to those words and thoughts without any reference to the thera-

---

[1] For more on this, see chap. 5, sect. 4, of my *Heidegger and* Being and Time.

pist's own. We can see here a form of dying to the self to which philosophy seems congenitally averse (whilst simultaneously being unable entirely to eradicate a sense of its seductiveness, from Plato's Socrates onward); do we also see—as many claim to see in Socrates' Platonism—a certain kind of desire to deny the human?

The Christian will, of course, be inclined to see the desire to deny the human at work in all three thinkers, in two related ways: insofar as each avowedly emancipatory philosophical practice transposes divine predicates onto human agents, and insofar as each practice represents Christianity as an expression of the enigmatic perversity it aims to acknowledge and neutralize (for from the Christian viewpoint, to relate oneself to God just is to fulfil one's humanity). She will further be inclined to regret that the inherent bleakness of these secularized displacements of her own conception of our wretched condition necessarily dispenses with the inherent optimism of their original; for their rejection of any divine transformative source of redemption also deprives them of any coherent prospect of achieving thoroughgoing redemption, and hence of what one might call "the joy of being wrong"—the indissociability within Christianity of a conception of oneself as originally sinful and the knowledge that one is redeemed.

Nevertheless, as we have seen, these thinkers are not only prepared to take seriously, but are in various ways forced to endorse, a conception of the human as structurally perverse beyond any full accounting, our desires and self-interpretations systematically turned against themselves and away from the truth of our nature and of our world. As a consequence, they necessarily take their readers to the limits of a wholly secular, Enlightened conception of the human creature and its place in the universe—compelling our thinking to the point at which it threatens to subvert our sense of the self-sufficiency of its bases. What they accordingly share with the Christian is a sense of the true modality of our tendency to turn away from our own best selves; for both, our repeated aversiveness to the true and the good is not a sequence of accidents, a sheerly contingent series of events that might equally plausibly have been otherwise, but something more like a necessity of the very nature that aversiveness subverts. Seeing this perversity as closer to essence than accident may not compel anyone to adopt a Christian understanding of its sources and cure—particularly since that understanding ultimately asks us to see even this essential perversity as open to overcoming; but without such an initial reattunement of our sense of the modalities of human existence, Christianity cannot possibly appear as a viable, humanly inhabitable, intellectual and moral stance.

At the very least, then, Nietzsche, Heidegger, and Wittgenstein hold open the possibility of taking religious points of view seriously, by making it clear that a wholly secular perspective is not a necessity—that the human condition might be understood otherwise without condemning ourselves to a libel against human modes of being altogether. And such a reorientation of our contemporary sense of cultural possibilities would be no small thing.

Index

Adam, 1–3, 7, 15, 51, 104, 115–16
animality, 42, 47, 67–84; domesti-
    cated vs. wild, 77
Aquinas, 4–6, 8
Aristotle, 3–5, 8
asceticism, 3, 6–7, 39–40, 41, 107–8
Augustine, 85–116
authenticity, 49–56, 59, 60–61, 63,
    65, 74, 83, 121

Bach, J. S., 116
Barth, K., 31
Being and Time, 46–70, 122
benumbment, 71, 74–75, 81
boredom, 79–82
Buddha, 27
builders, 108–12

Cavell, S., 16–18, 23n, 93, 100n,
    101, 110–12
Christianity, 10–11, 16–18, 122–24;
    Nietzsche's critique of, 26, 29–31,
    32–36, 38–39, 44; Heidegger's re-
    lation to, 47–48, 55–56, 56–66;
    Wittgenstein's relation to, 108,
    114–16
conscience, 36–39
conversion, 89, 95, 103, 115
criteria, 93–96

Darwin, C., 34
death, 59–66, 69–70, 76, 80
Derrida, J., 68, 74
desire, 34, 41–42, 80–84, 101–2,
    103–6, 109, 111, 113–17,
    119–20
Desmond, W., 23n
discourse, 47, 51, 75
dying to the self, 32, 36, 63, 108,
    122–23

Easter, 29–31, 80
enigma, 12, 14–15, 55–56, 66, 68,
    83, 112, 119–24
Enlightenment, 3–9, 27–28, 123
Eve, 1–3, 115

Fall, the, 1–3, 28–29, 38–39, 43,
    49, 66, 67–68, 84, 115–16
falling, 28–29, 49–56, 81
form of life, 32, 62–63, 96, 107,
    118
Freud, S., 34
Fundamental Concepts of Metaphysics,
    70–84

Gay Science, 18–31
genealogical method, 32–34, 122
Genealogy of Morality, 32–45

Girard, R., 112–17
God, 1–3, 6, 19, 21–22, 58, 62–63,
    94–95, 108, 120
grammar, 93–96

Hegel, G.W.F., 110, 118
Heidegger, M., 13–15, 31, 46–
    84, 88, 93, 107, 109, 111–12,
    118–24

Incarnation, the, 30, 44

Jungel, E., 31

Kant, I., 12, 94
Kierkegaard, S., 15–16, 16–
    18, 31, 47–49, 56–60, 61–
    64, 66
Krell, D., 73–75, 76
Kuhn, T., 88–89

language, 17–18, 37, 72–75, 85–
    113, 119
Lewis, A., 31n

Macbeth, 23–26
MacIntyre, A., 3–6, 11, 71–
    73, 76
madman, 18–31, 45, 63, 114
Marx, K., 34
master morality, 34
morality, 3–9, 32–45, 57–58

negation, 14, 63, 65–66, 74–75,
    80, 120
Nietzsche, F., 4, 13–15, 16–45, 63,
    104, 106, 107–8, 109–10, 114,
    116, 118–24
nothingness. See negation
nullity. See negation

original sin, 6–12, 14, 15–16, 38, 44–
    45, 86–87, 95, 104–6, 113–17,
    118–24

Paul, Saint, 41
perfectionism, 10
perversity, 11–12, 39–40, 41, 43, 51,
    53, 55–56, 66, 83–84, 112, 118–24
phenomenology, 47, 59, 64–66
Philosophical Investigations, 86–117
pictures, 87–89
Plato, 27, 91, 123
priests, 42–43
primitive, 110–12
projection, 78–79, 82

Rawls, J., 7, 107
redemption, 6–10, 43, 53, 56, 115–
    16, 118–24
religion, vs. morality, 6–11, 36–37

sado-masochism, 35, 36, 120
Sartre, J-P., 13, 31
scapegoat, 26, 114–17
scepticism, 93–96, 98–99, 121
slave morality, 35–36

terror, 22, 82
theology, 46–47, 56, 68, 113, 116,
    121
therapy, 95–96, 106–8, 122
Tractatus Logico-Philosophicus, 88, 108
Trinity, the, 30

wholeness, 57–61, 65–66
will to power, 17, 35–36, 39, 104
will to truth, 36–37, 39–40
Wittgenstein, L., 7, 13–15, 86–117,
    119–24
worldliness, 53–55

Working with Parents of Exceptional Children

A Guide for Professionals

Working with Parents of Exceptional Children

A Guide for Professionals

Richard M. Gargiulo
The University of Alabama in Birmingham

HOUGHTON MIFFLIN COMPANY   **BOSTON**
Dallas   Geneva, Illinois   Hopewell, New Jersey   Palo Alto

Printed in the U.S.A.
Library of Congress Catalog Card Number: 84-81345
ISBN: 0-395-35767-5
ABCDEFGHIJ-FG-8987654

Excerpts from the following material have been reprinted by permission of the publishers:

Charles W. Telford, James M. Sawrey, *The Exceptional Individual*, 4th ed., © 1981, pp. 18, 164–166. Reprinted by permission of Prentice-Hall, Inc., Englewood Cliffs, N.J.

Lawrence M. Brammer, *The Helping Relationship: Process and Skills*, 2nd ed., © 1979, pp. 40, 45, 50–51, 52, 58, 61, 75, 156, 157. Reprinted by permission of Prentice-Hall, Inc., Englewood Cliffs, N.J.

From A. W. Combs, D. L. Avila, and W. W. Purkey, *Helping Relationships: Basic Concepts for the Helping Professions.* Copyright © 1971 by Allyn and Bacon, Inc. Reprinted with permission. Adapted from A. W. Combs et al., *Florida Studies in the Helping Professions* (Social Science Monograph No. 37), by permission of University Presses of Florida.

John Bryant, "Parent-Child Relationships: Their Effect on Rehabilitation," *Journal of Learning Disabilities*, 1971, 4, 325–329. © 1971 by The Professional Press, Inc. Reprinted by special permission of The Professional Press, Inc.

Contents

Preface   ix

Chapter 1   Introduction   1
              A historical perspective on exceptionality   2
              Who is exceptional?   3
              The parent-professional relationship   4
              Purpose and plan of the book   7

Part one

Parents and families of exceptional children

Chapter 2   States and stages of
              parental reactions   13
              The myth of the perfect child   14
              The psychology of adjustment   18
              Patterns of parental reactions   19
              A final word   37

Chapter 3   **Understanding family dynamics**   **41**

Developmental perspectives of the family   43
The handicapped child and the family   46
A final word   63

Chapter 4   **Parents speak out**   **69**

A final word   110

Part two

Helping and helpers

Chapter 5   **Understanding helping**   **117**

A definition of helping   118
Helping—art or science?   119
The helping process   120
Concepts held by good helpers   123
Helping—for whose benefit?   126
The helper as a person   127
How effective helpers view themselves   128
Characteristics of an effective helper   129
A final word   135

Chapter 6   **Helping skills**   **137**

Listening   138
Attentiveness   146
Leading   147
Questioning   154
Barriers to effective helping   159
A final word   166

Chapter 7   **The helping relationship**   **169**

Understanding the helping relationship   170
The helper's purpose   173
Helping goals   174
The helping setting   176
The helping interview   177
Referrals   188
Helper ethics   189
A final word   190

Chapter 8   **Helping approaches**   **193**

Dimensions of helping theories   196
Representative helping viewpoints   197
Toward a personal theory of helping   215
A final word   216

Appendix   **Resources for parents and professionals**   **221**

Author/source index   **227**

Subject index   **231**

Preface

Since the mid-1970s the field of special education has undergone tremendous change. Many of the changes have been a direct consequence of court decisions, the passage of the Education for All Handicapped Children Act of 1975 (Public Law 94-142), and the activities of various parent and professional associations. One particularly important change that has taken place is in the relationship between parents and the professionals who provide services to exceptional children and their families. Parents are no longer on the periphery of the process by which decisions are made about their children. They are now accorded equal status with professionals and participate directly in the planning of their children's education.

Audience

The primary audience of *Working with Parents of Exceptional Children: A Guide for Professionals* is teachers, both preservice and practicing professionals. Because parents of exceptional children are usually involved with a variety of professionals (speech therapists, social workers, health practitioners, counselors, physical therapists, school psychologists, as well as teachers), this text is also intended for individuals in the helping professions. It is my belief, and the premise of this book, that all professionals who work with parents of exceptional children should possess the skills needed to establish and maintain a productive helping interaction.

Purpose

The success of the collaboration between parents and professionals depends not only on the professionals' sensitivity to the parents' needs but also on the professionals' ability to interact with parents. The purpose of this book is to promote professionals' understanding of and sensitivity toward parents of exceptional children. It is also the book's intent to develop the skills needed to establish an effective helping relationship. Helping parents necessitates the development of both dimensions within the professional. Consequently, the organization of the text reflects these concepts.

The text opens with an introductory chapter that examines the theme of the book—working with parents of exceptional children. The remaining seven chapters are divided into two parts. Part One contains chapters that focus on the handicapped child's impact on his or her family. Chapter 2 describes a three-stage model of parental response to an exceptional child. Family relationships and sibling reactions are the focal point of Chapter 3. The first part concludes with Chapter 4, which is a collection of personal anecdotes from parents of exceptional children. Part Two comprises four chapters that cover the major concepts and theories of helping. Chapter 5 discusses helping in its various forms and focuses primarily on the role and characteristics of an effective helper. Chapter 6 outlines requisite helping skills for professionals, and Chapter 7 describes the components of a helping relationship, including the four stages of the helping interview. An overview of some of the major helping theories is provided in Chapter 8. The two-part presentation of content is designed to enable the reader to develop more fully into an empathetic and effective helper.

Features

Several features have been incorporated in the text to facilitate students' understanding of the concepts presented. Parental and sibling anecdotes provide first-hand accounts of the effects that a child's exceptionality may have on the lives of family members. Throughout Part Two, examples of parent-professional dialogues apply specific helping skills from different professional perspectives. The text reflects a generic philosophy: chapters are not arranged according to categorical labels (for example, "Counseling Parents of Mentally Retarded Children") or levels of disability (for example, "Working with Parents of Severely Impaired Children"). The intent of this approach is to develop helping skills that are appropriate for professionals working with parents of any exceptional child. Bibliographical references for all in-text citations appear at the end of each chapter. An appendix provides a listing of different groups and associations concerned with individuals who have special needs.

Acknowledgments

I am deeply grateful to the many individuals who have contributed to the development of this book. Numerous colleagues provided constructive criticism and useful suggestions that helped shape the text. Their recommendations greatly enhanced the presentation of the material. I wish to thank:

> Anita L. Archer, San Diego State University
> Nancy K. Klein, Cleveland State University
> Cleborne D. Maddux, Texas Tech. University
> Alec F. Peck, Boston College
> Donald Potter, University of South Dakota
> Sheryl L. Roesser, University of Northern Colorado
> Donald Sellin, Western Michigan University
> John F. Toker, Kearney State College

My sincere appreciation is also extended to Judy Maxey, Lory Pratt, Sheryl Sabo, Carol Terry, and Major Marks for their rapid and accurate typing of the manuscript. A very special thank you is reserved for the editorial staff of Houghton Mifflin Company, who provided continued assistance throughout the development of this manuscript. My acknowledgments would be incomplete without recognizing the immense contributions of my wife Lisa. Her editorial assistance, typing, proofreading, and belief in this project deserve special recognition. In addition, my two daughters, Christina and Cara, each of whom is truly exceptional in her own unique way, also shared in the production of this book. Their patient understanding of why their daddy was always so busy was greatly appreciated. This book is dedicated to my family.

Richard M. Gargiulo

It is not enough to give the handicapped life, they must be given a life worth living.
—Helen Keller

Working
with Parents of
Exceptional Children

A Guide for Professionals

Chapter 1:
Introduction

> *Predictions are very difficult to make, especially when they deal with the future.*
>
> —Mark Twain

We live in a society that embraces the normal or average person, a society that easily recognizes and supposedly accepts individual differences but is mainly organized around the concept of similarity. When an individual does not correspond to society's standards for normalcy, we become disconcerted and tend to reject and categorize individuals on the basis of supposed aberrations. Americans, by and large, relate to and judge people on the basis of the labels attached to them—for instance, labels that describe a person's occupation, religion, or race. Likewise, terms identifying someone as handicapped or disabled generally produce a variety of verdicts and assumptions in addition to a wide range of reactions and emotions. Handicapped citizens are frequently portrayed as deviant, incompetent, or helpless (Gliedman & Roth, 1980). A disability label often leads to social isolation and assigns inferior status. As a consequence, many people fail to realize that a person with a handicap is first and foremost an individual. A disability should be secondary to a person's needs as a human being.

Most people have a poor idea of the problems encountered by handicapped children and their parents. Understanding of these difficulties, although grievously inadequate, is increasing (Ward & Reale, 1972); in fact, concern for children who are handicapped or have special needs is at an all-time high. In the past decade, a flurry of activity has arisen on behalf of exceptional children and their parents. This thrust has been spearheaded by the activities of parent and professional groups and associations, legal mandates, legislative enactments, and, in general, a moral awakening to the exceptional person's right to live his or her life to its fullest potential. As a result, society has become increasingly observant of the unique characteristics and assets of its handicapped citizens. Today, the exceptional child and his or her family find themselves propelled from the background to the foreground of social awareness.

A historical perspective on exceptionality

Although a great deal of attention and concern are currently focused on the special needs person, progress in this area has been very slow. The programs, practices, and facilities available to handicapped people at any given time reflect the prevailing social climate. As people's ideas and attitudes about exceptional individuals change, so do the services (Blackhurst & Berdine, 1981). Change in attitudes is generally a prerequisite to change in the delivery of services.

Since ancient times, societies have dealt with deviant or defective citizens in various ways. Early Greek and Roman cultures considered handicapped people to be cursed and nonproductive. In order to preserve the strength of their civilizations, such individuals were destroyed. In medieval times, handicapped people were both feared and revered because they were thought to possess magical powers. In other instances, defective individuals found their way into castles, where as court jesters or fools they were mocked and ridiculed while being protected and shown favor. During the periods of the Renaissance and Reformation, two distinct beliefs emerged. On the one hand, handicapped children were often called *les enfants du bon Dieu* ("the children of God"). Others persecuted handicapped people and thought mentally retarded people to be "filled with Satan." Even within the recent past, mentally retarded or emotionally disturbed individuals have sometimes been considered dangerous and treated as criminals (Blackhurst & Berdine, 1981; Mandelbaum & Wheeler, 1960).

In a similar vein, Kirk and Gallagher (1983) delineate four stages in the development of society's attitude toward handicapped individuals:

1. during the pre-Christian era the handicapped tended to be neglected and mistreated;
2. during the spread of Christianity they were protected and pitied;
3. in the eighteenth and nineteenth centuries institutions were established to provide separate education;
4. in the latter part of the twentieth century there has been a movement toward accepting handicapped people and integrating them into society to the fullest extent possible. (p. 6)

American attitudes toward the exceptional person parallel these stages. Initially, there were no public provisions for handicapped persons. Often they were relegated to poorhouses or kept at home with no educational opportunities. In the mid 1800s, many states established institutions that provided training as well as protective environments. The introduction of special classes for the exceptional student in the late 1800s characterized the third phase. The current and final stage in the development of American attitudes is reflected in the integration of the handicapped child with his or her nonhandicapped peers (Kirk & Gallagher, 1983). One could safely speculate that there will be a continuation of the trend toward recognizing both the potential and the rights of all individuals regardless of their abilities or disabilities.

Who is exceptional?

There have been many attempts to answer the question, "Who is an exceptional person?" Responses range from the very general—

someone who deviates from the average or norm—to the very specific, often reflecting a professional bias or orientation (for example, a psychometric, social, educational, or medical viewpoint). A pragmatic approach to defining exceptionality may be an appropriate compromise between general and specific interpretations. The following definition proposed by Telford and Sawrey (1981) appears to be especially relevant. "The term *exceptional individual* usually refers to those people who differ from the average to such an extent that they are perceived by society as requiring special educational, social, or vocational treatment" (p. 1 Additionally, Ross (1964) suggests that the modification of anticipated child-rearing practices, whether necessary or simply thought to be required, also qualifies under the rubric of exceptionality. This dimension introduces the importance of the parents' perception of their son or daughter, for anything that affects the child also has an impact on the parent and vice versa. As Ross (1964) keenly observes, since parental attitudes and behavior are affected by their perception of the child's condition, it is irrelevant whether the handicap actually exists and genuinely necessitates a revision in child-rearing practices or simply arises from the parents' perception.

Furthermore, differences between handicapped and nonhandicapped individuals are differences only of degree and not of kind. This quantitative outlook (Telford & Sawrey, 1981) suggests that exceptional individuals are more like the typical person than they are different. Moreover, exceptionality is always relative to the social environment in which it exists. Thus, deviations become disabilities only when they interfere with the realization or attainment of one's full potential, whether social, vocational, or educational.

The parent-professional relationship

Parents have often represented an untapped resource for professionals who work with exceptional children. Inasmuch as parents are capable of making valuable contributions, their involvement with professionals is important to the development of the handicapped person. In comparison with professionals, parents have a greater investment in their children, not only of time but also of emotion. No other person will know the child as well as the parents do. Their experiences predate and exceed those of any professional (Webster, 1977). As a consequence, they have more influence and are capable of assuming a more positive and active role than traditionally accorded to them (Feldman, Byalick, & Rosedale, 1975). Despite this fact, the history of parent-professional partnerships has been counterproductive and gloomy (Gallagher, Beckman, & Cross, 1983). Only recently have the contributions of parents been recognized. No longer are they excluded from active involvement and participation. Rather, parents should be considered as full-fledged partner with professionals. If this alliance is to be successful, it will require a realignment of professionals' attitudes toward and about parents. The concept of a collaborative relationship infers an equality in the partnership.

Optimal results are often achieved when parents and professionals work together for the betterment of the exceptional individual. Perhaps nowhere else is this partnership more evident than in the education of handicapped children. In the past, parental involvement with the educational process was vague. The parents' role was usually restricted to attending conferences and providing assistance with social or extracurricular activity. Educators were very willing to accept and were even grateful for the parents' help, but most were reluctant to allow parents to participate or to assume any larger responsibilities. Parents of handicapped children were often perceived as problems with which teachers had to contend. Some parents were even blamed for causing, or at least not preventing, their children's disabilities (Seligman, 1979). All too often parents were considered more of a nuisance than a resource (Seligman & Seligman, 1980). They were frequently analyzed, criticized, or made to feel responsible for their children's problems. It was not unusual to hear of parents being called lazy and stupid, demanding, greedy, conniving, or angry and defensive (Rubin & Quinn-Curran, 1983). Indeed, Blackhurst and Berdine (1981) believe that some education professionals are afraid to admit that they need the parents' assistance. Other educators claim that the discipline of education is far too complex for parents to comprehend, and some view parents as incompetent; hence, little would be gained by directly involving them in the educational process. These notions, according to Barsch (1969), are indeed ironic, for parents often regard special educators favorably and consider them to be specialists.

In all fairness, part of the blame for less than positive interaction falls squarely on the shoulders of the parents. In some instances, parents have condemned the professional for not recognizing the disability sooner and occasionally have even accused the professional of causing the handicap. Some parents have inhibited the growth of the relationship with professionals by withdrawing. They have judged professionals to be insensitive, offensive, and incapable of understanding their situation because professionals themselves are rarely parents of an exceptional person. And so, barriers between the two groups have been erected.

Fortunately, the pendulum is now swinging in the other direction. Today, few educators would suggest that parent participation is unimportant to the success of most educational programs. Parents have learned to assume new responsibilities, partly as a result of legislative enactments, legal mandates, and social pressures. A prime example of this is the 1975 landmark legislation Public Law 94-142, the Education for All Handicapped Children Act, which requires, in an unprecedented fashion, that parents participate fully in educational decisions concerning their children. PL 94-142 not only mandates parental participation in the decision-making process but stipulates when and how parents are to be involved. Parents no longer speak of privileges; instead, they speak of rights. Consequently, the education of the special needs child is no longer the exclusive domain of the trained educator. As Smiches (1975) points out, parents have successfully involved themselves in securing equal educational opportunities for handicapped children, ensuring the students' right to due process, and establishing educational accountability.

PL 94-142 ushered in a new era in parent-professional interaction. It has, according to Turnbull (1983), involved parents to an unparalleled degree in the education of their children. As parents begin to interact with professionals, their status changes from that of mere recipients of services to that of active participants. In effect, PL 94-142 constructed a two-way street that allows parents both to receive and to share information about their children. The one component of PL 94-142 in which this exchange is particularly evident is the individualized education program (IEP). The IEP is the primary vehicle for assuring that a handicapped student receives an education appropriate to his or her unique needs and abilities. Turnbull (1983), in citing the *Federal Register*, states that one of the main purposes of the IEP is: "The IEP meeting serves as a communication vehicle between parents and school personnel, and enables them as equal participants, to jointly decide what the child's needs are, what services will be provided to meet those needs, and what the anticipated outcomes may be" (p. 22). The IEP, however, is more than a meeting of parents and educators and the subsequent development of a document; these are only parts of the IEP process, not its culmination (Fiscus & Mandell, 1983). The IEP process is predicated on parents and professionals working together with shared responsibilities through the following six stages identified by Fiscus and Mandell: "information gathering, decision making, identification and assessment, placement and program planning, program implementation, and program monitoring and evaluation" (1983, p. 21). Thus, the IEP process requires that educators and parents formulate decisions in a cooperative manner.

It is apparent that professionals can no longer ask the question, "Should we form a partnership?" but rather, "What kind of partnership can be established?" Clearly, the best partnership is a positive, meaningful one. A meaningful parent-professional relationship relies heavily on the professional's ability to understand parents and to communicate effectively with them (Mandell & Fiscus, 1981). Although not easy, a task of this magnitude can be accomplished. The extent to which professionals are successful in meeting this challenge influences the parents' perception of the professional and, consequently, their joint achievements.

Purpose and plan of the book

Being a parent is a complex and demanding responsibility. It is a role filled with many challenges and rewards. Some families, however, encounter unique situations and difficulties, particularly if one of their members is exceptional. At the same time, society's ability to assist these families with special needs is often limited. Professionals concerned about helping families with handicapped children are frequently faced with a shortage of knowledge and understanding about the topic. Many have completed their training without the benefit of exposure to this subject (Barsch, 1968; Gallagher, Beckman, & Cross, 1983). Yet the concept of parent counseling is considered an integral part of almost every program that provides services to the child with special needs (McDowell, 1976). Likewise, McWilliams (1976) argues that *all* professionals concerned with the exceptional individual and his or her family should be well versed in helping skills. Obviously, many professionals, each offering different areas of expertise and functioning in different environments, are frequently involved in varying degrees with parents of exceptional persons. As a rule of thumb, when in need of assistance, parents of children with exceptionalities will often seek out those individuals who are the direct service providers for their children rather than licensed or certified therapists (Heisler, 1972). Consequently, teachers, social workers, speech therapists, rehabilitation counselors, nurses, school psychologists, and physical and occupational therapists, among other skilled individuals, become the first line of defense for parents of children with special needs. It is for this audience that the book is written. I firmly believe that these individuals are sufficiently capable of providing a meaningful helping experience for parents. The purpose of this book, then, is to help develop skills for interacting with parents of exceptional children and to aid the professional in bridging the gap between the family's need for sensitive, competent help and his or her ability to effectively provide that assistance.

Helping parents of exceptional children requires empathetic understanding coupled with proficiency in the basic helping skills. This fundamental premise is applicable to *all* parents. Neither the type of disability nor the severity of the handicap itself is solely responsible for the adjustment and reaction of parents and siblings. Rather, the response of the family and its individual members is best understood as a reciprocal, complex phenomenon incorporating numerous factors. In other words, parents of a visually impaired person do not necessarily exhibit patterns of reaction different from those shown by parents of a retarded child or, to a greater or lesser degree, from those of parents of an orthopedically impaired youngster. Notably absent from this book, therefore, are chapters arranged according to categorical labels (for example, cerebral palsy, gifted, mentally retarded) or level of severity (for instance, mildly impaired or severely impaired). This book is intended to produce within the reader those helping skills necessary to develop and promote a helping relationship appropriate to parents of children with any of a variety of disabilities. As Webster (1977) observes, helpers need to "select the principles on which they will operate and apply these in all their contacts with parents; they need not seek unique principles to apply to unique situations" (p. xvii). This generic philosophy requires that the reader learn how to use himself or herself effectively in a helping relationship.

Part One of this book addresses the various types of parental reactions to handicapping conditions and their impact on the family. In addition, it provides in the parents' and siblings' own words their views, feelings, and impressions. The intent of this strategy is to give "a view from the other side of the mirror," the twenty-four-hour reality of living with an exceptional individual. Part Two presents concepts and theories of helping, appropriate helper attitudes and characteristics, essential helping skills, and an overview of the components of an effective helping relationship. It is hoped that this dual vantage point of theory and practice will facilitate the development of both competency and sensitivity.

> *There is a destiny which makes us brothers; none goes his way alone. All that we send into the lives of others, comes back into our own.*
>
> —Edwin Markham

References

Barsch, R. (1968). *The parent of the handicapped child: The study of child-rearing practices.* Springfield, IL: Charles C Thomas.

Barsch, R. (1969). *The parent-teacher partnership.* Arlington, VA: Council for Exceptional Children.

Blackhurst, A., & Berdine, W. (1981). *An introduction to special education.* Boston: Little, Brown.

Feldman, M., Byalick, R., & Rosedale, M. (1975). Parents and professionals: A partnership in special education. *Exceptional Children, 41,* 551–554.

Fiscus, E., & Mandell, C. (1983). *Developing individualized education programs.* St. Paul, MN: West.

Gallagher, J., Beckman, P., & Cross, A. (1983). Families of handicapped children: Sources of stress and its amelioration. *Exceptional Children, 50,* 10–19.

Gliedman, J., & Roth, W. (1980). *The unexpected minority: Handicapped children in America.* New York: Harcourt Brace Jovanich.

Heisler, V. (1972). *A handicapped child in the family: A guide for parents.* New York: Grune & Stratton.

Kirk, S., & Gallagher, J. (1983). *Educating exceptional children* (4th ed.). Boston: Houghton Mifflin.

Mandelbaum, A., & Wheeler, M. (1960). The meaning of a defective child to parents. *Social Casework, 41,* 360–367.

Mandell, C., & Fiscus, E. (1981). *Understanding exceptional people.* St. Paul, MN: West.

McDowell, R. (1976). Parent counseling: The state of the art. *Journal of Learning Disabilities, 9,* 614–619.

McWilliams, B. (1976). Various aspects of parent counseling. In E. Webster (Ed.), *Professional approaches with parents of handicapped children* (pp. 27–52). Springfield, IL: Charles C Thomas.

Ross, A. (1964). *The exceptional child in the family.* New York: Grune & Stratton.

Rubin, S., & Quinn-Curran, N. (1983). Lost, then found: Parents' journey through the community service maze. In M. Seligman (Ed.), *The family with a handicapped child* (pp. 63–94). New York: Grune & Stratton.

Seligman, M. (1979). *Strategies for helping parents of exceptional children.* New York: Free Press.

Seligman, M., & Seligman, P. (1980). The professional's dilemma: Learning to work with parents. *Exceptional Parent, 10,* 11–13.

Smiches, R. (1975). The parent professional partnership. *Exceptional Children, 41,* 565–566.

Telford, C., & Sawrey, J. (1981). *The exceptional individual* (4th ed.). Englewood Cliffs, NJ: Prentice-Hall.

Turnbull, A. (1983). Parent-professional interactions. In M. Snell (Ed.), *Systematic instruction of the moderately and severely handicapped* (2nd ed.) (pp. 18–43). Columbus, OH: Charles Merrill.

Ward, S., & Reale, G. (1972). Survey. *Exceptional Parent, 2,* 28–29.

Webster, E. (1977). *Counseling with parents of handicapped children.* New York: Grune & Stratton.

Part one:
Parents and families of exceptional children

Chapter 2:
States and stages of parental reactions

Chapter 3:
Understanding family dynamics

Chapter 4:
Parents speak out

Chapter 2:
States and stages
of parental reactions

> *Parents may find comfort, I say, in learning that their children are not useless, but that their lives, limited as they are, are of great potential value to the human race. We learn as much from illness as from health, from handicap as from advantage— and indeed perhaps more.*
>
> —Pearl Buck

"There is something very magnificent and very wonderful about having a child, unless that child is handicapped. Parents of handicapped children face something that is not wonderful, not magnificent" (Michaelis, 1980, p. 61).

Being parents of a handicapped child is not a role people choose for themselves. No one asks to be the parent of an exceptional person, nor is anyone ever prepared for the awesome responsibility. Parenting an exceptional child is a difficult, demanding, and often confusing and demoralizing task (Wentworth, 1974). It is ironical that although a specialized education is necessary for a multitude of occupations and positions, no formal training is required for the role of parenting, much less available for the unwelcome role of parenting an exceptional child.

Our society is becoming increasingly aware of the needs of exceptional persons (Ward & Reale, 1972). Yet parents of handicapped children are still faced with inadequate understanding and a society that is generally intolerant of deviations from the norm. It is important to remember that a handicapped child is first and foremost a child. Parents of handicapped children encounter situations and conditions that parents of nonhandicapped children may never experience, but their role is the same as that of any other parent.

One mother of a handicapped daughter observes that although help is available to the families of exceptional children, the focus is usually on helping the child through the parents (Wentworth, 1974). But parents of exceptional children often need help in sorting out their emotional reactions. This chapter will examine both parental and societal expectations of children and investigate a variety of parental reactions to having an exceptional child.

The myth of the perfect child

People choose to have children for various reasons. Many couples look forward to having children as the culmination and fulfillment of their marriage. As Begab (1956) points out, long before the baby is born the parents invest all the emotions of their unfulfilled wishes and anticipate the birth with feelings of hope and anxiety. During the pregnancy, the parents, especially the mother, develop an image of what their unborn child will be like (Ross, 1964). This image is usually a composite representation of the self, the spouse, other children, and other loved ones (Solnit & Stark, 1961). This psychological preparation, with its associated anxiety, is a normal process and usually involves the wish for a perfect baby and the fear of giving birth to a handicapped child. Parents do not initiate a pregnancy with the thought that their child will be handicapped.

In fact, for some parents this possibility is so painful and frightening that it is blocked from awareness.

A couple awaiting the birth of their child have cherished dreams and fantasies about their child's future, including a cultural stereotype of the ideal child who possesses all the attributes needed to compete successfully in life (Ross, 1964; Moses, 1977). Society fosters this expectation; as children, we learn to anticipate success, achievement, status, and love (Roos, 1977). With the birth of a handicapped baby or the realization at a later date (for example, during the early school years) that their child is exceptional, the parents' expectations are cruelly contradicted by reality, and their hopes, dreams, and fantasies die. This discrepancy between parental expectations and reality poses a major hurdle for the parents' coping abilities (Ross, 1975).

Children are important to their parents. They can be a source of joy or sorrow. A child represents a way for the parents to fulfill their own dreams of accomplishment and achievement. For some, the child is an extension of themselves; they live their lives vicariously through the life of the child. For others, the child is a means of affirming their success and ability to be parents; in still other instances, the child is a step toward immortality.

From a different perspective, Ross (1964, 1975) observes that a child may, quite literally, be considered as a "product of love," a personal achievement or accomplishment. Hence a normal child may be regarded as a reflection of personal adequacy ("See how good I am—see what I made"), while a handicapped youngster may be seen as an internalized indication of the parents', especially the mothers', worthlessness, inadequacy, and failure ("I've failed, I'm no good"). Ross (1964) cites the following syllogism as an example:

If I am a good parent I shall be blessed with a perfect baby.
The baby is not perfect.
Therefore, I must be bad. (p. 59)

Mothers often wait with mild anxiety for the husband's first impression of the newborn child. If the child is handicapped, the wife may view her husband's disappointment as disappointment in her for having produced a defective infant. This belief can add tremendous strain to the marital relationship. In some relationships, having a baby is an attempt to salvage the marriage and bring the two partners closer together; in other marriages, the child is considered to be external proof that a marriage does indeed exist.

A child may also be viewed as a gift, a presentation to the husband or grandparents. If the baby is handicapped, the value and the meaning of the gift are diminished or destroyed, for we have been taught that one does not give imperfect presents.

Ross further suggests that another way of viewing a baby is as a gift from God, a sign of grace, proof that the parents are worthy to be parents. A handicapped child is often considered to be an indication of heavenly dissatisfaction, a punishment for sins and proof of unworthiness and personal shortcoming. However, depending on the parents' religious faith or orientation, the birth of a handicapped child could also be interpreted as a special indication of grace, part of a divine plan, an honor reserved only for the most worthy and capable of individuals.

The various meanings that a child has for his or her parents are not limited to the infant or very young child. As the child grows and develops and passes through each stage, the parents anticipate the next level of development and plan accordingly. The first word, the first step, the first day of school, and the first date are all developmental milestones that bring pleasure and joy to most parents. They also provide order and a sense of direction for the parents' lives. However, a child who is exceptional, whether observed as such from birth, during the early years, or upon entry to school, may not be able to fulfill these expectations. There are no road maps to follow; the child becomes an exception to the normal rules of growth and development, and the rewards of parenthood may be diminished.

With the dream of the perfect child destroyed, their aspirations frustrated and egos threatened, parents are often left with guilt and self-recrimination. Having an exceptional child has been interpreted as an indication of a serious deficiency in one or both parents, a source of shame (Roos, 1977). "When a child fails to meet society's expectations, he is blamed and so are his parents. Often, parents are their own harshest critics, taking all the blame for their children's failure to meet expectations" (Brown, 1969, p. 98). Barsch (1969) acknowledges that our society demands conformity. A sense of urgency for achievement seems to prevail despite visible or invisible handicaps. When an individual is unable to reach developmental landmarks, explanations are demanded.

When these are provided, society may grant a reprieve, but does not absolve the parents of their obligations. What is more disheartening, however, is the unspoken accusation that somehow the parent is personally at fault. "Ultimately, you [the parents] are left with the feeling that because you produced the child, you are to blame for the problems. After all, there would be no problems if there was no child" (Schleifer, 1971, p. 3).

Society does not view exceptional children as worthy investments. The social message communicated to parents in any number of subtle ways is that those individuals who obviously need more help will receive less because they are worth less to society (Gorham, Des Jardins, Page, Pettis, & Scheiber, 1975; Michaelis, 1977). Because society places such an emphasis on intellectual adequacy, physical beauty, competitiveness, and self-sufficiency, parents often find themselves stigmatized due to the child's inability to meet societal demands of normalcy. When these standards are violated, the children are considered to be "bad" children and the parents are seen as "bad" parents. Likewise, society has perpetuated the myth that to be a parent is a good thing, but to be a parent of a handicapped child is a bad thing (Zuk, 1962). One father of a handicapped daughter notes:

Many of the basic problems with which parents of handicapped children have to deal come directly from society. Such problems originate in society's perpetration of certain myths or frauds, to put it bluntly. We are especially susceptible to these myths as we are growing up. One myth encouraged by the romance magazines that teen-agers read is that marriage is "eternal bliss." Another more pertinent myth is that out of this eternal blissful union will come children who are both physically and mentally beautiful and perfect. Therefore, the parents of a handicapped child have not lived up to the "ideal" and have produced an imperfect replica of themselves. This may cause much unconscious, if not conscious, guilt as well as feelings of inferiority. At the same time, if the parents are unfortunate enough to have a handicapped child (which society says subtly they are not suppose to do), society then hypocritically says they must be *superparents*. They must supply enormous additional amounts of care, love, and attention to their child. They must do this, additionally, on a 24 hour a day, 365 day a year basis; otherwise, they are *superbad*. (Greer, 1975, p. 519)

This father, who is a handicapped special educator, further comments on the difficulty of living up to and meeting society's expectations:

In the back of parents' minds, then, is a vague awareness that society is looking over their shoulders and judging if they are carrying out their pre-scribed duties, giving much love, attention, and devotion, not missing any treatment appointments, providing the best possible care, etc. This is a "goldfish bowl" type of existence which eventually takes its toll in energy, strength, and courage. (Greer, 1975, p. 519)

It has also been suggested that the world can be partitioned into three distinct groups of people:

There are those who can tolerate the everyday stresses and strains of life; they say little, and these are the average people. There are those who can-not tolerate the everyday stresses and strains of life; and they shout, and these are our leaders. Then, there are those who cannot tolerate the stres-ses and strains of life and they whisper, and these are our victims. Society has generally demanded that families of disabled children whisper. Society has implicitly blamed and punished those parents and professionals who have attempted to shout about their pain and anguish. (Schleifer, 1971, p. 5)

The psychology of adjustment

The realization that their child has a disability, regardless of when it is discovered, places tremendous stress on the parents' psychological coping mechanisms. The awareness that they will be unable to fulfill their dreams and aspirations may produce a wide range of emotional responses (such as shock, guilt, grief, and anger) and a feeling that a part of themselves has been lost forever. Parents have the right to exhibit these emotions; they are natural and normal. It would be unrealistic to expect parents to be glad about having a handicapped child. It should be recognized that parental reactions and responses are independent of when the exceptionality is first observed. In some instances, the handicap is identifiable at birth; in other cases, the emotional responses can be precipitated by a handicap resulting from an accident during the early childhood years or elicited when the child is labeled exceptional by the schools. It does not matter when the parents find out. The emotional repercussions are the same; only the duration differs.

Having an exceptional child affects parents in varying ways. Each situation is unique. More important are the parents' attitudes and the way they face the many problems and situations that confront them. Although an understanding of the child's handicap will not cause the disability to disappear, professionals who work with the parents and their child have the responsibility of assisting the parents not only in understanding their feelings, but also in better understanding the child and planning for his or her future. A handicapped child's prognosis is greatly enhanced if the parents have accepted both the child and his or her disability.

It is inaccurate to stereotype parents of handicapped children as a pathological group or to assume that all parents suffer emotional damage and require help (Schild, 1976; Stewart, 1978). Some parents cope in a constructive fashion, accepting the realities and dealing with the challenges in a manner that is helpful to the child (Smith & Neisworth, 1975). Roos (1977) asserts that stereotyping and general lack of knowledge about disabilities often leads to much professional mishandling of parents.

Parental reactions to children with different handicaps, although not identical, resemble each other to a considerable degree (Mac Keith, 1973; Drotar, Baskiewicz, Irvin, Kennell, & Klaus, 1975). It is a false assumption that the emotional responses of parents differ according to the child's handicap. Reactions differ more in degree than kind (Baum, 1962). Barsch's (1968) evaluation of parents of children with five different disabilities failed to find significant differences among the parents that could be attributed to the child's type of disability. While similarities may exist, reactions will differ, and professionals must consider each situation as highly individualistic.

Patterns of parental reactions

There are many different patterns of parental reaction. It is difficult, if not impossible, to predict what types of reactions parents will exhibit. In some families, having an exceptional child is a tragedy of the utmost magnitude; in other families, it is a crisis, but one that can be resolved; for still others, it is not considered a problem in itself, but rather one element in a daily struggle for survival (Begab, 1966). Still, most parents have had no previous experience with disabilities and are often unprepared to deal with them. For some individuals, this may be their initial exposure to a disability label. For example, some parents may encounter such terms as *learning disabilities, educable mentally retarded,* or *cerebral palsy* for the first time.

The traditional way of viewing parents of a handicapped child is to assume that they will pass through several stages in their adjustment process. Generally, one moves through stages of initial shock and guilt toward a final goal of acceptance and adjustment. One parent, however, writes:

My own experience as the father of a retarded child did not fit this pattern. Instead, it convinced me that most people seriously misunderstand a parent's response to this situation. The standard view does not reflect the reality of parents' experience or lead to helpful conclusions.

Professionals could help parents more—and they would be more realistic—if they discarded their ideas about stages and progress. They could then begin to understand something about the deep, lasting changes that life with a retarded son or daughter brings to parents. And they could begin to see the negative feelings—the shock, the guilt and the bitterness—never disappear but stay on as part of the parents' emotional life. (Searl, 1978, p. 27)

Similarly, a Canadian mother of a blind boy relates:

When our son was born my husband and I were told that the parents of handicapped children move through certain stages of reactions: shock, guilt, reaction, and anger, all culminating in the final blissful state of adjustment. I do not believe in this pattern. I know too many parents of handicapped children to be a believer in any set pattern.

I feel that we do move through these emotions, but just because we have come to adjustment (which I prefer to call "acceptance" because we spend our whole lives adjusting although we may at one point accept the situation), that does not mean we never return to the other emotions. We may continue to feel any of these emotions at any time, in any "order."(West, 1981, p. 10)

Another parent relates that a psychiatrist she knew suggested that helpers stop insisting that parents accept their child's disability. Adaptation would be a more realistic goal than acceptance. "Anger, guilt and unhappiness at having a disabled child are to be expected. Professionals must try to help parents adapt to the fact that a child is handicapped, but they cannot expect them to be happy about it" (Eisenpreis, 1974, p. 8).

Parents need to realize the universality of their emotions and that their reactions are legitimate, automatic, understandable, and normal. They are also necessary. Parental responses to a handicapped son or daughter are generally not abnormal but represent common reactions of people to frustration and conflict (Telford & Sawrey, 1981). Both Greer (1975) and West (1981) remind parents that their reactions are natural and do not indicate that they are bad parents.

Although many researchers and authors have speculated about the various stages of parental responses to having an exceptional child, it should be noted that not all parents follow a sequential pattern of reaction according to a predetermined timetable. These stages should be viewed as fluid, with parents passing forward and backward as their individual adjustment process allows. Some individuals may never progress beyond hurt and anger; others may not experience denial; still others accept and adjust rather quickly to their child's abilities and disabilities. Also, both parents do not necessarily go through these stages together. Each parent will react in his or her own unique way. It is possible, for example, that one partner will make great personal sacrifices and exhibit total dedication to the child, while the other spouse may escape any responsibility by becoming totally involved in his or her work.

The following stages of parental reactions represent a composite model based on patterns of response developed by both professionals and parents of handicapped children. Wentworth (1974) describes a model derived from her experiences as the mother of a multihandicapped daughter. Although writing about mental retardation, Roos (1977, 1978), a professional in special education and the father of a mentally retarded girl, details stages he believes are not specific to retardation but are typical of the reactions experienced by most people. The response of parents to the birth of a child with congenital malformations (for example, Down's syndrome, cleft palate, heart disorders) was investigated by Drotar and his colleagues (Drotar et al., 1975). Their findings were generated from parent interviews conducted within a few days after the birth of the child to as long as five years later (one interview was thirteen years later). Despite the variation of abnormalities, a number of common themes emerged from their investigation. The parents appeared to struggle with common issues and experience similar emotional reactions. The writing of Kübler-Ross (1969) provides the framework for the final source of the parents' adjustment process. Both Duncan (cited in Seligman, 1979) and Moses (1977) have taken Kübler-Ross's developmental stages of reaction to dying (denial, bargaining, anger, depression, acceptance) and applied them to the "loss" encountered by parents of handicapped children. It should be noted, however, that the following descriptions, conceptualized according to primary, secondary, and tertiary phases of parental responses, do not necessarily represent reactions to the handicapped child per se but may be reactions to family and friends, toward oneself or to poor treatment by professionals.

Primary phase

Shock   Most parents of handicapped children experience an initial response of overwhelming shock and disbelief, a period of irrational behavior characterized by excessive crying and feelings of numbness and helplessness. Many parents say that they were totally unprepared for the news of their child's handicap. For example:

We were first informed of her condition when Sally was twenty-two months old. We felt that the bottom had dropped out of our world. We felt utterly alone, helpless and convinced that no one else had ever faced this particular tragedy. (Schult, 1975, p. 6)

It was like a slap in the face. . . . At first I cried a lot. I choked out words. It was very upsetting to try to talk to anybody. . . . When you're first told, you feel you are all alone, that everybody's against you. I really have to say I cried an awful lot and prayed a lot. (Gargiulo & Warniment, 1976, p. 475)

Denial   Some parents attempt to escape the reality of the child's handicap and cushion its impact by *denial*—by refusing to recognize the child's disability, by rationalizing the deficiency, or by seeking professional confirmation that there isn't anything wrong with the child. Parents may also evidence denial, a basic human reaction, in a more subtle manner, one that may easily be over-looked. They may deny the impact of the disability by quickly becoming too cooperative with professionals.

Denial, which is a defensive posture, may be exhibited due to fear of the unknown—the uncertainty of the child's future potential, doubts about being able to cope with the added responsibilities brought on by the handicap, and the unanswerable question, "What will happen to our child?" Denial can be positive, for it buys time and allows the individual an opportunity to reorganize and rebuild. At this stage professionals need to be supportive and sensitive and communicate an attitude of acceptance.

Grief and depression   Parents, according to Roos (1978), are typically disappointed about having a handicapped son or daughter and are realistically concerned about the future. For some, a handicap is symbolic of the death of the ideal child and may precipitate a grief reaction similar to that associated with the loss of a loved one. Grief is a necessary and useful reaction and should not be avoided. It provides the parents with a transitional period whereby former dreams and fantasies about the "perfect child" are readjusted to present-day reality. Grief also makes it possible for the parents to progress from the state of initial shock and disbelief to that of awareness of the disappointment. Yet there is no definite ending to the grief and depression—some parents will continue to experience grief and disappointment throughout their lives.

Depression is often a consequence of the grieving process. Depression is anger turned inward, anger toward oneself. Moses (1977) believes that most people possess an internalized sense of omnipotence, of being all-powerful. All those awful things that could happen in the world will happen to someone else. When one of these events does occur, like the birth of a handicapped child, parents realize they are not omnipotent but vulnerable, and this depresses them. They become angry at themselves and enraged at their weakness and impotence. Parents may also believe that they are still as omnipotent as ever, that they could have prevented the event from occurring but didn't. This too produces depression. Society considers depression to be inappropriate, a feeling that is not to be tolerated. Yet it is part of a normal, natural, and necessary process. Professionals have to relate to the parents' depression as an appropriate and reasonable reaction. It allows the parents an opportunity to accept that which cannot be changed.

Withdrawal, or the severing of oneself from social contacts with others, may also be a component of the third stage. It provides parents with a recuperative period. Withdrawal can also be a state of mind: parents can mentally remove themselves from their emotional environment. Extended withdrawal, however, is not productive, healthy, or helpful. It could evolve into a defense mechanism, an attitude by which, according to Wentworth (1974),

the parents build up their emotional stamina against the onslaught of despair and fear which full recognition of the reality of their child's handicap might bring. Like grief and guilt, withdrawal is a personal emotion, for it concerns self; like denial and hostility, the individual's state of mind can greatly affect those around him. (p. 56)

Either process can be counterproductive, affecting the entire family and blocking progress toward acceptance and adjustment.

Secondary phase

Ambivalence   A child with disabilities is capable of intensifying the normal emotions of love and anger experienced by most parents toward their child. The greater the parent's frustration, the more common the feelings. Some parents may even wish the child were dead. These negative feelings are usually accompanied by guilt, to which certain parents respond with total dedication and others with rejection. Parents who react to the guilt via self-sacrifice may assume a martyr's stance. This posture frequently involves the neglect of other family members and may result in marital discord. The following case study exemplifies the martyr syndrome and its impact on the family.

Jerry, eight years old, has cerebral palsy. His parents have filed for a divorce. How did it come about? To go back to the beginning: According to Jerry's mother, she didn't really want a baby. "I knew something was wrong during my pregnancy. Sometimes I think this is God's punishment, although I really know that is crazy," she reported. When the initial state of shock wore off, the mother took over. She never asked anyone what she should do; she just plunged in to work with her son. She read everything she could find on cerebral palsy and became an authority on the topic. Initially the husband approved and was proud of her.

Slowly but surely the entire family life became organized around Jerry and his special needs. This did not bother the husband until he noticed that their daughter was badly in need of new clothes. When he asked his wife to buy their daughter some new clothes, she gave him a blank stare but said and did nothing. The husband finally asked his sister to help his daughter buy some new clothes. The wife became angry and complained to her sister-in-law about her spoiling the girl and how useless the husband was around the house.

For a while after his son's birth, the husband tried doing things for the handicapped child. However, he decided it would be better if Jerry tried to do more for himself, and began doing less for him. The wife took up the slack by doing more and more for her son. The husband felt that the only way he could be useful to his family was to earn more money. Consequently, he began working longer hours, and weekends as well. After a few years he gradually came to the realization that their marriage had come to an end. They no longer did anything together—never went out or visited friends; and no longer had any sex life. Half the time the wife slept in Jerry's room. At other times, husband or wife or both were too tired.

The wife was at her son's call twenty-four hours a day. At his slightest sign of distress she would rush to his side. When Jerry was seven the family moved to a house in the suburbs, nearer the hospital. The husband did not complain, even though it increased his commuting time from twenty minutes to an hour. A year later, he came home one evening, told his wife it was all over, and asked for a divorce.

The divorce came as a surprise to everyone. There had been no fighting, quarreling, or bickering. The wife was too preoccupied and tired to be involved with her husband, and the husband had ceased bothering her. Although the request for a divorce came as a shock to the wife, in some ways she was relieved by it. For a long time the husband had been just one more mouth to feed and one more person to work for and clean up after. Their divorce settlement was amicable; very little explanation was given to other people.

About a year later, the former husband married again and took his daughter to live with him and his new wife. The former wife offered no objections to this arrangement. She was still completely wrapped up in Jerry, and had little time or energy to spend with her daughter. (Telford & Sawrey, 1981, pp. 164–166)

The American Heritage Dictionary defines *rejection* as a refusal to consider, refusing to give affection or recognition to a person, discarding something as useless or defective. Rejection is the parents' last-ditch effort against accepting the permanence of the child's handicap. Rejection of the child is part of the parents' defense against their pain.

Wentworth (1974) speculates that rejection can be shown in several ways. First, parents may reject the reality of the disability by refusing to acknowledge the extent of the handicapping condition. Often parents develop an inaccurate picture of the child's achievements and abilities. Some parents may believe that the child is not performing up to his or her level of ability ("She's just lazy") and therefore will exert undue pressure on the child to perform at levels he or she is incapable of. On the other hand, parents may consider the child "hopeless" and thus refuse any plans for training and therapy. These parents believe that little will be gained due to their son's or daughter's limited capacities.

Rejection can also be a consequence of the parents' anticipation of the constant demands of lifelong emotional and financial responsibility. Faced with these burdens, parents can easily fall prey to resentment, which can lead to rejection of the child. In a few instances, actual physical rejection may occur. The parents may institutionalize the child and effectively forget about him or her. Or one parent, generally the father, may abandon the home.

A more subtle type of rejection, one often hidden behind other emotions, occurs when the child's physical needs are met while his or her emotional needs are neglected. However, some parents, especially mothers, may also ignore the child's physical wants. Finally, rejection can take the form of exclusion, whereby the handicapped child is denied participation in family activities.

Guilt   Guilt is perhaps the most difficult reaction for parents of handicapped children to overcome. Moses (1977) believes that it is not the guilt itself, but rather what preceded the guilt, that causes the pain. Parents may believe that somehow they caused their child's handicap or that they are being punished for past wrongdoings. A pediatrician and the mother of a severely retarded, nonverbal daughter, writes:

I mentally went back over my pregnancy. I mentally reviewed what I did, persons I was in contact with, what type of exposure I possibly had to things that could not be tested for. I tried to calculate how much radiation I might have been exposed to. We had bought a large order of meat from a supermarket, and I theorized that the meat might have had preservatives which might have affected my child. I had used cyclamates which had not been removed from the markets at the time, and I thought this might be the cause of my child's abnormality. (Ziskin, 1978, p. 75)

Guilt generally adheres to an "if only" pattern of thinking. For example, if the disability is recognizable at birth, mothers may say, "If only I'd quit smoking," "If only I'd stayed on my diet," "If only I hadn't painted the nursery." Fathers may reminisce, "If only I'd helped her more," "If only I'd gotten her to the hospital sooner." Parents whose children are handicapped due to accident or illness are also sensitive to "if only" thoughts. However, these thoughts are often more definite, with a clearer cause-and-effect relationship. Common thoughts are "If only I hadn't let Johnny go to the store alone," "If only I hadn't ignored her cries for help," "If only I'd taken her to the doctor sooner," "If only I'd kept the cabinet locked."

During the guilt stage, overcompensation is a common reaction. Parents try to "make it up" to the child. Nothing is denied that might bring a moment of happiness. Overcompensation is an attempt to appease the parents' feelings of guilt. The handicap becomes more important than the child. Some parents become martyrs, displaying self-sacrifice and self-denial for some assumed need of the child.

When parents feel guilty, they usually do not yield to reason or argument. They become obsessive and emotional and constantly ask why these things happen. Professionals therefore must send a reassuring message that it is all right to feel guilty. Guilt is a normal and necessary reaction; it does not always have to be irrational or inappropriate. If parents understand and accept their guilt, they can move beyond it.

Anger   Anger is a roadblock in the parents' journey toward acceptance. Anger can be manifested in two ways. The first type, which is generally acceptable, is often expressed in terms of fairness and the question, "Why me?" The second form is displaced anger, rage directed toward others, away from the source where it might belong. In order to feel hostile toward someone, a reason must be found to blame that person. Doctors are often the initial victims of the parents' anger because of perceived incompetency, because they served as the bearer of bad news, or because they failed to inform the parents of a suspected deficiency. Teachers and therapists may also bear the brunt of parental hostility. Some parents legitimately feel anger toward their handicapped children for disrupting their lives, but society says that such feelings are criminal and incorrect. Thus, the parents, unable to directly vent their anger, displace their rage on the spouse or siblings. Wentworth (1974) observes that blame accomplishes nothing. It is a destructive force. Parents therefore need guidance and direction in order to realize that the object of their hostility is not other individuals or the child but the handicapping condition. If the parents are to experience growth, they will need an environment that is supportive and that considers their feelings as part of a normal and natural process.

Shame and embarrassment   Most parents demonstrate feelings of pride in their children's accomplishments. Parents of a handicapped child, however, learn to anticipate the social rejection, pity, and ridicule that others in society have for their child. Their love, according to Roos (1978), is only partial protection against the feeling of shame that is produced when their son or daughter is laughed at or singled out as defective.

A child's public actions are often a reflection of how well the parents have upheld their responsibility. For some parents, the fear of embarrassment due to the child's behavior is so great that they will not venture away from home with the child; consequently, social withdrawal is a common reaction.

Closely aligned with the feelings of shame and embarrassment is loss of self-esteem. Since parents usually identify with their children and often perceive them as extensions of themselves, a defect in the child could easily be interpreted as a defect in oneself. Thus, a handicapped youngster is likely to threaten the parents' self-esteem and may force them to radically modify lifelong goals. One parent writes:

I felt I was a nobody. Any credits of self-worth that I could give myself from any of my personal endeavors meant nothing. Graduating from college and a first-rate medical school, surviving an internship, practicing medicine and having two beautiful sons and a good marriage counted for nil. All I knew at this point was that I was the mother of an abnormal and most likely retarded child. (Ziskin, 1978, p. 75)

Tertiary phase

Bargaining   Bargaining is one of the final stages in the adjustment process. It is very personal and rarely seen by others. Bargaining is a strategy whereby parents hope to "strike a deal" with God, science, or anyone who promises to make their child normal. They may make statements like, "If you cure my child, I'll devote my life to the church." It is regarded as the final attempt to cure the child.

Adaptation and reorganization   Research (Drotar et al., 1975) has indicated that progress toward adaptation is a gradual process requiring varying lengths of time and a reduction in the feelings of anxiety and other intense emotional reactions. Parents become increasingly comfortable with their situation and express confidence in their parenting abilities, which in turn leads to a period of reorganization during which parents encounter a more rewarding level of interaction with their child. Another aspect of reorganization is the parents' increased ability to deal with their responsibility for the child's problems. Positive, long-term acceptance of the child also requires that spouses support and communicate with each other. Support is not always evident in all instances, however. Some couples rely heavily on each other and are drawn closer together, while in other situations partners become estranged. As an example, in interviews conducted with mothers of learning disabled children, Gargiulo and Warniment (1976) observed the following two conflicting scenarios:

At first, Susan's problem did affect my marriage. My husband acted as though he was ashamed of her, and I became overly protective. As we became more aware of her problem and what we could do to help, we began pulling together, realizing that our daughter needed both of us. In the long run it has strengthened our marriage. (p. 475)

My marriage was, and still is, very much affected by Bruce's problem. My husband does not want to accept the responsibility associated with our son's learning disability. He very much ignores it. His solution is to be very, very firm with Bruce. I'm too easy. This has led to terrific disagreements about our son. At times, the situation is so desperate that I have often thought of taking Bruce and leaving my husband. My marriage is better if we both pretend that Bruce doesn't have a learning disability or that he doesn't even exist. (pp. 475–476)

Acceptance and adjustment   Acceptance is the goal that most parents strive for. It is an active, ongoing process, a state of mind in which a conscious effort is undertaken to recognize, understand, and resolve problems. But previous negative feelings are never completely resolved. They can occur and recur, requiring the parents to subdue these obstacles constantly. As parents overcome these stumbling blocks, they grow and learn about themselves and others. Parents learn that acceptance involves not only accepting the child but also accepting themselves as they are and acknowledging their individual strengths and weaknesses.

An adjunct to the concept of acceptance is adjustment, which by definition implies action. It is action precipitated by the individual rather than action that is done to or for the person by others. This action is both positive and forward moving. Adjustment is not a stage that abruptly begins on the day the parents learn to accept the reality of the child's handicap, nor is it a battle that is ever completely finished. Instead, adjustment demands change and a realignment of goals and ambitions. It is a difficult and lifelong process influenced by attitudes and to a great extent by individual personality traits. Wentworth (1974) reminds parents that up until the time they reach acceptance, their adjustment has been subtle, for not until they recognize the permanence of the disability do they realize the need to adjust. Until now the parents have been adapting; now they begin adjusting.

Other aspects of parental reaction

The following four topics, chronic sorrow, shopping behavior, parental rejection, and compensating parents, are expanded discussions of behaviors related to the primary, secondary, and tertiary stages of parental reaction. These aspects of emotional response are frequently observed by professionals when working with parents of exceptional children and consequently deserve additional comment.

Chronic sorrow   Olshansky (1962, 1966) describes chronic sorrow as a natural and understandable response of parents to a tragic fact, the birth of a mentally retarded child. He views this as a nearly universal reaction among parents whose children are moderately or severely mentally handicapped. Although the quality of response will vary according to such factors as the parents' religion, social class, and ethnicity, parents will suffer chronic sorrow throughout their lives regardless of whether the child is at home or institutionalized. Release from chronic sorrow may be obtained only through the death of the child. Chronic sorrow is the by-product of "the permanent, day-by-day dependence of the child, the interminable frustrations resulting from the child's relative changelessness, the unesthetic quality of mental defectiveness and the deep symbolism buried in the process of giving birth to a defective child" (1962, p. 192).

Historically, professionals have viewed chronic sorrow as an abnormal rather than a legitimate reaction. Olshansky advises, however, that this attitude is not in the parents' best interest. The emphasis placed on acceptance by helpers may cause the parents to resent and resist the helper's efforts. "Parental acceptance will come in time if they are helped to deal with their chronic sorrow and if concrete services are available to help them in managing and living with the child (1966, p. 22).

On the other hand, Solnit and Stark (1961), using a psychoanalytical explanation, consider the reaction to the birth of a handicapped child to be similar to mourning the death of a child. With the birth of a mentally retarded child, the mother suddenly realizes the loss of the anticipated perfect child and the birth of a feared, guilt-producing, and anger-evoking child. Parents are left in a state of acute grief as a result of this catastrophe. Consequently, the immediate demand to love the handicapped child leaves too little time for grief over the loss of the imagined ideal child.

The main distinction between the two mourning reactions is their effect on the parents' treatment of the child. The child will realistically require much care and attention for an indefinite period of time. At one extreme, the parent, motivated by excessive guilt feelings, dedicates his or her life exclusively to the welfare of the child. At the other extreme, the parent demonstrates intolerance of the child and attempts to deny his or her relationship to the child.

Olshansky (1966) refutes Solnit and Stark's hypothesis on the basis of the following four points:

1. The death of a dream child is not equivalent to the death of a real child.

2. The hypothesis takes insufficient account of the fact that for many parents identification of mental deficiency does not take place at birth.

3. Those parents who are beyond the period of mourning should be free of sorrow and should be able to attend to the needs of their child. [However, Olshansky believes that chronic sorrow exists as long as the child lives.]

4. [The hypothesis] keeps the problem neatly encapsulated within the psyche, when it is clearly both in and outside the psyche (p. 21).

Shopping behavior   Anderson (1971), writing about parents of mentally retarded children (although her thesis would be applicable to any handicapping condition), sees "shopping behavior" as a learned parental response. *Shopping behavior* is defined as "making visits to the same professional or to a number of different professionals or clinics in such a manner that one visit follows another without resolution of a resolvable problem" (p. 3). Other parents may become therapeutic shoppers, endlessly searching for new treatments, techniques, or programs. These responses are "maladaptive in that it is frequently costly in time, parental energy, and money; it is disruptive of family life, sometimes even involving a family making long trips or changing its place of residence; and it takes the parents' focus off constructive efforts to work with their child" (p. 3).

Shopping behavior is usually seen as an act originating within the parents and precipitated by parental guilt. "In the parent's attempt to absolve himself from the guilt he feels over having a retarded child, he projects the blame for his child's condition, or his child's not responding readily to professional attempts to help, onto the helper" (p. 3). Thus, by shopping, the parent hopes to prove that the professionals are not only wrong but also responsible for the child's handicapping condition. Professional workers usually react by seeing the parent as trying to manipulate them. Yet shopping requires two individuals, the parent and a service provider. Anderson believes that the shopping act is a direct result of professionals' failure to assist parents in their sorrow over having a mentally retarded child.

Anderson enumerates four possibilities that may account for parental dissatisfaction with their initial professional contact:

1. The professional does not suspect retardation or does not mention it as part of the clinical picture when talking to the parents. For example, a child may initially be diagnosed as having cerebral palsy with no mention of retardation. Only later will the parents be informed of the child's limited intellectual ability.

2. The helper, aware of the child's disability, initially decides not to inform the parents about their son's or daughter's handicap and thus spares them the truth.

3. Although suspicious, the professional, not wanting to cause undue alarm, does not tell the parents about his or her suspicions.

4. The helper recognizes the condition and attempts to inform the parents but is not heard. This is perhaps the most common explanation for parental dissatisfaction.

According to Anderson, helpers can assist in eliminating shopping behavior according to how they conduct the initial informing interview. She suggests that both parents be present and jointly informed about their child's disability and that a professional team approach be used, although this suggestion is subject to controversy. The interview should be structured in such a fashion that the parents take the lead. Feelings generated by this contact should be expressed and dealt with openly. Help should be offered on a continuing basis. It is easier to successfully conduct an informing interview than to terminate a well-established shopping pattern with its accompanying feelings of hostility toward professionals.

Rejecting parents   Gallagher's (1956) classic article on parental rejection, although written almost three decades ago, is still relevant today. Gallagher states that parental rejection is a concept familiar in special education but that it has become an overused term laden with negative connotations. It is defined as a "persistent and unrelieved holding of unrealistic negative values of the child to the extent that the whole behavior of the parent towards that child is colored unrealistically by this negative tone" (pp. 273–274). Gallagher lists the following ways that rejection can be expressed.

1. *Strong underexpectations of achievement.* Parents view the child as useless and without any attributes. They undervalue the child's capabilities, minimize the assets, and establish unrealistically low goals. This underestimation may then be manifested by the child, who begins to behave and act as if he or she was worthless, thereby creating a climate for the self-fulfilling prophecy.

2. *Setting unrealistic goals.* Rejection of this type results when parents set unattainable goals, generally in the area of social and emotional maturity. The child, unable to obtain these goals, provides the parents with an avenue for justifying their negative feelings toward the child. It also allows the parents to punish and reprimand the child because he or she has failed to meet prescribed goals.

3. *Escape.* Rejection can also be overtly demonstrated by desertion and abandonment or, in a more subtle fashion, via placement in a school or institution a great distance from the parents even though comparable facilities are closer to home. Parents rationalize their behavior on the basis of their inability to properly care for the child even though the evidence may be to the contrary.

4. *Reaction formation.* This form of rejection represents a complex defense mechanism. The parents, unable to admit their negative feelings toward the child because it is counter to how they see themselves, deny their feelings and portray to the world the opposite image. Rather than admitting that they hate the child, which is contrary to their self-image as warm, loving individuals, the parents verbalize feelings of love and acceptance for the handicapped child. This is not a hypocritical position, for the parents actually believe in the image they publicly project.

As a type of reaction, rejection places the parents in a no-win situation. If the parents are honest and admit to their negative feelings, they are condemned for being rejecting parents. On the other hand, if they camouflage their feelings and acknowledge love for the child, they are suspected of manifesting a reaction formation.

As a result of the negative implications that parental rejection has for helpers, Gallagher finds it necessary to distinguish between primary and secondary rejection. Primary rejection is a consequence of the unchangeable nature of the handicapped child. "In primary rejection, the personality dynamics of the parent rather than the behavior of the child often determine the parents' attitudes" (p. 275). Secondary rejection, which is the more common of the two, is a product of the behavioral manifestations of the child, which result in negative parental attitudes. Primary rejection, therefore, requires the alteration of parental attitude, while secondary rejection necessitates modification of the child's behavior. Parental attitudes, however, are not conveniently identified as primary or secondary rejection, and there are no easy criteria to follow. Gallagher suggests that it is safe to assume that negative attitudes reflect secondary rejection unless the parents indicate otherwise.

Compensating parents   Three different parent-child relationships, acceptance, rejection and compensation, are hypothesized by Bryant (1971) to affect a child's rehabilitative progress. His comments are specifically aimed at the interaction of mothers and speech disabled children, but could easily apply to almost any type of handicap. In addition to the conventional reactions of acceptance and rejection, Bryant considers compensation to be the third most common parent-child relationship. Compensation develops from a combination of acceptance and rejection of the child and the disability.

Bryant characterizes the accepting parent as being conscientious about keeping appointments, seeking advice, and following through on suggestions or recommendations. The rejecting parent "forgets" appointments and is minimally involved in the rehabilitation of the child. The compensating parent, although easily recognized, hinders habilitation and rehabilitation.

She keeps all appointments, making it clear from her emotional and physical state that she is exhausted. She is rushed, worried about the child's progress, harried about what else she must accomplish before the day's end, and most probably in bad humor.

The parent who compensates, who attempts to accept her child over feelings of rejection, is often too involved in the rehabilitative program. She is overanxious about progress, suspicious of the quality of the program and of the qualifications of the specialists on the team. (p. 327)

A compensating parent will attempt to replace rejecting attitudes with ones of acceptance. The result often reflects both acceptance and rejection and is evidenced by behavior that is harmful to the child's emotional well-being. Bryant's example (p. 328) demonstrates this substitution process.

Acceptance		Rejection		Compensation
Love	+	Indifference	=	Possessiveness
Empathy	+	Selfishness	=	Sympathy
Forgiveness	+	Fault finding	=	Overpermissiveness
Gentleness	+	Cruelty	=	Smothering
Caution	+	Carelessness	=	Suspicion
Activity	+	Apathy	=	Overactivity

Children of compensating parents are often anxious, tense, and fearful of their mother's disfavor. Not only might these children fail to progress with their therapy, but also poor school performance and antisocial behavior are possible consequences.

Bryant suggests, therefore, that early counseling is important with the aim of assisting the parents in understanding that:

1. They have a responsibility to their children, not to themselves, and that if the rehabilitative program is to be at all successful, they must allow their children the emotional freedom to profit from the program.

2. The [treatment] program is not designed to prove that they are worthy parents, but rather to help their children in their adjustment to society.

3. They must maintain a consistent and accepting attitude and not become discouraged or overzealous by slow or rapid progress.

4. They must understand that . . . it is the parents' responsibility to help prepare the child for a life that is as normal as possible. (p. 328)

The results of these suggestions, it is hoped, are better adjustment for both parent and child and maximal benefit from the rehabilitative program.

A final word

As we conclude our examination of various patterns of parental response to handicapping conditions, it is important to remember that no one can predict how parents will respond, just as one cannot predict one's own response. Reactions are based on emotions. The magnitude of the parents' feelings and reactions reflects *their* perception of the problem. Thus, each situation is unique. Parents' progress through the primary, secondary, and tertiary phases of reaction will vary. For some, progress will be exceedingly slow; others will experience minimal disruption; for still others the pain, sorrow, and disappointment, although diminished by time, will always be there. All parents may recycle through earlier stages at critical milestones in their life or in the child's life: for example, when parents anticipate retirement, when their teen-ager is not invited to the junior prom, or when their child is unable to play school sports. Parents feel these emotions, and to deny them is wrong. Helpers, therefore, are once again cautioned against stereotyping parents and are urged to see the parents' reactions as legitimate, normal, human responses.

I am not responsible for my feelings, but for what I do with them.

—*Hugh Prather*

References

Anderson, K. (1971). The "shopping" behavior of parents of mentally retarded children: The professional person's role. *Mental Retardation, 9,* 3–5.

Barsch, R. (1968). *The parent of the handicapped child: The study of child-rearing practices.* Springfield, IL: Charles C Thomas.

Barsch, R. (1969). *The parent-teacher partnership.* Arlington, VA: Council for Exceptional Children.

Baum, M. (1962). Some dynamic factors affecting family adjustment to the handicapped. *Exceptional Children, 28,* 387–392.

Begab, M. (1956). Factors in counseling parents of retarded children. *American Journal of Mental Deficiency, 60,* 515–524.

Begab, M. (1966). The mentally retarded and the family. In I. Phillips (Ed.), *Prevention and treatment of mental retardation* (pp. 71–84). New York: Basic Books.

Brown, G. (1969). Suggestions for parents. *Journal of Learning Disabilities, 2,* 97–106.

Bryant, J. (1971). Parent-child relationships: Their effect on rehabilitation. *Journal of Learning Disabilities, 4,* 325–329.

Drotar, D., Baskiewicz, A., Irvin, N., Kennell, J., & Klaus, M. (1975). The adaptation of parents to the birth of an infant with a congenital malformation: A hypothetical model. *Pediatrics, 56,* 710–717.

Eisenpreis, B. (1974). My child isn't like that. *Exceptional Parent, 4,* 5–9.

Gallagher, J. (1956). Rejecting parents? *Exceptional Children, 22*, 273–276, 294.

Gargiulo, R., & Warniment, J. (1976). A parents' perspective of learning disabilities. *Academic Therapy, 11*, 473–480.

Gorham, K., Des Jardins, C., Page, R., Pettis, E., & Scheiber, B. (1975). Effect on parents. In N. Hobbs (Ed.), *Issues in the classification of children* (Vol. II, pp. 155–188). San Francisco: Jossey-Bass.

Greer, B. (1975). On being the parent of a handicapped child. *Exceptional Children, 41*, 519.

Kübler-Ross, E. (1969). *On death and dying.* New York: Macmillan.

Mac Keith, R. (1973). The feelings and behaviour of parents of handicapped children. *Developmental Medicine and Child Neurology, 15*, 524–527.

Michaelis, C. (1977). Imperfect child—Cause for sorrow. *Special Children, 4*, 39–48.

Michaelis, C. (1980). *Home and school partnership in exceptional education.* Rockville, MD: Aspen.

Moses, K. (1977). Effects of the developmental disability on parenting the handicapped child. In M. Rieff (Ed.), *Patterns of emotional growth in the developmentally disabled child* (pp. 31–52). Morton Grove, IL: Julia S. Molloy Education Center.

Olshansky, S. (1962). Chronic sorrow: A response to having a mentally defective child. *Social Casework, 43*, 190–194.

Olshansky, S. (1966). Parent responses to a mentally defective child. *Mental Retardation, 4*, 21–23.

Roos, P. (1977). Parents of mentally retarded people. *International Journal of Mental Health, 6*, 96–119.

Roos, P. (1978). Parents of mentally retarded children—Misunderstood and mistreated. In A. Turnbull & H. Turnbull (Eds.), *Parents speak out* (pp. 12–27). Columbus, OH: Charles Merrill.

Ross, A. (1964). *The exceptional child in the family.* New York: Grune & Stratton.

Ross, A. (1975). Family problems. In R. Smith & J. Neisworth (Eds.), *The exceptional child: A functional approach* (pp. 179–193). New York: McGraw-Hill.

Schild, S. (1976). The family of the retarded child. In R. Koch & J. Dobson (Eds.), *The mentally retarded child and his family* (pp. 454–465). New York: Brunner/Mazel.

Schleifer, M. (1971). Let us all stop blaming the parents. *Exceptional Parent, 1*, 3–5.

Schult, M. (1975). I'll never do that! *Exceptional Parent, 5,* 6–10.

Searl, S. (1978). Stages of parent reaction. *Exceptional Parent, 8,* 27–29.

Seligman, M. (1979). *Strategies for helping parents of exceptional children.* New York: Free Press.

Smith, R., & Neisworth, J. (1975). *The exceptional child: A functional approach.* New York: McGraw-Hill.

Solnit, A., & Stark, M. (1961). Mourning and the birth of a defective child. *Psychoanalytic Study of the Child, 16,* 523–537.

Stewart, J. (1978). *Counseling parents of exceptional children.* Columbus, OH: Charles Merrill.

Telford, C., & Sawrey, J. (1981). *The exceptional individual* (4th ed.). Englewood Cliffs, NJ: Prentice-Hall.

Ward, S., & Reale, G. (1972). Survey. *Exceptional Parent, 2,* 28–29.

Wentworth, E. (1974). *Listen to your heart: A message to parents of handicapped children.* Boston: Houghton Mifflin.

West, E. (1981). My child is blind—Thoughts on family life. *Exceptional Parent, 11,* 9–11.

Ziskin, L. (1978). The story of Jennie. In A. Turnbull & H. Turnbull (Eds.), *Parents speak out* (pp. 70–80). Columbus, OH: Charles Merrill.

Zuk, G. (1962). The cultural dilemma and spiritual crisis of the family with a handicapped child. *Exceptional Children, 28,* 405–408.

Chapter 3: Understanding family dynamics

> *We have learned not to stunt a child's growing body with child labor; we must now learn not to break his growing spirit by making him the victim of our anxieties.*
>
> —Erik Erikson

An exceptional child, regardless of whether he or she is cerebral palsied, learning disabled, or gifted, is first and foremost a child. So, too, the family with an exceptional youngster or adolescent is first of all a family. If Boggs (1969) is correct in stating that parents of handicapped children are drawn from the ranks of normal parents, then it follows that families with handicapped children are also extracted from the ranks of typical families. Furthermore, many of the problems in families with an exceptional child are essentially no different from difficulties found in any family (Meyerson, 1983).

"A family," according to Ross (1964, p. viii), "is a dynamic system of interacting individual personalities who live together in a complex and changing society." Hence, within the family constellation, the exceptional member should not be viewed as an isolated entity. He or she can only be seen and fully understood in the context of the family unit. Whatever affects the individual affects the family—and, conversely, whatever happens to or affects the family also affects the individual family members. As one sibling commented:

All of the members of my family are disabled. But most people recognize only the disability of my deaf sister. They do not realize that the disability of one member affects the entire family. Parents realize this to some extent because they themselves are affected—their attitudes, their priorities, their life styles. But sometimes they become so involved with the problems directly related to their disabled child that they lose sight of the effect upon the other children. (Hayden, 1974, p. 26)

If the family is considered as an interdependent system in which common needs and purposes are met by the interaction of members (Schild, 1976; Seligman, 1979), then the problems of exceptionality can be seen and treated as concerns of the entire family.

Like people, families vary one from another, although they still have many things in common. Certain families are exposed to and experience unique circumstances and situations. This is especially true for a family in which one or more members is, in some way, exceptional. These families generally encounter many complex problems—problems that are only compounded by society's negative and stereotypical attitudes toward those who are "different." In many instances, families are significantly affected emotionally, socially, and financially. The impact, however, is not always negative (Schild, 1976; Dunlap & Hollingsworth, 1977). As one parent noted, "a child's toy held too close to the eye will block out the view of a mountain. If held too close to the mind's eye, a child's disability can negate the life of the whole family. It is essential to develop a perspective toward it" (Behmer, 1976, p. 37).

Begab (1966) points out that exceptionality, like parenthood, has different meanings in each family. There is no easy way to answer the question of how an exceptional child affects the lives of the various family members. Gordon (1977) suggests, however, that although the needs of a handicapped child are great, the needs of the family are even greater. Yet, although the child's needs are frequently met, those of the family are seldom recognized or satisfied. As a whole, the family is often confronted with many multifaceted problems but few solutions. Invariably, problems involving an exceptional person are also family problems. There is little doubt that the presence of a handicapped child significantly affects the structure, function, and development of the entire family (Simeonsson & Simeonsson, 1981). Helpers, therefore, need to be concerned with the total family (Goldie, 1966; Telford & Sawrey, 1981).

When assessing the effect that a handicapped son or daughter has on the family, one must handle each situation individually. Some of the variables associated with the family's ability to cope with a handicapped member are the marital integration of the parents, social class, degree of impairment, financial and educational attainments, religious beliefs, and the child's sex, among others. The purpose of this chapter is to examine the effect that an exceptional person has on the dynamics of family life—remembering, of course, that every family is both special and different and that only general statements can be proposed.

Developmental perspectives of the family

The same social forces that most families deal with also affect families with handicapped members—in some instances jeopardizing the integrity of the family unit. As Lillie (1981) observed, the American family has been subjected to a variety of social pressures and change. Lillie cites, for example, the vagueness and lack of commitment to parental roles, the increased importance attached to personal self-fulfillment (which is generally found outside the family and home), and finally, learned parenting skills and values that may conflict with present-day social mores and lifestyles. Still, the family is the foundation of society and the cornerstone of our social fabric.

Changes that affect the family are transactional in nature: one change evokes another, which in turn generates additional alterations. The Simeonssons (Simeonsson & Simeonsson, 1981), using a developmental perspective, have identified three factors that influence family transactions and consequently affect the handicapped child and his or her family. These factors, which acknowledge the conventional as well as unique problems of a family with an exceptional person, are the additional developmental tasks encountered by the family, various developmental crises, and the modification of developmental goals. Figure 3.1 illustrates the interrelationship of these factors.

Simeonsson and Simeonsson speculate that exceptional individuals and their families contend with the same developmental tasks common to the majority of families, besides struggling with extraordinary or prolonged demands. A family's ability to deal with these developmental requirements depends on the type and severity of the disability as well as the availability of family resources. Mac Keith's (1973) theorizing, as well as the writing of Seligman (1979), provides the framework for the Simeonssons' concept of developmental crises. Four major crisis periods are identified: (1) an initial awareness of the child's exceptionality, (2) the realistic acceptance of the youngster's academic capabilities, (3) upon termination of schooling, the adaptation of the individual and his or her family to the limitations of future independence, and (4) the adjustment to the independence of the handicapped person's adult status in relationship to aging parents. Acknowledgment of the existence of these four stages provides a foundation for viewing the family constellation and also gives direction to and assistance in understanding family functioning. The final component of the Simeonsson model focuses on developmental goals appropriate for helpers and parents. Specifically, helpers should assist parents in setting priorities for the family and arriving at a realization of their son's or daughter's assets and deficits. Parents, meanwhile, require detailed information and data concerning both their child's handicap and the availability of specialized services.

The reciprocal nature of family interactions is also assessed in an earlier, and now classic, paper by Farber (1959). Farber describes the effect of an exceptional child on family stability. His concept of a family life cycle resembles in many ways the stages of developmental crises posited by the Simeonsson model. Although his study focuses only on parents of severely retarded children and suffers from methodological deficiencies, Farber's findings represent an important contribution to understanding family relationships.

Farber hypothesizes that families progress through various stages. The cycle commences with marriage and the birth of the first child. The second period continues throughout the preschool years, becoming the third stage when the youngest child is a preadolescent. The sequence continues when this individual becomes an adolescent,

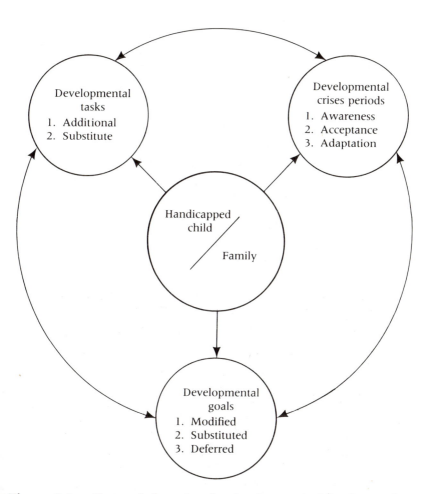

Figure 3.1   Factors influencing the development of families with handicapped children. From "Parenting Handicapped Children: Psychological Aspects" by Rune J. Simeonsson and Nancy E. Simeonsson, in *Understanding and Working with Parents of Children with Special Needs,* edited by J. Paul. Copyright © 1981 by Holt, Rinehart and Winston. Reprinted by permission of Holt, Rinehart and Winston, CBS College Publishing.

is maintained when all children become adults, and ends when all of the children marry. This cycle is unfulfilled or arrested when one of the children is severely impaired. Regardless of the birth order, he or she assumes the social role of the youngest child. Thus, Farber speculates, the family is unable to emerge from the prepubscent life cycle stage and consequently family integration is reduced. The presence of a severely handicapped child not only impedes movement through the life cycle, but also prevents the family from reaching the final stages. Parental roles remain fairly constant, but sibling relationships are greatly hampered. Farber further finds that family integration is related to the marital integration of the parents, the family's social status and religious beliefs, and the availability of a psychological support system.

The common developmental theme expressed in both the Simeonsson model and Farber's investigation is the importance of the interactional, reciprocal nature of family dynamics. Armed with this knowledge, helpers should be in a better position to support and enrich the lives of the handicapped child and his or her family.

The handicapped child and the family

The emphasis so far has been on the family as an interactive social system. The presence of a child with special needs alters, either directly or indirectly, the nature of family interactions. In addition, an exceptional child tends to disrupt the family structure. This disruption is considered a natural phenomenon requiring the family to maintain, as nearly as possible, a "normal" lifestyle (Chinn, Winn, & Walters, 1978). Yet these families, and the parents in particular, are confronted with a puzzling dilemma. Others demand and expect that lives should continue as if nothing abnormal or uncommon has occurred, but, as one mother observed:

The fact of life for parents of handicapped children which is least understood by others is this: It is difficult and exhausting to live normally, and yet we must. To decide on the other route, to admit that having a disabled child makes us disabled persons, to say no to the ordinary requirements of daily living is to meet the second enemy—loneliness [the first is fatigue]. It means drifting slowly out of the mainstream of adult life. In a very real sense, we are damned if we do make the extraordinary effort required to live normally, and damned if we don't. (Morton, 1978, pp. 144–145)

Understanding the impact of a handicapped child on family dynamics is perhaps best accomplished by examining individual aspects of family life—specifically, the parents' marital integration and sibling attitudes.

Marital relationships

Being the parent of a handicapped child tends to shake the entire family tree. The husband blames the wife, the wife accuses the husband, no one is without suspect (Begab, 1966). Families even blame one another for "bad blood" (Pieper, 1976). These recriminations eventually take their toll on the stability of the marriage. The research literature tends to support the clinical impression that the presence of a handicapped child greatly adds to the everyday stresses and strains of married life. A handicapped child may aggravate existing marital tensions or even precipitate conflict between husband and wife. The number of desertions and divorces in families with exceptional children far exceeds that found in the general population (Telford & Sawrey, 1981). Block (1978) reports that in addition to marital difficulties, the problems of suicide and alcoholism occur more frequently in families with disabled children.

The special needs youngster is sometimes blamed for exacerbating old wounds or parental anxieties that may have been dormant for many years. Consequently, he or she is held responsible for the poor quality of the parents' married life (Cohen, 1962). The child may also be viewed as the source and cause of all family problems, thus acquiring the role of the family scapegoat. On the other hand, the child may become a negative bond, binding together the partners of an unhappy marriage. No matter how unsatisfactory the relationship, the marriage must be preserved at all costs. To desert one's spouse or dissolve the marriage would be socially and morally unthinkable (Abrams & Kaslow, 1977). Thus parents may be required to subordinate their marital difficulties and arrive at temporary solutions for the well-being of the handicapped child and the family. This might explain why some couples claim to be drawn closer together by their exceptional child. In some instances, however, parents are estranged from one another, especially if each blames the other for the child's condition. In any event, the maintenance of a satisfactory marital relationship is an important aspect of the parents' adaptation to their exceptional child (Drotar, Baskiewicz, Irvin, Kennell, & Klaus, 1975).

While it appears that an exceptional child greatly upsets marital equilibrium, this is not true for all couples. Great diversity exists within individual families and even within and across categories of exceptionality. A reduction in marital stability is not necessarily an inevitable consequence of having an impaired child in the family. As previously alluded to, the stress that accompanies the parenting of a handicapped child can bring spouses closer together and strengthen their marriage. As an illustration, one mother of a learning disabled child did not believe that her son's handicap adversely affected her marriage. In fact, she responded:

I think it brought us closer together. It was harder for my husband to realize that there was a problem. I think he knew it was there, but he just didn't want to admit that something was wrong with his son. I think it made us come closer to each other, if that is possible. It made a stronger marriage because we both knew that we had to work with this child in order to get him through life so that some day he could marry and have a family of his own (Gargiulo & Warniment, 1976, p. 475)

Even researchers who evaluate families at risk report contradictory findings. Farber's investigations (1959, 1960) indicate that retarded boys, especially those from lower-class families, have a greater negative influence on their parents' marriage than do retarded girls. Likewise, Love (1973) observes that parents of mentally retarded persons are three times more likely than parents of nonretarded children to have their marriages end in divorce. Yet Fotheringham and Creal (1974) conclude from their research that the inclusion of a severely retarded child in the family does not seriously hamper marital integration.

Variability of marital relationships is not limited to households with retarded children. Scientists investigating families with physically handicapped youngsters have found that some marriages suffer irreparable harm, while in other instances spouses claim that their child's affliction actually strengthens their marriage (Walker, Thomas, & Russell, 1971). More recently, Martin (1975) reports that the incidence of divorce or separation among parents of spina bifida children is no higher than that of the general populace. Marriage stability has also been examined among families with children manifesting sensory impairments. The general conclusions of both Gregory (1976) and Jan, Freeman, and Scott (1977) are that some marriages deteriorate—however, others improve, and most parents indicate minimal consequences due to raising a deaf or blind child.

The preceding research evidence certainly differs from the gloomy clinical opinions expressed by the majority of professionals. Perhaps these findings will assist helpers to turn their attention away from the negative aspects of parenting the child with special needs. An unrealistically optimistic view is not called for, but helpers would do well to see parents in a more balanced light, with problems, weaknesses, *and* strengths (Seligman, 1979). Echoing this thought, Gallagher and his co-workers (Gallagher, Haskins, & Farran, 1979) urge helpers to focus on outlining and enhancing those variables associated with positive family adaptation.

Sibling attitudes

Until recently, the majority of research literature examining families with special children has focused almost exclusively on the parents and the child with the disability. By and large, researchers have either neglected or consigned to secondary importance the effect the handicapped child has on his or her nonhandicapped or normal siblings. It is as if, according to Chinn et al. (1978), investigators have forgotten that these siblings share in the anticipation and excitement of a new child in the family. They also share in the grief and pain when their brother or sister is atypical.

An exceptional child affects the entire family. In fact, there is a common belief that a handicapped child contaminates the family and generates considerable psychological stress (Grossman, 1972; Seligman, 1979). In some instances that may be true, since a special child is indeed very capable of being a disruptive influence in the lives of all family members, including brothers and sisters. In other families, however, the effect on siblings is minimal. Researchers have consistently found that the effect of a handicapped child on his or her nonhandicapped siblings is largely due to the parents' attitude and reaction toward the disabled child (Graliker, Fishler, & Koch, 1962; Grossman, 1972; Kew, 1975; Klein, 1972a; Wolfensberger, 1967). Normal siblings tend to mimic and adopt the feelings and behaviors expressed by their parents (Begab, 1966; Chinn et al., 1978; Wentworth, 1974). The father's reaction in particular—that is, his acceptance or rejection of his handicapped son or daughter—has been shown to greatly influence the overall family demeanor (Love, 1970; Seligman, 1979). Hence the parents' attitude is crucial to sibling adjustment.

Many times nonhandicapped siblings suffer from neglect or a lack of attention as both parents become overly involved with the special needs of the exceptional child. However, brothers and sisters need attention in their own right. According to Chinn and his co-workers (Chinn et al., 1978), these children have the same basic needs as any other youngster. In addition, they have some special needs that must be attended to if a positive adjustment is to be made. Some of the reasons that normal children encounter decreased parental attention are:

1. The parents may be overwhelmed with the responsibility of caring for the special needs child.
2. The parents are filled with guilt, consequently all of their time and energy is devoted to the handicapped child.
3. Sometimes parents attempt to escape from the entire family due to a threat to their self-esteem.
4. The parents may be operating under the false assumption that they are unfit to be parents because they have produced a defective offspring.
5. The parents may withhold attention because they truly are incompetent, therefore, inadequate attention is manifested regardless of the circumstances (Chinn et al., 1978).

Emotional responses   Siblings are capable of experiencing a wide variety of emotional reactions toward a handicapped brother or sister. Wentworth (1974) believes that these reactions are primarily directed toward the self and how life is influenced by a handicapped sibling. As a result, nonhandicapped siblings are affected more by their perception of how the parents treat them in comparison to the handicapped sibling than they are by the reality of the condition itself.

There are few, if any, sibling reactions that can be labeled typical of all nonhandicapped siblings. For a variety of reasons, children's emotional responses differ, as do those of their parents. The following reactions are identified by Chinn et al. (1978) and Wentworth (1974) as characteristic of some of the reactions and feelings sustained by brothers and sisters of exceptional children.

Resentment   Perhaps this is the most common reaction experienced by normal siblings. It is a natural by-product of being angry about having a handicapped brother or sister. Resentment may develop because the exceptional child might require a disproportionate amount of the parents' attention; the special needs child may prohibit the family from participating in certain experiences or excursions; special treatments and/or therapy may contribute to family financial hardship; older siblings may resent having to babysit, or having social constraints placed upon them by their younger atypical brother or sister.

Jealousy   Jealousy can easily develop from resentment, especially if the handicapped sibling perceives that he or she has lost "favor" with the parents. The handicapped brother or sister sometimes becomes a rival or competitor for the parents' attention and affection. Often this will result in the normal sibling's engaging in acts or behaviors designed to secure parental attention: for example, experiencing academic or behavioral problems in school, telling lies, or exhibiting unusual mischievousness.

Hostility   From feelings of jealousy often comes hostility, which is a perfectly natural reaction. Unlike objective adults, children are subjective and consider events in terms of how they are personally affected. They may view their atypical brother or sister, rather than the handicapping condition, as the source of all their problems. Therefore, feelings of hostility are usually aimed toward the handicapped sibling. These feelings may manifest themselves in physical aggression or verbal harassment and ridicule. In some instances, hostility is directed toward the parents through acts of disobedience or impertinence.

Guilt   Normal siblings frequently evidence feelings of guilt; however, these reactions differ from the guilt their parents suffer. Siblings' guilt may stem from their negative feelings about their handicapped brother or sister (which they realize are wrong), or it could be a consequence of having mistreated the handicapped child. Furthermore, when viewing their atypical sibling, some children experience guilt because of their own good fortune to be normal.

Grief   Siblings do grieve for their handicapped brother or sister. Their grief is often a reflection of their parents' sorrow. They grieve not for what they have lost, but for what will be denied to their afflicted sibling.

Fear   Nonhandicapped siblings may also encounter fear. They may be fearful of acquiring a disability, or of their own future children being handicapped. A further worry is that someday they will have to assume total responsibility for the care of the disabled child.

Shame and embarrassment   Shame and embarrassment are common emotional responses of normal siblings. A child may be ashamed of his mentally retarded brother or sister and embarrassed to have friends visit or to be seen in public with his or her atypical sibling. Wentworth theorizes that the degree of embarrassment is related to the degree of disability and the ages of the impaired and nonimpaired children.

Rejection   In certain families a normal sibling may reject the exceptional sibling. He or she may reject the reality of the impairment. More commonly, however, rejection is shown by withholding affection or ignoring the sibling's existence.

Wentworth (1974) concludes her analysis by reminding parents that in a given situation not all children react in the same manner or with the same intensity. Furthermore, the emotional impact of a handicapped sibling does not automatically have to be harmful. In fact, in most families, siblings display a certain degree of negative feeling toward each other.

Research findings   In recent years investigators have begun to turn their attention to siblings' reactions to having a handicapped brother or sister. The literature suggests that, in general, nonhandicapped siblings experience a wide variety of problems. One of the problems encountered by these children is the unrealistically high expectations that some parents place upon them in an attempt to compensate for the limitations of the handicapped child (Schild, 1976). Michaelis (1977) relates that one daughter was told that she had to "achieve for two" in order to compensate for the parents' disappointment in her brother. While some nonhandicapped siblings believe that they need to overachieve, other may find their academic progress impeded, possibly as a result of feeling guilty about being normal (San Martino & Newman, 1974). In other instances, normal siblings may exhibit excessive participation in extracurricular activities. Van der Veen and Novak (1974) speculate, however, that this might be an attempt to avoid close contact with the handicapped brother or sister.

The mental wellness of typical siblings has also been an area of research concentration. Poznanski (1973) observes that normal children, in comparison with their handicapped siblings, frequently have more severe emotional problems. She attributes this to the decreased amount of attention given by parents to their normal offspring. In another study, siblings of children with spina bifida were found to have a significantly higher incidence of maladjustment than siblings of controls (Tew & Laurence, 1973). In families in which one child is mentally retarded, Gath (1974) reports that older sisters demonstrate increased behavioral disturbance, perhaps due to the extra burdens of having to care for their retarded sibling. Mothers of deaf children relate that jealousy is a common problem among siblings (Gregory, 1976). Shere (1956) found in her early work with thirty pairs of twins in which one was cerebral palsied that the nonhandicapped twin was easily frustrated, more excitable, less cheerful, and more prone to emotional outbursts than the cerebral-palsied twin. She concluded that, from a mental hygiene viewpoint, the behavior of the cerebral-palsied twin was more desirable. Carr (1974) cautions, however, that many sibling studies suffer from methodological deficiencies. Interpretation of the research literature is further qualified since the emotional impact of a handicapped brother or sister is mediated by the age and sex of the nonimpaired sibling (Gath, 1973, 1974; Graliker, Fishler, & Koch, 1962; Schwirian, 1976).

Frances Grossman's (1972) work with brothers and sisters of mentally retarded children has attracted a great deal of attention.

Her research suggests that siblings of atypical children respond to their brothers and sisters in significantly different ways. A review of her investigation details this differential effect.

Grossman studied eighty-three college students, each of whom had a retarded sister or brother. These volunteers were matched with a control group of students who had nonretarded brothers or sisters. Fifty percent of the students in each group attended a highly competitive, expensive, eastern university, while the remaining students were enrolled in a local community college. All students were individually interviewed about their experiences and also completed several written tests. The severity of the retarded siblings' disabilities ranged from mild to severe; approximately 25 percent had Down's syndrome.

Grossman's data indicate that some students profited from the experience of growing up with a retarded sibling, whereas several others were adversely affected by this experience.

The ones who benefited appeared to us to be more tolerant, more compassionate, more knowing about prejudice and its consequences and they were often, but not always, more certain about their own futures, about personal and vocational goals, than comparable young adults who had not had such experiences.

The ones we judged to have been harmed often manifested bitter resentfulness of their families' situations, guilt about the rage they had felt at their parents and at the retarded sibling, and fear that they themselves might be defective. Often they had been deprived of attention that they needed to help them develop, simply because so much family time and energy had been given to the handicapped children. (p. 84)

Children of higher sociocultural status (SCS) who attended the private university were inclined to be protected or shielded from the inconveniences of having a retarded sibling. Sons from upper-SCS families were exempted from the responsibility of caring for their retarded brother or sister. Daughters, however, were not as immune from this duty. A similar contrast was observed in lower-SCS families, although young women from these families were expected to assist in child-care responsibilities from the time they were quite young.

Grossman found that the differences in lifestyles affected her subjects to an extraordinary degree. For example, the financial resources available to the upper-SCS families allowed for private residential care or the hiring of domestic help, a luxury unavailable to lower-SCS families. Yet Grossman notes that:

The striking difference between lower-SCS families and upper-SCS families is found in the primary impact of a retarded child. In an upper-SCS family, the major impact can be seen in the interactions of family members over their attitudes toward the handicapped child. In a lower-SCS family, the primary impact is seen quite simply in the degree and kind of hardship inflicted upon the family by the retarded child. (p. 103)

Thus, according to Grossman, sociocultural status has far-reaching consequences for families with retarded children. In upper-SCS families at least, the parents' attitudes and reactions, especially the mother's, were the single strongest factor influencing the normal siblings' acceptance of their retarded brother or sister. Grossman concludes that it is the family's perception or definition of the problem that most directly affects how individual members adjust to the presence of a retarded child.

It should be pointed out, however, that Grossman's subjects were volunteers. One could speculate that some nonretarded siblings declined to participate—possibly those who possessed negative feelings about their retarded siblings. Grossman acknowledges that her sample is highly biased in favor of well-adjusted siblings. In addition, her subjects reflect a select group of siblings of retarded children—those enrolled in college and comfortable enough to provide information about their family situation.

Concerns and questions   Invariably, siblings ask questions or express concerns about their handicapped brother or sister. Most parents attempt to respond to their children in an honest and straightforward fashion. Yet, for a variety of reasons, their best intentions sometimes fall short of the mark. As a consequence, siblings have unanswered questions or concerns that require resolution. The following list of concerns, some of which have been previously alluded to, was prepared by Cansler and Martin (1974, p. viii).

1. Siblings wonder about the cause of their brother's or sister's handicap, and sometimes fear that something may be wrong with themselves.

2. Siblings sometimes feel that having to help take care of the handicapped child interferes with their own activities.

3. Siblings may want to talk with their parents about the handicapped child's problems but do not know how to bring up the subject.

4. Siblings may feel upset and angry when parents have to spend a lot of time with the handicapped child. Sometimes siblings try to get attention from the parents by acting like the handicapped child.

5. Some siblings feel that they have to work extra hard (in school, sports, etc.) to make up to the parent for the handicapped child's deficiencies.

6. Siblings worry about how to tell their friends that they have a retarded brother or sister and wonder if their friends will make fun of them or their family for being different.

7. Siblings wonder if they will be able to get married and have children.

8. Siblings may worry about whether or not they will have to take care of the handicapped child in the future; they may wonder if they will be *able* to take care of him or her if anything happened to their parents.

9. Siblings may want to know how they can get along better with their handicapped brother or sister—how to help him/her learn to do things, how to play with him/her, what to do when baby-sitting.

Schreiber and Feeley (1965) conducted a group counseling experience for adolescent siblings of mentally retarded children. These teenagers had many questions about mental retardation and its impact on their lives and those of their families. Some of the questions that emerged from this experience are as follows:

1. How do you tell your friends about your retarded brother or sister, especially friends of the opposite sex?

2. How do you deal with your parents who have not discussed the problems of mental retardation in the family and its implications for you?

3. How do you deal with friends and people in school when you are hurt by their talk of the retarded as nutty and crazy?

4. What are we to do when our parents do not really feel affection for our retarded brother or sister?

5. How can we deal with our feelings when our friends show off their brothers' and sisters' pictures and talk about their accomplishments?

6. How does a teenager really accept a problem that he will face the rest of his life?

7. How can a teenager plan for his adult life? (pp. 223–224)

Sibling viewpoints   In an interview with Stanley Klein, editor of the magazine *Exceptional Parent,* several college students who were brothers and sisters of handicapped individuals discussed their experiences, feelings, and relationships with their atypical siblings. Richard tells of his physically deformed and hearing-impaired brother; Diane is the sister of a 21-year-old severely retarded girl; Tracy speaks of her 24-year-old brother, who suffered a birth injury. Their recollections are poignantly depicted in the following excerpts.

Discussing the extra burdens and responsibilities that generally accompany a special needs child, Diane relates:

I resented it once in a while, I think. Well, there are five girls in my family so that we were fortunately able to take turns. Of course, there were arguments here and there. I think you will find that anywhere. But as I said, once in a while I do not know if I resented Cathy, or if I resented my parents. I am really not sure. I know I felt that the activities of our entire family, in terms of recreation, were restricted.

I was sort of active in grammar and junior high school doing a few things—playing basketball and being involved generally. It always hurt me when my parents were never able to come watch me participate. I felt that they did not care about what I was doing, what my so-called accomplishments were. Of course, the excuse always was, "Well, you know we cannot find a babysitter, and you will just have to accept that."

But I did not accept it at the time, and I really thought, "Well, they do not care. They just do not want to go, they could find a babysitter if they really wanted to, but . . . " (Klein, 1972b, p. 24)

Peer interaction was also an area that caused the panelists some discomfort. As Tracy recounts:

I was able to see the interactions between the other kids and my brother. When I began junior high as a seventh grader, my brother was a ninth grader. Seventh graders, like me, were not known on the bus, and I heard some guy talking in the back about Mark and how stupid he was, and you could make him do anything and he is so gullible, and all this kind of stuff. I walked back to the kid and slugged him in the face. I was getting really annoyed and he could not understand what was happening.

I always felt that I had to protect him from someone, from teasing, from fights and from any other kids trying to put things over on kids who are at a disadvantage to them. If you love somebody you cannot help but get emotionally involved in that. (Klein, 1972a, pp. 12–13)

Richard echoes these thoughts:

I remember one day standing in front of the house. I must have been in about the sixth grade or so. One of my friends had just related an incident to me about how some other kids were picking on my brother and how he felt very sorry and all this stuff. Then he turned to me and said, "By the way, what *did* happen to your brother?" Looking back now, I can say well, I should have explained to him. But I just kind of got raging and I said, "Don't ask me that and the first person who asks me that after this, I'm going to punch him in the face!" That was all there was to it, and I felt kind of strange. I questioned my sense of protectiveness of him and I wonder if it was not just really a denial of my own lack of understanding. (Klein, 1972a, p. 13)

Episodes of embarrassment are also discussed by Diane:

I would bring friends into my home, and I would introduce, particularly when I was dating, my family, then I would introduce Cathy and say, "This is my retarded sister." I can remember young men coming in and walking over and saying, "Hello, Cathy," and of course she could not talk. I had embarrassing moments. In fact there were times when I even wished that she would be in bed when my dates came over, because I did not want to explain. I was not so sure that I would be seeing these people again. I do not know, it was not that I felt that it was not any of their business. I thought that if this person is not going to be a friend, a close friend, why should they know, why should they be bothered with it? (Klein, 1972b, pp. 26–27)

When questioned if their families were strengthened by the presence of their disabled sibling, Richard and Diane described opposite experiences.

Diane:

I always felt that there was something very different about our family. Of course, you know, Cathy being that difference. Because of her difference there was a degree of specialness or closeness about us that, I do not know, it was sort of a bond that made us all very, very close. We all pitched in and helped each other out and Cathy was the one thing in difficult times that we could focus on.

Richard:

I think you are fortunate. I think that our family was somewhat torn apart for that very reason. I guess it is something that I have no right to understand.

My mother feels that it was her fault that my brother was born the way he was. Some kind of drug I think that was being given out at that time, the early 50's, I think Thalidomide, that she seems to . . . maybe she took it, or that has something to do with it, she really feels it is something in herself. Sometimes I feel that my father has not addressed himself to that. It enhances his role as father, as a protective figure. He has a watchful eye out all the time, for my brother's financial affairs, social affairs, and everything else. He really has not attended that much to my mother's feelings, which bothers me.

I remember one time we had an argument about religion because I did not want to go to church anymore. They kept telling me that I had to go, and I said, "Well, one thing is, why should I go when you don't go?" The conversation started to get a little bit intense. My mother kind of mumbled, but she clearly said, "Why? After what God did to me?"

She ran into the other room, and started crying. At the time, I could not handle her, I felt like going in there and kind of consoling her, and saying—I do not know what I would have said—"It's okay." (Klein, 1972b, p. 25)

Both Richard and Tracy speak of the possibility of having to provide for their brothers' future care.

Richard: I have said to myself—neither of my parents have ever mentioned it to me—as a matter of fact recently too, that I would be quite willing to take my brother and have him live with myself and my wife. I would not take, I really would have to be pressured before I would take either my wife's mother or my own parents to live with us the rest of our lives. But my brother—I feel a lot differently about that.

Tracy: I think that it is something that we all probably have thought about. I had never really thought about it until my father did take me aside one day, and said, "Listen, I want you to look at my will." I said, "Do I have to?" He said, "I think that it is time you realized that you are the executrix of the will, even though you are the younger daughter, and you are in charge of your brother, and his protection." I never thought of it before, but it had never been really all laid down on paper before me that I would be responsible, which I do not mind. (Klein, 1972b, p. 26)

In the following selection, another college student (Hayden, 1974, pp. 26–28) recapitulates her life with her younger deaf sister.

THE OTHER CHILDREN

I first remember having a sense of special responsibility for my deaf sister when I was three. It was my duty to keep her out of danger and mischief—a seemingly normal responsibility for an older sister. But the responsibility has at times felt unbearably heavy. As a two-year-old, Mindy was not only typically rambunctious, she lived in a bizarre and often dangerous world all her own—separated from the rest of us by her deafness and her inability to communicate. It was a world of fascinating objects to handle, of races with Mother, Daddy and big sister—a world, even, of nocturnal romps in the street while the rest of the family slept. And once, it was a world of pretty colored pills in the bathroom medicine cabinet.

"Second mother" to Mindy

When Daddy spent a year in Korea, I became Mother's sole helper. My role as a second mother to Mindy held some prestige and much responsibility. It took away from play-time with children my own age. And, just as a mother serves as an example for her children, I was expected to be an exceptionally "good" little girl. The high standards my mother set for my behavior, though, had not only to do with my setting an example; her reasons were also practical. Mindy's impetuous behavior left her with little patience, energy or time to put up with shenanigans from me.

As I got older, problems resulting from my having a deaf sister increased. My mother began to attend college, and the new pressures and demands caused her to be demanding and dependent upon me. I did not understand why I would be severely chastised for the same behavior that Mindy, who embodied the behavior problems of three children, "couldn't help." My friends' parents seemed less critical of their children than my parents were of me. Mother and Daddy "expected more" from me, but it seemed to me that they gave me less.

The responsibility I felt for Mindy was tremendous. One year, when my "babysitting" duties involved periodic checking on my sister, Mindy wandered away between checks. After a thorough but fruitless search of the neighborhood, my mother hysterically told me that if anything happened to Mindy I would be to blame. I felt terrified and guilty. I was seven.

Competition and rivalry

Mindy's achievements always met with animated enthusiasm from our parents. In contrast, it seemed, Mother and Daddy's response to my accomplishments were on the pat-on-the-back level. I was *expected* to perform well in every circumstance. I wanted my parents to be enthusiastic about my accomplishments too. I didn't want to have to beg for praise. I didn't want to be taken for granted. I wanted to be noticed.

Babysitter and manager

When I was not baby-sitting there was my role of "fetch and carry"—sometimes literally. Mindy's deafness prevented my parents from calling to her so I was appointed official messenger. "Go tell Mindy to come to dinner." "Go tell Mindy to come inside." "Go tell Mindy to clean up her room." At first I probably gloried a bit in my "authority." But that soon grew stale. I was expected to stop whatever I was doing and bear some message to Mindy. And I discovered that like the royal messengers of old, bearers of orders or bad tidings are not cordially received. In retaliation against the inconvenience and hostile receptions, I made a point of being as bossy in my deliveries as possible—which resulted in acute mutual aggravation.

Love and respect

In my junior year of high school, Mindy and I began to grow close as sisters. Our increased maturity and the circumstances of our father's being away in Vietnam caused us to turn to one another for companionship and comfort. In the process, we began to discover one another as individuals. We took time to understand our mutual antagonisms and to forgive each other a little. Mindy now understands that as a child my responsibility for her was immense and often intolerable, and that she thoughtlessly made it more difficult for me. And she has forgiven me for the hurt resentment caused her. Differences between us will always exist, but Mindy and I now understand and respect each other's needs without resentment.

The impact a disabled child has upon the other children in a family is tremendous—in both a positive and negative sense. Parents must not expect sainthood from their "other children." Most likely many years will pass before their nondisabled children fully understand why their sister or brother "couldn't help it," why they were expected to be model children, why attention from their parents was rationed and why their parents sometimes seemed unduly critical and impatient. Until the "other children" do understand, their reactions may be "thoughtless" or "unfair." Before love can replace misunderstanding and intolerance, resentment must be recognized and accepted as a legitimate and even inevitable part of the struggle of growing up together.

Chinn et al. (1978) believe that a family with a handicapped child is capable, by members' own efforts and those of relatives, friends, and helpers, of "returning to balance." Parents should strive to maintain an equilibrium, meeting their needs and those of all their children. As a result, the family is reintegrated and can realistically and effectively function as a complete unit.

A final word

By and large, most people have little understanding of and even less appreciation for the psychological, economic, and social demands and obligations encountered by parents of an atypical child. It should be obvious that a handicapped child can affect, either beneficially or detrimentally, the entire family. Helpers, therefore, should show concern for the parents and *all* the children, for whatever affects an individual member affects the total family. However, since not all families are affected in the same way, individualized assistance consistent with the needs of the family is required. If helpers are able to demonstrate sensitivity to each family's uniqueness, then this perspective will go a long way in promoting the development and full functioning of the family unit.

> *Children begin by loving their parents; as they grow older they judge them; sometimes they forgive them.*
>
> Oscar Wilde

References

Abrams, J., & Kaslow, F. (1977). Family systems and the learning disabled child: Intervention and treatment. *Journal of Learning Disabilities, 10,* 27–31.

Begab, M. (1966). The mentally retarded and the family. In I. Phillips (Ed.), *Prevention and treatment of mental retardation* (pp. 71–84). New York: Basic Books.

Behmer, M. (1976). Coping with our children's disabilities: Some basic principles. *Exceptional Parent, 6,* 35–38.

Block, J. (1978). Impaired children. *Children Today, 7,* 2–6.

Boggs, E. (1969). Pointers for parents. In W. Wolfensberger and R. Kurtz (Eds.), *Management of the family of the mentally retarded* (pp. 497–505). Chicago: Follett.

Cansler, D., & Martin, G. (1974). *Working with families: A manual for developmental centers.* Reston, VA: Council for Exceptional Children.

Carr, J. (1974). The effects of the severely subnormal on their families. In A. Clarke and A. Clarke (Eds.), *Mental deficiency: The changing outlook* (3rd ed., pp. 807–839). New York: Free Press.

Chinn, P., Winn, J., & Walters, R. (1978). *Two-way talking with parents of special children.* St. Louis: C. V. Mosby.

Cohen, P. (1962). The impact of the handicapped child on the family. *Social Casework, 43,* 137–142.

Drotar, D., Baskiewicz, A., Irvin, N., Kennell, J., & Klaus, M. (1975). The adaptation of parents to the birth of an infant with a congenital malformation: A hypothetical model. *Pediatrics, 56,* 710–717.

Dunlap, W., & Hollingsworth, S. (1977). How does a handicapped child affect the family? Implications for practitioners. *Family Coordinator, 26,* 286–293.

Farber, B. (1959). Effects of a severely mentally retarded child on family integration. *Monographs of the Society for Research in Child Development,* No. 71.

Farber, B. (1960). Family organization and crisis: Maintenance of integration in families with a severely mentally retarded child. *Monographs of the Society for Research in Child Development,* No. 75.

Fotheringham, J., & Creal, D. (1974). Handicapped children and handicapped families. *International Review of Education, 20,* 355–369.

Gallagher, J., Haskins, R., & Farran, D. (1979). Poverty and public policy for children. In P. Brazelton and V. Vaughn (Eds.), *The family: Setting priorities* (pp. 239–269). New York: Science and Medicine Publishing.

Gargiulo, R., & Warniment, J. (1976). A parents' perspective of learning disabilities. *Academic Therapy, 11,* 473–480.

Gath, A. (1973). The school age sibling of mongol children. *British Journal of Psychiatry, 123,* 161–167.

Gath, A. (1974). Sibling reactions to mental handicap: A comparison of the brothers and sisters of the mongol child. *Journal of Child Psychology and Psychiatry, 15,* 187–198.

Goldie, L. (1966). The psychiatry of the handicapped family. *Developmental Medicine and Child Neurology, 8,* 456–462.

Gordon, R. (1977). Special needs of multihandicapped children under six and their families: One opinion. In E. Sontag (Ed.), *Educational programming for the severely and profoundly handicapped* (pp. 61–71). Reston, VA: Council for Exceptional Children.

Graliker, B., Fishler, K., & Koch, R. (1962). Teenage reaction to a mentally retarded sibling. *American Journal of Mental Deficiency, 66,* 838–843.

Gregory, S. (1976). *The deaf child and his family.* New York: Wiley.

Grossman, F. (1972). Brothers and sisters of retarded children. *Psychology Today, 5,* 82–84, 102–104.

Hayden, V. (1974). The other children. *Exceptional Parent, 4,* 26–29.

Jan, J., Freeman, R., & Scott, E. (1977). *Visual impairment in children and adolescents.* New York: Grune & Stratton.

Kew, S. (1975). *Handicap and family crisis.* London: Pitman.

Klein, S. (1972a). Brother to sister. *Exceptional Parent, 2,* 10–15.

Klein, S. (1972b). Brother to sister, sister to brother. *Exceptional Parent, 2,* 24–27.

Lillie, D. (1981). Educational and psychological strategies for working with parents. In J. Paul (Ed.), *Understanding and working with parents of children with special needs* (pp. 89–118). New York: Holt, Rinehart and Winston.

Love, H. (1970). *Parental attitudes toward exceptional children.* Springfield, IL: Charles C Thomas.

Love, H. (1973). *The mentally retarded child and his family.* Springfield, IL: Charles C Thomas.

Mac Keith, R. (1973). The feelings and behaviour of parents of handicapped children. *Developmental Medicine and Child Neurology, 15,* 524–527.

Martin, P. (1975). Marital breakdown in families with spina bifida cystica. *Developmental Medicine and Child Neurology, 17,* 757–764.

Meyerson, R. (1983). Family and parent group therapy. In M. Seligman (Ed.), *The family with a handicapped child* (pp. 285–308). New York: Grune & Stratton.

Michaelis, C. (1977). Imperfect child—cause for sorrow. *Special Children, 4,* 39–48.

Morton, K. (1978). Identifying the enemy—A parent's complaint. In A. Turnbull and H. Turnbull (Eds.), *Parents speak out* (pp. 142–147). Columbus, OH: Charles Merrill.

Pieper, E. (1976). Grandparents can help. *Exceptional Parent, 6,* 7–10.

Poznanski, E. (1973). Emotional issues in raising handicapped children. *Rehabilitation Literature, 34,* 322–326, 352.

Ross, A. (1964). *The exceptional child in the family.* New York: Grune & Stratton.

San Martino, M., & Newman, M. (1974). Siblings of retarded children: A population at risk. *Child Psychiatry and Human Development, 4,* 168–177.

Schild, S. (1976). The family of the retarded child. In R. Koch and J. Dobson (Eds.), *The mentally retarded child and his family* (pp. 454–465). New York: Brunner/Mazel.

Schreiber, M., & Feeley, M. (1965). Siblings of the retarded: A guided group experience. *Children, 12,* 221–225.

Schwirian, P. (1976). Effects of the presence of a hearing-impaired preschool child in the family on behavior patterns of older "normal" siblings. *American Annals of the Deaf, 121,* 373–380.

Seligman, M. (1979). *Strategies for helping parents of exceptional children.* New York: Free Press.

Shere, M. (1956). Socio-emotional factors in families of the twin with cerebral palsy. *Exceptional Children, 22,* 197–199, 206–208.

Simeonsson, R., & Simeonsson, N. (1981). Parenting handicapped children: Psychological aspects. In J. Paul (Ed.), *Understanding and work-*

ing with parents of children with special needs (pp. 51–88). New York: Holt, Rinehart and Winston.

Telford, C., & Sawrey, J. (1981). *The exceptional individual* (4th ed.). Englewood Cliffs, NJ: Prentice-Hall.

Tew, B., & Laurence, K. (1973). Mothers, brothers and sisters of patients with spina bifida. *Developmental Medicine and Child Neurology, 15,* (Supp. 29), 69–76.

van der Veen, F., & Novak, A. (1974). The family concept of the disturbed child. A replication study. *American Journal of Orthopsychiatry, 44,* 763–772.

Walker, J., Thomas, M., & Russell, I. (1971). Spina bifida and the parents. *Developmental Medicine and Child Neurology, 13,* 462–476.

Wentworth, E. (1974). *Listen to your heart.* Boston: Houghton Mifflin.

Wolfensberger, W. (1967). Counseling parents of retarded children. In A. Baumeister (Ed.), *Mental retardation* (pp. 329–400). Chicago: Aldine.

Chapter 4:
Parents speak out

The deeper that sorrow carves into your being, the more joy you can contain.

—Kahlil Gibran

Many times when reading about helping, helper characteristics, and stages or patterns of emotional responses, it is very easy to lose sight of the parents' involvement and investment in their handicapped child. Helpers can become very glib in their professional pronouncements and maintain an air of detachment, yet it must be remembered that lives of entire families can be changed, sometimes for the worse, when a child is labeled handicapped. Not only do helpers need to possess good qualities and skills—they must also be sensitive to the human aspect of parenting an exceptional child. Helpers need to maintain the perspective that the handicapped individual is first and foremost a person, and then someone who happens to be exceptional. Likewise, the family is first a family and second a family with a handicapped member.

The following selections, written by parents and about parents, lucidly present the view from the other side of the coin. These articles tell of the human toll and triumphs, not from a clinical viewpoint, but as seen through the eyes of people whose dreams were destroyed, who were shunted away by society, who fought "the system" and sometimes won, but sometimes both they and their child lost because the professionals with whom they had contact did not want to help, know how to help, or care to help. While reading these vignettes, one might try, just for the moment, to change places with these mothers and fathers and imagine how it would feel to have a son or daughter in this situation.

WHAT IS TO BECOME OF KATHERINE?

During the more than 20 years of her life, Katherine Jamieson has been diagnosed as retarded, borderline retarded, borderline, borderline normal, and every possible gradation in between. Her IQ has tested between 70 and 90 over the years, and as the AAMD definition of retardation fluctuated, so did the diagnosis. She has been in special classrooms, in sheltered workshops for adult retarded, in various types of training programs, in the mental hospital, and in a residential facility—the list is endless. The pile of material collected by her father is remarkable for what it includes. Perhaps more remarkable is that it exists at all.

The material Mr. Jamieson has collected falls into several categories. There are the myriad little pieces of paper with lists of places and telephone numbers, presumably places that Mr. or Mrs. Jamieson called in an effort to find placement for Katherine. When I gave up counting, I had deciphered 20. There are many letters received over a period of years from counselors, therapists, and supervisors giving reports on Katherine's progress or, usually, the lack of it. At one point there is a letter to Katherine from her father, full of anguish and rage. "What will you do if you don't make it here? There is nowhere else for you to go; we have tried everything. Do what they tell you." Between the lines is the un-

From "What Is to Become of Katherine?" by M. de Boor, 1975, *Exceptional Children,* *41*, pp. 517–518. Reprinted by permission.

written note, "Do it for us. We can't do any more for you." At the end of the file there is a series of letters from a workshop. The letters say things such as "On the bottle washing detail Katherine was unable to apply herself, likewise on the dishwashing detail, but she has done adequate or above adequate work in some other detail." There is the reply from her father, "Thank you for your nice letter. It was so good to hear something positive about Katherine for a change."

There are letters from Katherine, long (13 pages) at times, barely legible, but coherent—letters home from a growing girl. Invitations designed for a spring party but never filled out and never mailed. A drawing, a long story. Notebooks with her algebra assignments and doodles. Signs of a girl growing up. Postcards to her brothers. Shoes put on layaway and never paid for.

Then there are all the bills, bills that every parent has (dentists, orthodontists) and bills that only Katherine's parents have. Mental health bills from psychologists and statements from the state hospital. Coupled with these are insurance forms, long letters to various agencies and insurance companies about forms that must be filled out. A statement from the state that Katherine is not qualified for disabled aid. A long letter to a state agency about the fact that the Jamiesons really cannot pay all these bills because they have other children who must not be deprived because of Katherine. The underlying message is clear; she is not their fault.

There are reports from many agencies. "Katherine is retarded." "Katherine will never be able to live alone." "We can't help her any more." "She's untrainable and always has been." A school for the retarded wants extensive information before they will even consider Katherine. Could the parents go and look at the facility before they once again do all the work involved in collecting files? No, says the school, only afterward when it is possible that she will be admitted will they be allowed to look. So they do all the paperwork and the school turns them down.

An indication of the impotent rage appears in a letter to a bus company demanding refund for a ticket purchased for Katherine but never used. Mr. Jamieson has asked for this before but was sent a long form. He writes back an enraged letter about their "stupid form" and their "stupid rules" and says that if he does not get his money back he will go higher. When one is dealing with important questions, it is the little annoyances that really do one in.

When Katherine was evaluated this week at our facility, the conclusion was that she is not retarded at all. So what is she? Is she the victim of growing up in the 1950's when *learning disability* was just a word? Could she have been helped had she been born in 1970? Possibly. But instead there is Mr. Jamieson and his file, which he marched in with and deposited.

The fact that this file exists says a great deal. Many of us have files on our children, but we do not save every scrap of paper on which we have scribbled notes to call so and so, arrange this or that. Mr. Jamieson did. Most of us with children have doctor bills of all sorts, but we do not put them in a file marked with the child's name. Mr. Jamieson did. Most of us do not make copies of the letters we send to our children, or the notes we send to teachers, or the insurance forms we file when our child breaks his arm. Mr. Jamieson did, and the question is why?

I think it is a matter of quantity. Katherine Jamieson had a problem that became evident at the age of 2. Presumably with confidence, the Jamiesons went to the first professional for help and were told something negative such as "She is retarded," but they were not told what to do about it. Perhaps they were told "There's nothing to do; it's very sad."

This file picks up the last 4 or 5 years, by which time everyone the Jamiesons talked to was telling them (a) "We will only look at your child after you have filed 47 forms and let us look at everything concerned with Katherine, down to and including whether her grandmother had five toes or six," and then (b) either "Yes we will look at her" and "She is retarded and there is nothing to do" (not "We don't know what to do") or "No, we will not look at her." By this time Mr. Jamieson has started to keep a file. At least he will have that to show for all his labors, since his daughter has not benefited by them. He reaches the point where he exchanges notes with the state hospital about the wording of the records. This is after he has decided that he will keep the records himself so that he can send them out to each agency instead of always going through the red tape of release forms.

The final impression gained from his file is that here is a father for whom the system has become the adversary. Rather than helping him and Katherine, the system is at war with them. If the time comes for the trial of the system against Katherine, Mr. Jamieson will have the evidence in his file. And he also has

Katherine, now 21, unable to hold a job, promiscuous, unstable, happy only with her guitar. And the question which the Jamiesons asked 15 years ago is still unanswered: What is to become of Katherine?

A SOCIETY THAT IS GOING TO KILL YOUR CHILDREN

I know a beautiful woman who is in her sixties. She is as stable, intelligent, kind, caring, interested and interesting, vital and loving a woman as I have ever met. She is the mother of an autistic person, a man nearing forty. She and her son have been mistreated, malpracticed upon, legally stolen from, taken advantage of, denied services, denied rights, the object of verbal and physical abuse, and generally ignored or treated as fools by a small army of doctors, psychiatrists, bureaucrats, researchers, administrators, and other leaders in the various states in which she has lived.

Why? Because her son was autistic. None of it would have happened if her son had been born with the ability to function in the fashion that people call "normal." If he had, she would not have suffered in the manner that she has at the hands of those who have caused her pain. Her crime was that she did everything she knew how to do to help her son.

When the boy was very young, she noticed he was not developing as he should and that he was doing peculiar things such as screaming all night long, endlessly wriggling his fingers along the periphery of his vision, making funny little nonsense noises instead of talking, refusing to wear clothing, refusing to be comforted when upset, not looking people in the eye—all those sad and confounding, amusing, bittersweet and heart-rending little things that autistic children do in those early years. (Remember, parents? You remember. We remember. Doesn't it jolt tears into your eyes to remember? Doesn't it make you laugh and cry inside to look upon those strange and fearful days and see that beautiful child—yours—mine—in diapers, running aimlessly, laughing in the sun-

Excerpted from "A Society That Is Going to Kill Your Children," by F. Warren, 1978, in *Parents Speak Out*, (pp. 181–183) edited by A. Turnbull and H. R. Turnbull, Columbus, OH: Charles Merrill. Copyright 1978 by Charles Merrill. Reprinted by permission.

shine of a far-off, time-lost day, glimpsed fleetingly through the mist of long-gone years; amused at sounds unheard by us, at thoughts unknown, unknowable; terrified to lost, abandoned wailing at horrors unperceived and unperceivable to us—we who loved so long and painfully and unavailingly.)

So, with rising fear, she took the child to all the places from which help is said to come in our society—doctors, psychiatrists who probed with knowing smiles into the deepest personal regions of her life, specialists, treatment centers, hospitals, clinics. This went on and on through years of waiting rooms and corridors, through examinations, diagnostic tests, and lab reports, before a hundred polished desks, a hundred men in white until they both, she and her son, grew old and tired. (Remember, parents? Remember? For she is us and we are her.)

And what did the hundred (more or less, give or take a dozen or so, it doesn't matter) important, knowledgeable, people do?

They cleared their throats importantly.

They smoked their cigars and cigarettes casually.

They looked at her over smart bifocals wisely.

They wrote jargon in their secret files so knowledgeably.

They cruelly stamped a dozen labels on the child.

They sent her bills which she paid and paid and paid religiously.

They sent her away unaided and alone.

They did other things, too.

They held the struggling child down, drugged him senseless, and cut out part of his brain; they called it lobotomy, and she paid for it.

They tied him to a table, sent fierce jolts of electricity through the tender, already faulty, already damaged tissue inside his skull; they called it treatment, and she paid for it.

They said he was emotionally disturbed, they said she made him that way, they called her insulting names in a code language they made up themselves, to serve their own purposes. They said what they were doing was therapy, and she paid for it.

Finally, when the child had been reduced to a shuffling, drooling, brainless, hopeless creature who could not speak a single intelligible word, could not keep from soiling his pants with feces, could not attend to his simplest human needs, and was given to wild fits of self-destruction in a pathetic effort to rid himself of the burden of life, they took him away, tied him to a chair in a dreary, cold, and stinking ward in a crumbling, overcrowded "hospital." They called it care and she paid for it.

My God, isn't that enough? Oh, no, it isn't—not nearly enough. The bond between mother and child is strong. It is flesh caring for flesh, blood reaching out to blood, and does not end when institution doors clang harshly shut. My friend never stopped trying—she is trying now. She never stopped hoping—she is hoping now.

Sometimes when she drove 100 miles to visit her son, the staff at the institution sent her away. She asked them why, and they called her a nuisance. She wrote scores and scores of letters—asking, pleading, demanding, searching, cajoling to improve the conditions of his existence—and they said she interfered.

She saw him sitting, neglected, in his own feces and they rationalized this outrage. "We don't have the staff. . . . We do our best, but there isn't enough money. . . . The legislature won't. . . . The administration won't. . . . The rules won't. . . ." and so on.

She learned that he was never taken out to walk in the sunlight. She saw his skin grow pale, his muscles wither from lack of use, his body sagging and old when it should have been young and strong, his broken mind untended, unstimulated, wasted.

Her conversations, condensed from a hundred meetings with administrators, directors, staff people, bureaucrats, "service providers," over the span of twenty years went something like this:

"Can you put him in a better ward?" "No." "Can you get him out to walk once a day?" "No." "He loves to swim. Can he swim sometimes?" "No." "Can you build a swimming pool? All the residents could use it. It would be good for them." "No." "Can you provide him some education, some training?" "No." "The community college is nearby. They will provide trainers if you will identify twelve people. Call it adult education and draft a program for them. Will you take the time?" "No." "The institution a mile away has a swimming pool. Can he go there once a week?" "No."

Once, in the 1960's, she escalated her simple requests into demands, drawing upon the strategy of black action groups. When she was rejected, she went in utter desperation—a lone, weary, aging woman—and lay her body in the street at the "hospital" where she caused a flurry of disruption until she was taken away.

Why, you might ask, did she not just take her son home, keep him there, and care for him herself? There are many reasons, not the least of which is that she did for years until her resources—financial, physical, and emotional—were drained.

Another is that she believed the myths, expounded by professionals, that somewhere in their heads, hidden in their books, behind some closed and secret doors beyond her knowing, was help and hope and care—if only she would trust and lay her burdens in their hands. She did, and they killed her son.

There is no pleasant ending to this story. There cannot be. A living corpse still rocks behind closed doors. A good and loving mother tends her wounds and keeps on trying.

YES, OUR SON IS STILL WITH US

In this account of my son's life in our family circle, I hope to present a strong case for the preservation of every human being and the inclusion of every child in a loving family when possible.

Stephen is 11 years old, profoundly retarded, cerebral-palsied and epileptic. He doesn't walk or talk and he probably never will. He does not understand speech and has few ways to communicate his needs. Stephen also has both visual and auditory perceptual impairment and a variety of seizure disorders. Although some of the disorders are well controlled, he has dozens to hundreds of small drop seizures daily.

Stephen is a handsome boy, although he has a wasted, underdeveloped and poorly muscled body. He does not whine, whimper or cry except when in extreme pain. He has a very sweet expression and a gentle personality.

In this account of his life, I would like to emphasize that I realize that the qualities of each child make him or her—to a greater or lesser degree—easier to take care of in the home. I am not foolish enough to think that every severely handicapped child will be as comparatively easy to take care of as Stephen.

I have longed many times to be able to describe to a doctor how we feel about our handicapped child. I am in my late 40s and my husband is in his early 50s. We have a 20-year-old son and

From "Yes, Our Son Is Still with Us," by C. Hosey, 1973, *Children Today*, pp. 2, 14–17, 36. Reprinted by permission.

two daughters, aged 16 and 18, living at home, as well as a married daughter. The children were 11, 9, 7 and 5 when Stephen was born. My husband and I married young and adopted our first two children after several childless years. Then I gave birth to our third child, a normal and very intelligent daughter. A short time later, we adopted our fourth child. And then, when I was 37, I gave birth to Stephen after an uncomplicated pregnancy. But the delivery was induced and precipitate, and much later we were told that lack of oxygen was the probable cause of enormous damage to his central nervous system.

Stephen's color was not normal following birth; his lethargy was profound and his sucking ability was so poor that his weight fell almost a full pound during his first five days. Nevertheless, Stephen was discharged from the hospital to us as "a normal male infant."

As his first year came to an end, however, I realized that his inability to turn over, sit up, or crawl was not to be explained by his chubby weight or crossed eyes. When he was 14 months old, we asked for comprehensive testing. I stayed in the hospital with Stephi during the week of tests. Each evening the pediatrician would come and tell me the results of the tests and, because I was naive, I was pleased as he reported each negative result. It was only at the end of the week, when he explained, that I started to understand the horror of the situation. The doctor said he had done the tests hoping to find something, anything, that was correctable. But as each of the tests were negative, he realized that we were faced not with a thyroid deficiency or something of that nature but with an undeterminable amount of brain damage and a very crippled little boy.

During that week in the hospital I had spent many hours fighting panic—swinging upward when I got the details of a test result, and then down again when I made myself face the facts, as I had begun to face them the day I first called the pediatrician before one of Stephen's well-baby check-ups and told him I thought Stephen was retarded and asked him to talk honestly with me.

I was told there was nothing to be done but wait and see how he developed. I took Stephi home from the hospital to the family. We were in a better position than many young couples who have this experience. First of all, we had raised four normal children, which was a comfort. Secondly, we were both of a mature age, not a young couple untested by problems. But I will always remember my feeling of numb despair. I didn't cry or give much external sign of my inner hysteria but I felt that I would never be able to adjust to this situation.

The shock of the birth of child like this doesn't come all at once. It's worse in some ways than the death of a child because you gradually realize that this child is never going to live in the fullest sense of the word. It is only after months or years pass that you find out how your family will be affected.

It was difficult for us to absorb the first shock, which is truly physical as well as mental. We were numb, we could scarcely walk about and do our normal day's work, or talk to other people. Still, we had no agonizing decision to make at this point. We loved Stephi, he had been a part of our family for more than a year, and no one would have suggested, even if it had been possible, to allow him to die. He was living and he was healthy then. The shock consisted of knowing that we had a child who would never grow up. He might have a very long life, but he would not experience any of the pleasures of a normal life.

I feel strongly that no couple, no matter what their age or experience, can make a wise or even a fully conscious decision at a moment like this. I feel that unless a decision is absolutely imperative because of life or death alternatives, it should be postponed. I am firmly convinced that parents' assertion of their instinct to love and cherish their child is essential to a family's mental health. I think that at the moment of first knowledge of their child's damage this instinct may be stunned by the pain they are experiencing. But I know that if someone stands by and encourages them to love the child and, if possible, to take the child home, it is going to help in many ways for the rest of their lives. If this instinct to love and cherish the child asserts itself, then I think that they can make a loving decision about him later on. This may be later in terms of a week, or years, but if they have allowed their natural parental instinct to be developed, they are going to make it because they love the child and they will not, instead, have to live with a memory of rejection. It is better to remember in the years to come that you did everything out of love for your child, and not because you lacked courage. If parents have to institutionalize the child, soon or years later, it may be very painful, but they will be comforted by knowing that they loved him.

Because we had to travel with my husband's job in the years following Stephen's birth, we had the opportunity to see more doctors with Stephi than the average family could or would. We found that, as time passed and Stephen's disabilities became more apparent, doctors were still explaining to us that he was retarded. Since this would have been obvious to anyone at first glance, we could only conclude that they were really saying, "Why do you still have this retarded child with you?" Or they would be more forthright about it and say, "A child like this is damaging to your other children. You should see about an institutional placement for him. Do you have him on a waiting list? You have your own lives to live."

From the time we were given our first child, our lives had involved our children and they were never to be separated totally from any of them. So now we questioned why our lives and emotions should be separated from the most helpless of all of our children. Doctors did at times express pity and I have heard many other parents of retarded children say rather belligerently that they don't want pity. I don't feel this way. There's nothing wrong with pity as far as I'm concerned; in fact, I feel very sorry for myself at times. I think that honest parents of a child like ours do feel that they and certainly their child have had a damn poor shake out of life. It is a tragedy! It's heartbreaking. But our children are here. They live. They must not be rejected like broken toys.

I've often wondered why doctors didn't give me credit and support for an intelligent decision to give my child the safe-keeping that I knew I could give him for as long as it was possible for me to give it to him. But so many times I've been made to feel that I love Stephen almost illegally and certainly unintelligently. We were told by one doctor that Stephen was not a productive member of society; therefore we did not have the right to take family time, money and energy away from our other four "productive members of society" in favor of Stephi. We had a strong family feeling that each child, as in all families, naturally gets the time and money and energy that he or she needs from parents. As far as society goes, I think one of the greatnesses of our country is that the benefits, the fruits of our country, don't go just to the taxpayer, but to all the people. And it is the same in a family. As far as our other children are concerned, we couldn't believe that his presence was going to be detrimental to them. They seemed to be growing normally. They dearly loved Stephen and still do. They don't hesitate to bring their friends home and to discuss their little brother. In fact, when one of our daughters was in the fourth grade and her class was discussing mental retardation she asked me if she could take Stephen in for "Show-and-Tell." The teacher agreed, and I felt that it was beneficial to the children. Handicapped children have been kept in back rooms and in special classes, hidden away, so naturally they are objects of curiosity to be stared at. When they are permitted to enter as much of normal social life as possible, there will be a greater understanding of their problems.

The sorrow of Stephen's condition is a lasting thing, something that flares up at strange times. It hits both of us, my husband and me, many times. Once when I was driving through the mountains of Switzerland, it overpowered me—knowing Stephi would never feel the beauty of approaching evening in the mountains. And at other times, perhaps during a beautiful piece of music that I know that he will never understand . . .

The day-to-day care of Stephen is not the difficult part. I guess the most difficult thing about these children is facing their future. We can protect him now, but unlike most couples who enter their later years with a fair amount of serenity, looking forward to retirement and the easing of family responsibility as their children leave home, we have one child who will never be independent. We are able to care for him lovingly now, but this isn't enough. He shouldn't be well cared for only during our lifetime, but for all of his. And most families probably find this the worst of the nightmare, wondering where their child will live out the end of his life, praying that he won't be neglected, malnourished or cared for by insensitive people.

I often wondered when Stephen was very young and not having any medical problems how I would have felt if I had had a child who had been diagnosed as gravely damaged at birth and I had had to make a life-or-death decision. Later in Stephen's life, we went through a series of medical crises—several episodes of chain epileptic seizures, months of allergic drug reactions, weeks of forced feedings when he lost his swallowing reflex and wasted almost to death, and, just a year ago, a day and a night of almost fatal hemorrhages after surgery. It was a testing period for me because, as I saw him through those periods, there was no doubt about my feelings. I wanted him to live, just as I would want my normal children to survive.

Stephen is currently enrolled in the Intensive Training Unit for retarded-multihandicapped students at the Montgomery County Association for Retarded Citizens in Silver Spring, Md. We found through the years that meeting Stephen's need for training in the basic life skills required the most determined effort on our part. Less damaged children are sometimes accommodated in public school systems, but we had to insist repeatedly that he not be ignored because of the multiplicity of his problems. The quality of his adult life was going to depend on our being able to do something about our conviction that feeding himself was better than being fed, and learning to sit upright in a wheelchair was preferable to lying in a crib for the rest of his life.

In writing all this, I have tried to present the problems of a family with a handicapped child. This is easier to do than to explain the plus side of our life. There is so much more of that, but it is harder to put into words. Stephen has given us a great deal of positive happiness. He isn't just tolerated. When he is ill, we pray that he will survive. We had a family celebration at the end of his ninth year, the first year he had not had a stay in a hospital. The family was thrilled when he brought his first bite of food to his mouth by himself, and when he learned to stand up from his wheelchair. I think our children have gained in compassion and maturity. They are more aware than many of their contemporaries of how precious a normal life is, how wonderful an undamaged intellect, and how lucky they are to have whole bodies. Great patience with a slow child can leave you with a sense of warmth and pride.

I am sure it is difficult even for a doctor who works with children like Stephen every day to try to imagine himself a parent of a seriously damaged child. I couldn't do it before I had Stephi. I was totally unprepared. But there are no regrets now. I wish very much that Stephen was a normal child. But as long as he is the way he is, I am glad he is ours. I wish that every father and mother who has a handicapped child born to them could be given a chance to love their child.

WHO CARES WHAT HAPPENS TO MIRIAM?

The following selection is a transcription of an interview originally conducted on public television in New York City (WNET-TV). It was part of the popular series, "How Do Your Children Grow." Hosted by Eda LaShan, the interview presents a discussion of the difficulties and successes experienced by Miriam's parents, Mr. & Mrs. Dallas DeSoyza, in their attempts to secure services for her.

Eda: We are going to be talking about something called Down's Syndrome, which I think is probably better known to many people, including myself, as mongolism. With me tonight to discuss this kind of condition are Teddie and Dallas De-Soyza, who have a four-year-old daughter named Veronica, and another little girl who is 20 months old, Miriam, who has Down's Syndrome. Now, let us start right at the beginning.

Teddie: Miriam was born on a Tuesday evening, a Caesarian section. The doctor said, "Let me give you a spinal, so that you'll see the baby. It'll be a good experience." I said, "Fine!" I gave birth to the baby, and I remember seeing the *back* of her head.

On Wednesday morning, a doctor, a strange doctor, came into my room. He said, "I've seen the baby, I don't know how many pounds she is." I said, "I do, she's 5-12."

Then he proceeded, stumbling all along. "Well," I said, "how is the baby?" He said, "She's very oriental

From "Who Cares What Happens to Miriam?" by E. LaShan, 1973, *Exceptional Parent*, March-April, pp. 11–17. Reprinted by permission.

looking." "Well, my husband's oriental." He replied that she had a very high cheekbone and slanted eyes. "Well, my husband has high cheekbones and a slant to his eye." He kept stumbling, and I was becoming very suspicious. "Well, it's a very pronounced look, an oriental look." Finally, I asked, "Now, what are you trying to tell me? Is something wrong with the baby? Are you trying to tell me something?" "Uh, well, you want me to be specific?" I said, "You're damn right, I want you to be specific, it's my baby. And I want you to tell me what's wrong."

"Well, we have to take a chromosome test, and find out what's wrong; we think it's a chromosomal defect." And immediately I thought, what is a chromosomal defect? I never heard that expression, or associated it with anything. I said, "Are you telling me something about this baby?" And of course I became furious and angry with him, and frightened. He said, "Well, I can't give you the details at this point, uh . . ."

Eda:

Now that I've made you thoroughly anxious, that's all I can tell you.

Teddie:

Right. I said, "Tell me what you're trying to say, will you please tell me!" and of course I started to cry, and went to pieces. He said to me, "Now, now, that's life." I told him to get out of the room. I screamed at him.

Eda:

Where was Dallas all this time?

Teddie:

Dallas was at work.

Eda:

Had you received the information yet?

Dallas: I had gone to work, planning on visiting her during my lunch hour. The first I heard of it was the call that I received from Teddie—she was crying over the phone and said, "There's something wrong with the baby, a doctor said she has a chromosomal defect."

I was working with doctors at the time, so I went and spoke to one of them. He said it was probably mongolism. From there I went straight away to the hospital. I tried to see the baby—I saw this baby, naturally I knew—I had seen mongoloid children. I asked the nurse, "What's the condition?" She would not speak. I said, "Is the child mongoloid?" She did not say it, but from her reaction I gathered it was.

I had seen Ted before that, and that was it for that day. We met the obstetrician, a very nice, very understanding man. He said, "Well, this is something that happens." I did my best to console her, because she was the one who went through the agony of being confronted with this information when she was half-groggy from the anesthesia, all alone.

Teddie: That strange doctor coming in and telling me that. I had nobody to speak to. When one obstetrician came in, I was crying. He is a very sensitive man, I must say, and he was very upset about this whole thing—I blamed him immediately. "Why didn't you show me that baby? I know why you didn't show me her face. Because you knew she was a mongoloid!" He almost cried. I feel that he was very sincere and—and yet, there was no reference to what we should do. There was no service that I was told about where we live. As for referrals—there were no referrals made, no people came to my bedside—no one explained mongolism and told me about where we could find service within our own neighborhood. That was very disheartening, that whole thing.

The next day, they had put a new pediatrician on the case. He came bouncing in, very jolly, and said, "Well, I guess you'll leave the baby in the hospital." And I said, "My baby?" And he said, "Yes." I said, "Is she sick?" "No." "Give me one good reason why I would leave my baby with this hospital." I said I would be very fearful to leave that baby with the hospital. "I love my own baby and I am going to keep it. You have no right to assume that I am going to leave her in an institution." He quickly ran out of the room. When I came home from the hospital, I was on my own, trying to find out where the services were in our community.

Eda:

Did you bring the baby home immediately? Wasn't there some question about heart problems and physical disabilities?

Teddie:

Not yet. Her breathing was very bad at the time. They thought maybe they would have to keep her in for that. Also, she was not feeding properly, but when they saw I was so upset, that I did not want to leave the baby with the hospital, they decided to send her home with me.

Eda: What were the grounds on which they wanted to keep the baby?

Teddie: There were respiratory problems. They were taking X-rays. Lots of Down's Syndrome babies have respiratory problems, besides a heart condition—which we did not know about at the time.

Dallas: The pediatrician considered the possibility, but mainly assumed her ailment, or possible ailment, was because she was a Down's Syndrome or mongoloid baby—and there was the assumption that we would not want the child.

Eda: That is really what I was asking, whether they assumed that you did not want the child.

Teddie: They assumed that. He came into the room with the papers and said leave the baby with the hospital.

Eda: In other words, they were kind of assuming that you and they would hope that the baby would die, is that it?

Teddie: I think so, or at least that we would not be burdened with this terrible thing, the stigma attached to having a child—Dal and I never even thought about that. We just knew that this was our baby and it was a terrible thing to have happened, we were very sad about it, and we still are, we always will be. But we love our baby. We took her home, and we have loved her from the moment we took her home.

Eda: Could you tell us about what has happened with her and what her life history has been? Could you give a little more background for those who, like myself, do not have much information?

What are the characteristics of a child with Down's Syndrome?

Dallas: Well, they do have the looks.

Teddie: Slanted eyes, and the rather flat nose, and high cheekbones. However, you know, they are all different—when we say mongolism we think immediately of one category—yet, as I have learned myself, they are all very different.

Eda: What are some of the things you have learned about it?

Dallas: We have learned that there are certainly different levels of functioning among children; that they are very loveable children. We feel that if they are loved, and if they are stimulated, they will respond.

Eda: Is retardation the usual case with a mongoloid child, or is there great variation in that?

Teddie: There is not normal intelligence, say, for instance, the range of normal intelligence would be from one point to another. The mongoloid child is capable of a portion of that range. Within that portion there are different levels of intelligence.

Dallas: It is mainly a below-normal range, consisting of so-called educable, trainable, and non-trainable children; each group is identified, for one thing, by the level of their intelligence in terms of performing certain tasks. Apart from that, mongoloid children are also prone to many physical conditions. We read up as much as we could get at, from libraries, in books about the condition. We found that heart problems are fairly common;

there are other physical problems, like palate deformities. Also, the whole growth pattern, that is, the physical growth, is retarded.

Eda: Once you brought Miriam home, were there resources for you to turn to?

Teddie: When we left the hospital there were no referrals made; no one came in. I said to the doctor, "Well, where do we go? What are we supposed to do with the baby? What do we do with a retarded child?" He said, "Oh, you'll find some in the community. There will be something there." I called all the telephone numbers I could find. There were programs for children who were two years old, and programs for older children. And there was one referral to retarded infant service. By that time, I did not want to speak to any more professional people. I really did not. I wanted some place where they would demonstrate to me what to do with a mongoloid child. We are going to take our baby home, so show us what to do with her! She must have some potential. We felt that way, therefore, Dallas and I treated the baby as normally as we could. It was not until she was about two months old that we found the Rose Kennedy Center in New York.

Eda: Is that a clinic or a hospital?

Dallas: It is a community center for research in mental retardation and human development.

Teddie: We went there, and a team of a nurse, a doctor, and a social worker spoke to us. They described Down's Syndrome and showed us with charts just exactly what happens to the chromosomes. That was fine, they were very supportive. We were very happy to be able to go there.

We *were* a little dismayed when we felt that they assumed that we were poor, maybe ignorant, people who had to be told everything about what to do with the baby. I did not feel that I had to be told not to be ashamed, to go out with the baby—because we had done this already—I was just rather slighted by that. We did keep going back to Rose Kennedy Center because people there were very interested in *us* as people. I was dismayed because nobody demonstrated what to do with the infant who is mongoloid. There must be certain techniques to . . .

Dallas: The idea being that with a normal child, the child's learning development begins from birth. The child with Down's Syndrome has special needs. We did not want to wait until the child was three years old. Because the child is retarded we believe that the earlier we start, the better we can reach whatever potential the child has. That is what we seek in every normal human being; why not with a retarded child? Instead of waiting till they are three, do whatever you can, starting right away. We had lost faith, to an extent, in professionalism. We wanted to approach it more humanely, and do whatever we could to bring out the most of whatever potential she had, starting right at the beginning. This area is where we did not find resources.

Eda: Except yourselves.

Teddie:	And our friends.
Eda:	What did you do during those early months?
Teddie:	We played music in her crib—we used to bang the crib; she would look back, and she looked very alert to us. She would follow objects with her eyes. We had toys dangling. We used a ball, and little toys—manipulative little toys that she could try to grab for. It was very difficult because it took much longer than with Veronica, who is very alert, learns very fast at everything, more quickly than I suppose most children do. With Miriam, it took twice as long. I remember we used to try to make her laugh, and it took six months before she really had a knowing kind of smile.
Eda:	That must have been a moment. When did it happen?
Teddie:	Very exciting—it was in July.
Dallas:	But by that time we had gone through much else, because she had had heart failure when she was three months old. By chance, we found it out; because the doctor, the pediatrician looking after her, we felt, did not have much concern for this baby. When Teddie went to the pediatrician with the baby, he said she seems to have a heart condition. If you want to pursue this, you can see a cardiologist. *If you* want to pursue this!
Eda:	A lot of people have been giving up on this child. Was Miriam rehospitalized then?
Teddie:	Oh, we went to the doctor on Thursday, and he said try to see a cardiologist, if you wish to pursue it. He

did give me the name of one cardiologist whom I could try to contact, which I did immediately. She was booked until July, and this was in April. I called the pediatrician again and said I cannot get through to her, can you recommend somebody else? Or would you call? And he said, "Well, try again. And keep trying till you get one." At that moment I knew that he was not interested in our baby. This made me very angry. And I called all the hospitals that I could in the city, and doctors. Then, through a friend of ours, we did get a cardiologist who would see Miriam the following Friday.

In the meantime, Miriam was vomiting. She was very sick. We were very worried about it. We called the doctor the next day and said we have to come in to see you, we are frightened that the baby may not pull through this. We do not know what is wrong, she is vomiting. He said to come in. We got there and he said, "It's a good thing you brought her in, she's in heart failure. And she would not have made it through the day, I don't think."

Eda:	He hospitalized her?
Teddie:	He hospitalized her; she was in for a week. They gave her digitalis, and this pulled her through. And she's a tough little kid; I guess she wants to live.
Eda:	It sure sounds that way. I have a feeling she is getting help from a couple of adults, too.
Teddie:	At that time we were told that heart failure was due to a heart condition—they could not say exactly what it was

| | without a catheterization which subsequently she has had. We found that there is a fault, a hole in the septum (dividing wall) of the heart, and eventually she will have to have open-heart surgery, but not until she is big enough to survive the shock of an operation. Because of that heart condition, her circulation is impaired, and her growth is slowed down, retarded. But she is coming along. |

Eda: Tell me what she is like now. She is 20 months old.

Teddie: Twenty-months, and a "hotshot," I call her, because she gets in her walker and can go lickety-split down the hall. She plays games. She can play peek-a-boo. She teases you, pretends she is going to Dallas and then will turn her back to him and come to me. And she is saying, "Dada." I will say to her, "Where's Dada?" And she will turn around to Dallas.

Dallas: She practically smiles all the time.

Teddie: And is very happy.

Dallas: You know, she is extremely pleasant.

Teddie: Veronica and she—and I think this is very important, Eda, for us to bring out—it has not torn our family apart.

Eda: That was my next question.

Teddie: It has not broken up our marriage; unfortunately it has for some. And that is what I would like to get to next.

Eda: It is partly the unanimity of your sense of mission, is it not? I think what happens in some families is that perhaps one feels this sense of hope and the other may not.

Teddie: I think that is a very important point. I decided that I would write a proposal on just what I thought had to be done in the community for retarded children— retarded infants. And I did. We have a proposal which calls for "pre-enroll-ment," what I call pre-enrollment in the program would be to make a contact in the hospital with the mother who gives birth to a retarded child, and, well, we would at least give them an alternative to institutionalization. We want to let them know there is hope for a retarded child and to give the kid a chance.

Eda: How marvelous that would be, not to feel so alone as you felt at that moment.

Teddie: Not just the mother, it is the family. Be-cause it is the family that feels lost at this moment, all the hopes they have built up for the child are knocked off at the moment of birth. People tend to re-treat into a shell, they are ashamed of coming out, they are ashamed of having a child like this. They are depressed. So often we have seen families that either have been strained to the breaking point, or have barely managed to sur-vive, or have just broken up.

Dallas: I think one of the factors is, very fre-quently, the kind of totally primitive and irrational notion that somehow the parents are responsible. Isn't that one of the things that has an effect on many families?

Teddie: What I think, too, is that professionals make you feel that you are guilty.

Eda: How do they do that? What do they do?

Teddie: Well, as I said, this whole idea that there are certain reactions that you will necessarily have because you have had a retarded child—I had a furious battle with somebody, a professional person, who categorized me as feeling a certain way. I said I do *not* feel that way. I do not feel guilty; I feel very sorrowful. I am sad that my baby will not be able to function in a normal way; I feel sad that she has to live in a society that does not accept her, has to live among people who look upon her as something very odd.

I am very annoyed at this, although some people *do* feel guilty. I think that religion has a lot to do with it; people thinking they are being cursed by God—and some people *do* feel that way. I am grateful that I do not, I do not feel this way at all.

Dallas: Also, I think we live in a society that puts a premium on perfection and equates perfection with high intelligence or beauty rather than on humanity, on being human, on being social and on happiness, on becoming fully human. Whether one is retarded or one is normal, so-called normal, and intelligent—I think what is most important is that we develop to the maximum of our potential, whatever potential we have received from God and nature, that we are happy that we are able to relate to people, to make our contribution to one another.

Eda: I think you are so right, that the sort of climate in which we live is one in which you like to pretend there is no

	such thing as pain, and there is no such thing as imperfection, and there is no such thing as struggle and frustration.
Dallas:	Anything less than perfect is: "The less seen of, the better." They are ashamed.
Teddie:	That is what we are fighting right now. We have a day care center. It has been put together by parents.
Eda:	All this has happened since when?
Teddie:	All this has happened since I had Miriam.
Eda:	Before we go on to—I want to talk about that in much more detail. But before we do, I want to ask about something you mentioned before. How does Veronica relate to Miriam?
Teddie:	Veronica is a very loving child, though jealous at first of the baby, naturally.
Eda:	Imagine that!
Teddie:	We did have to give the baby a lot of attention. I remember holding the bottle for an hour with Miriam just to get her to drink two ounces of milk. Of course, Veronica resented that. But we worked it out. She knows we love the baby, and she knows we love her. I have tried to divide my time, not equally, I cannot say that, but I have given her enough time, and I have been away with her on Saturdays when Dal is home.
Eda:	What are they like together?
Dallas:	Veronica plays with toys, reads, shows pictures; Veronica cannot read. And they play peek-a-boo. But as Ted has done, she shows the baby pictures from the book. I think the baby has learned a tremendous amount through playing with Veronica.

Eda:	That is what I was wondering about. It is a great stimulation.
Dallas:	They get along well together. Miriam is tiny and we are a little bit afraid sometimes.
Eda:	How much does Miriam weigh?
Teddie:	We took her today to the doctor. She is 14 pounds, 9 ounces.
Eda:	At 20 months?
Teddie:	Twenty months, but she is strong! Her legs are getting stronger. She can stand, holding. And she has a strong grip. In fact, we have to watch her because she pulls Veronica's hair. She plays and taps her head, and she claps hands. She knows that if you're happy clap your hands.
Dallas:	She takes books. We read stories to her. She does not understand, but we point out the pictures. She rolls around on the floor, or in a walker, gets to a book and sits down, gets the book open, she can turn the pages, one by one. She babbles away, points to things and just babbles away as though she were reading. One would imagine, if one were a stranger to English or whatever language, that she were reading. But she babbles away, she imitates.
Eda:	She knows it has something to do with communication.
Teddie:	Yes.
Dallas:	And Veronica does that with her, we do that with her. Veronica plays with the ball, throwing the ball to her, and she throws it back. And, she likes to play with the xylophone, too.

Eda:	In other words the sounds of life are all around her, aren't they?
Teddie:	They are.
Eda:	That has something to do with growing, doesn't it? I diverted you—I do want to hear more about what you did, because I think you were able to mobilize some forces in the community, and that is great.
Teddie:	We were. It was through Kennedy Center; we called a meeting. We wanted to go into the hospital to visit mothers. From that meeting I made contacts with a lot of the parents who had infants. I told them about the day care center that I had in mind, that we had to really take up for our own children and do what we feel we have to do for them, that nobody else is going to, until maybe they are four years old. Educators tell us that with normal children you have to stimulate them from birth to three years. Those are the most important years now. The mothers became very enthusiastic. We had regular meetings with them. We had a pancake supper and raised money for our day-care center. It has progressed this way. We met in my apartment with the children and their mothers. The mothers have been getting out their feelings, frustrations.
Dallas:	And the fathers too.
Teddie:	And the fathers also. I forgot the fathers, they are a very important component. We have developed a program of our own, with our own expertise. This

is what I think is so important, that parents feel and believe that they have an expertise of their own, instead of just accepting everything that professional people tell them.

Eda: The day-care center is already functioning?

Teddie: Yes, it is functioning with children from infants to four years. We have professional consultants. The parents are there, doing the actual work. Friends and consultants give us some kind of direction. We have our own ideas of what we should do with the babies. We are hoping to get funding. But, as you know, it is a very difficult thing, because we want this to be a parent-controlled thing. I think that is where we will have difficulty. We have written letters to state departments, we have written letters to the City. And we have waited months and months, and we have not gotten responses. We have to call them again. There are always other people whom we are referred; we get a real runaround.

Eda: There seems to be a natural reluctance among experts, I am sorry to say, to suggest that maybe parents who live with a child 24 hours a day know a little something about children.

Teddie: Yeah. Let me give you one example. One mother has a two-year-old who cannot walk yet, but she is beginning to walk. She can play Simple Simon—she imitates. She does respond. She was playing ball with the other children and clapping hands, and making like "Patty Cake." This woman went to one of the institutions which has an infant service. There were psychologists, the nurse, the whole team. They saw the child for 45 minutes and claimed, then and there, on the spot, that the child was severely retarded. The mother was absolutely floored by this. There was no recourse, she had to accept what they were saying and was very broken up about this. This is what we feel we can avoid. We can give the parents that support, and urge them not to accept the judgments that are put upon their children by professional people. We know of another case, where a woman was told the same thing, and her child will be seven years old in November. Hannah is going to school, she is learning to swim, she does puzzles, she can play—she plays with Veronica. And she is functioning.

Dallas: She speaks, and she was a child who was diagnosed as severely retarded.

Eda: I can think of one of the reasons for this: there are a couple of subjects about which people get very confused, because they are very mysterious. One is the power of love, and the other is the power of some magical, instinctive life force involving tremendous inner struggle. These are things which are very hard to do research on, and they are very hard to quantify. You cannot make a statistical study of how much love and a sense of hope and mission and faith there is in a family. You cannot study them statistically—maybe they do not even exist. I think this is one of the kinds of things that you have been discovering; that is part of the whole picture.

Dallas: About this day-care program that we have all been working on: what we are seeking is that through this project we will help people in the community—people who have little or no contact with retarded children—accept them, as they would another normal child. Here is a child, a human being who has special needs. For that reason, the day-care program that we hope to have operating more efficiently, given the funds, would be one for normal as well as retarded children; there would not be isolation, relegation of these children to a separate facility. The normal children will accept these as fellow human beings, that they are different in some ways, yes, but they have humanity. Retarded children too would benefit by this contact with normal children.

Eda: Absolutely, absolutely.

Teddie: Already, we have normal children coming to our program. They play together. There are certain areas where we have to separate them for instruction, instruction in the sense that they have different needs than the normal child. However, there are certain areas where they play together. We have a boat, a rocking boat; they all get in it together, and they rock back and forth, and everybody is happy.

Eda: What you are really saying is that human beings of all kinds, whether they are children or grownups, have a lot to teach each other, even more, depending on how different they are. I wish we really believed that.

In more general terms, there is not only the question of the handicapped child and the physically normal child, but so many other areas in which the tendency is, in education and family life and community life, to categorize people and separate them, into types— even in school, there is a slow learner, the rapid learner, the genius. I think some of the most terrible damage is done to children who, let us say, happen to learn quickly academically, who are cut off from children who have different kinds of experiences—who may be more poetic, may be slower, may be more in touch with life and nature—actually the damage is to both.

I have got to tell everybody about a book which is very much the kind of story that you have told. It is a book called *The World of Nigel Hunt*. It was published in England. It is an autobiography written by a mongoloid child; a fascinating story of a child, same kind of situation as yours, in which the parents refuse to say no to life, and who believed that every human being has potential which must be realized—Dallas said it far more beautifully than I could. At any rate, they began to teach this child. They did not take no for an answer, and they taught him to read and write and to typewrite. The thing that is so fascinating about this book—is that even after this child had learned to read and write, and they could demonstrate it in the schools, the school still said, "I'm sorry, the diagnosis is mongoloidism, and he can't read and write."

Just simply shrugged it off as if it were not even real. You know, when you do not want to see something, you just do not see it.

There is one comment in the book which I think is so apt in terms of some of the things you have been saying. "About a fortnight after Nigel's birth, his mother and I were told that no matter how much trouble we went to, no matter how much love and care we gave Nigel, he would be an idiot, and that nothing we could do would alter that fact. If we had accepted this, it would have become true." I think that is one of the most beautiful and important things.

I think it is a great inspiration, just as Teddie and Dallas have been, for what is possible when people believe in human possibilities and believe that one never need give up hope.

A LOOK BACK: LEARNING TO LIVE WITH LEARNING DISABILITIES

Being a parent of a learning disabled child has made my life somewhat chaotic. I have often wondered if all the experts and specialists really know what it is like to live on a 24 hour basis with a child who has special needs. The educator leaves the problems at the schoolhouse door, the clinician only gets a glimpse of the child's abilities and disabilities, while the medical specialist often looks only at the child's physical or health needs. All of these professionals, however, generally fail to realize the child is part of a family unit. It is only the family members who never leave the problems behind them. Meeting the family's best interests should be part of any diagnosis.

B. Pigman, January 1983, personal communication.

Most people never realize the enormous impact that raising a disabled child has on every member of the family and not just the problems that occur for the child with the disability. One can almost consider the disability as another family member. After all, it consumes time, resources, energy, and emotions. If this seems a bit melodramatic, I suppose I would have thought so at one time. Now, however, after raising my son Steve these past eighteen years, I am not sure it is dramatic enough. Mere words could never convey an adequate impression of what living with, loving and raising a learning disabled child has been like.

What then is it like to be the parent of a learning disabled child? The first step is awesome for you sustain the loss of a dream. It is the dream of the perfect child, completely intact and healthy that all of us have been led to believe is our guaranteed right. When that dream is shattered you can deny, fill with rage, look for an instant cure and/or eventually come to grips with the fact that your child may never reach his potential without much work and many tears.

That lonely, empty feeling you experience before you finally hear a professional diagnosis of what is wrong with your child is fear and ignorance of the unknown. We have hidden handicapped children from the world until just recently. Few of us have any real experience in dealing with the first step of admitting our child is less than perfect. When you begin to recover from the shock that your child has special needs, you begin the endless route of seeking help. What you may find, however, is that there is insufficient training of those who are to provide you with aid. Also, they may not know the best means of delivering whatever help they offer. If one has the ability and stamina to actually get the needed help, at the time when it is most opportune and without attached judgmental values, then perhaps, with a bit of luck, raising a handicapped child will not present too great of a challenge. Yet, for most of us, the journey to secure a meaningful existence for ourselves, the child, and the rest of the family can be fraught with numerous pitfalls, countless detours, and the need to be able to chart and explore new routes where no clear paths presently exist. Eighteen years after exploring many dead ends at high monetary and emotional cost, my husband and I have found that there are no magic cures, only compensations. Along the way we experienced moments of bittersweet joy and sometimes even a bubble of unbridled exhilaration but these moments were far too few or too late to remove the sting of mishandling by experts in the field.

Looking back, I would recall two events that occurred during my pregnancy which would increase my guilt feelings when I later learned about probable causes of learning disabilities. As a result of medical complications and a death in the family I went into labor over-medicated after stopping labor for three days. Steve entered the world a shoestring baby, over 20 inches long, 6 pounds 10 ounces of bright yellow jaundiced skin and flaming red hair, squalling loudly. He would continue to cry day and night for the next six months.

Whatever confidence I had in my mothering abilities began to erode at this point. After all, his two-year-old sister had been the model child. After one marathon crying session of 15 hours, my self-worth as a mother had hit rock bottom. Steve had projectile vomiting which meant I couldn't leave him with a babysitter. Convulsions with every fever left me feeling incompetent. My resentment began to build. What twenty-year-old mother has been prepared to handle this? Doctors advised that Steve must not be allowed to cry until after surgery could repair internal problems. One very spoiled child, as well as one very up-tight, over-anxious mother, resulted from this advice. Extreme temper tantrums followed. Steve could hold his breath until he passed out and often did. I felt an utter failure in motherhood. Yet, the advice I was receiving from the medical profession was to relax.

The next few years are all a blur, filled with endless visits to emergency rooms and doctors' offices. Steve was a neat little boy who acted impulsively. He also had absolutely no fear of any situation. He walked out on rooftops, dismantled his crib while sitting in it, rode a bicycle down a flight of steps, tried to fly from the garage roof and even attempted to roll off the garage roof in a barrel. He frequently threatened running away. His assorted battle scars and numerous bruises led one pediatrician to a thinly disguised inquiry as to whether child abuse might have been the cause of so many accidents.

Sleep disturbances followed. Both Steve and I were basically worn out. The only thing that seemed to quiet Steve was continued rocking. I felt overwhelmed. This child consumed most of my time, energy, and waking hours. Andrea, his sister, was being pushed aside in a frantic attempt to meet her brother's needs. Yet, there seemed to be no name for this condition although by now the pediatrician began to suggest the possibility that something was wrong.

A period of relative peace and tranquility, the calm before the storm, followed babyhood and lasted until kindergarten. However, temper tantrums and the need for extreme order continued. If any item, toy, furniture, or clothes was moved, it would send Steve into a rage. I began to feel just like a little wind-up toy that was overwound. Steve's wondrous imagination however, love of wearing costumes and his imaginary friends made this period more joyful than painful.

The first year of school was a signal of what was to follow but we did not heed the warnings. Steve had the same excellent teacher that Andrea had. However, he kept running away, saying over and over, "It too busy, too noisy, no think time, I not going back there." The hazard of spending time in the principal's office loomed large. I kept sending Steve back with both of us upset over his lack of adjustment. Reversed letters, words and sentences also should have been clues but, because learning disabilities were just being discovered, these clues were not considered. "Late bloomer" and "needs a more structured environment" were the solemn pronouncements given to us. It seemed that Steve was forever disobeying me and the teacher and then insisting that, "You too did tell me I do can it!" Later we would find out that Steve did not always process word endings, thus the word "can't" to him became "can."

First grade is still hard for me to discuss. Two weeks into the school year, Steve began to develop giant hives and once again started to have temper tantrums and stomach aches. He would cry every morning. Extremely high fevers with no known source became common. Steve began to talk about killing himself. Rage resurfaced. Tears flowed in an endless river from both our eyes. Every morning Steve would hang onto the car handle in the school parking lot and scream, "You can't make me go in there. I'll lay down on the road and let a big truck hit me!" As I pulled his tiny fingers off the handle and bodily carried him in kicking and screaming to the front door, I felt I was running a gauntlet of disapproving eyes. What person in their right mind would believe one small child could carry on like this? Teachers would go by and shake their heads. I received more than one lecture on spoiled children and overprotective mothers. By now my only consolation was the fact that I was following the experts' orders. I'd be limp by the time I returned to the car but Steve was in school and I had not given in to his "school phobia."

The pediatrician sent us to a psychologist. The psychologist said that Mom and Dad seemed o.k., but Steve seemed to have a severe case of school phobia. This is the first time I was not made out to be the dragon so I thought the psychologist was great. Others had suggested that we take Steve out of school and have him tutored privately. On a bricklayer's salary, this was hardly feasible. So we tried in-depth child counseling. After some months, Steve still hated school and many dollars had been spent. I began to dislike experts and specialists who had no real answers, only impractical suggestions.

I really began to dread parent-teacher conferences during the first and second grade. I was told that I was rejecting the fact that some children are incapable of learning as fast as others and that Steve had an attitude problem and didn't spend enough time on his work. However, we were spending an average of three to four hours a night on his school work. It also seemed peculiar to me that he could correctly answer questions orally but miss all of them on his "messy written work." The teacher did not respond to my pointing out that correctly answering all the questions verbally might mean that his intellect was not low. She just stood up, leaving me with no answers, only questions. Steve and I walked slowly out to the car where he began to cry. I dried his tears, pulled him into my lap, and listened to him sob, "Mommy, I did too try!" "I did, really!" "Write a note to my teacher and tell her I try!" Steve believed that notes were magic. In later years I would find out that this same teacher would pick Steve up out of his chair by his hair, shake him, and call him lazy. Steve could never tell me about this. Once she paddled Steve for using an eraser and told the other students that Steve could do the work but he didn't like to try. In junior high, Steve mentioned this to me, remarking that he always thought he must have been a super bad kid and was afraid that I too would be mad at him if he had told me.

I can still feel the excitement I first felt when I read an article entitled "Dyslexia" in a popular women's magazine. I thought the author knew Steve personally. I gathered more articles and called the school to ask where he could be tested. They had no idea.

Steve and I went back to the local mental health center where an IQ test suggested a superior intellect. Steve, by this time however, felt he was a complete failure in life. He knew he was dumb but after the psychologist shared the test results, Steve began to think differently and I felt a heavy weight lift off my shoulders. Tests given at a university reading center were suggested. Since my husband was laid off before the appointment was made, there was a great debate over whether we could afford to have the test given and whether testing would be worthwhile. Four hours of testing revealed severe auditory and visual perceptual dysfunctions. At that time, I had no idea what that meant but a detailed report assured me that things were not hopeless. High intellect was confirmed and suggestions were made. With my hands tightly clutching those results, I went back to Steve's school. If you have ever watched a bucket of water being thrown over a smoldering fire, then perhaps you have an insight as to the reception I received. Of course, the school would not accept external test results and were not at all interested in a mere parent's presentation of what might be the problem. Their unspoken implication was that all too often they had had to deal with his over-anxious, up-tight young mother. After all, they were the educational experts. Seldom have I been as angry and frustrated. I watched their smug, know-it-all expressions and felt my hands begin to shake, but I managed to say in a tight little voice that my children would not be attending their school next year. We switched schools that week.

Third and fourth grade were the first real successes Steve encountered. Both teachers researched and followed the reading clinic's suggestions. Tantrums ceased and learning began. A tutor and the ACLD (Association for Children with Learning Disabilities) also helped to reduce the isolation I had felt up until this time.

Trouble began once again in the fifth grade. By this time I felt as if I should be a partner in Steve's educational process. Unfortunately, the teacher did not. I knew she hated to see me drop in. Even a visit from Steve's tutor made little impression. His nightmares began again. Threats of suicide were not uncommon. During one routine morning tantrum, Steve began to tremble and yelled, "I'm not going to that school!" He opened up the car window and threw out his books and eye glasses. As I slammed on the brakes, Steve leaped out of the car and started to run. A railroad track lay just ahead. I could hear the whistle of an approaching train. I caught up with and tackled Steve just before he reached the tracks. To this day I occasionally wake up after having dreamed that I did not make it to Steve in time. In my dream, the train wins the race!

Back to the psychologists, more therapy, more expense. Always questions and more questions, but seldom, if ever, any answers, are my main remembered impressions of those early years. Everyone seemed so free with advice yet so little advice was practical or workable.

Steve's tutor began to train me so that his outside program would not be interrupted when she moved away. It was about this time that guilt began to set in as I learned more and more about probable causes that can often result in learning disabilities. Depression followed this awareness. Feelings of anger and guilt did not abate until many years later.

Another real bright spot was sixth grade. Steve's potential was again confirmed after hard fought permission was granted to take a standardized test orally as well as written. The results showed Steve was learning even if paper and pencil tests failed to show it.

Junior high and high school were a mixture of triumph and despair. Excellent on the football field, Steve had to work twice as hard to keep from reversing the numbers of football plays, handle homework and keep up his in-class assignments. We would often sit up late into the night going over and over school work and football plays. Diligence paid off however as he won a number of sports awards. Physical activity was a real outlet for all the frustration he felt.

I found myself torn into a thousand pieces as we put in an average of two and one-half hours of work each evening. I read the texts and wrote out his dictated answers so he could recopy them. By this time, and for the first time, Steve could receive help in school but, for the most part, he preferred trying on his own with just my help as this did not make him feel as different or to seem less whole than his friends. Most of his teachers were quite supportive once they were aware of his problem. I've spent countless hours on the telephone and in teachers' rooms acquainting Steve's instructors with his learning style, arranging for extended test time or oral testing privileges. It was during this time that Steve began to increasingly take charge of his own educational needs. A quantum leap in reading ability occurred coinciding with puberty.

A learning disabled student isn't just disabled during school hours. The discovery of girls generated a new sort of dependency on mom. How can you talk to girls on the telephone or take messages when thoughts are garbled between the mind and the mouth? How does one write a note or settle an argument caused by the failure to process that favorite person's words correctly? I became a sounding board. It is hard to break ties, to be grown-up, when you are so dependent on another person.

I have taken a long hard look at what our life was like. My marriage had suffered from all those years of intense involvement with meeting Steve's needs. Andrea had been forced to become very independent; no time to share leaves few bridges to cross. After having worked with Steve all these years, I knew I wanted to teach so I applied for college admission. My husband and daughter must have felt left out. I can understand that as I also had some unfulfilled dreams.

At times, I am still angry over the missed diagnosis, the unrealistic advice and the judgmental attitudes of professionals. Yet, in the end, I feel that only by sharing these negative encounters and the feelings associated with them, as well as the final triumph of seeing Steve accepted for college, can I realistically help other parents to feel less alone, less guilty, and less angry when they experience some of the same common frustrations that occur when dealing with a handicapping condition. I would consider myself a complete success if, after reading this, only one professional would stop and consider what it is like to be the daily caretaker of even a mildly handicapped child. Professionals can help by learning to listen and talking to the parents, not "at" or "down" to them. By remembering that the parent is often too tired, too broke and too emotionally spent to always appear concerned, the professional can cue in on what stage of acceptance the parent is in and thus best meet the family's and child's needs.

If I could have one wish fulfilled, prevention of handicaps would, of course, be foremost. Barring this, I would try to insure that no additional blame is implied, covertly or overtly, when the parents seek help; or if they fail to seek help, understand that they may not have known that help exists or may not be at a stage where they can accept the offer of assistance. Even if the parents know where to go, they may be ill-equipped to deal with specialists who use jargon and phrases, offer unrealistic suggestions and seem not only to have all the answers but also sit in judgment on the parents' abilities. I would ask each professional to consider the family's needs along with those of the child and to walk in their shoes for just a short moment. Then, and only then, will their assistance be both practical and humane.

A final word

The preceding vignettes may appear to some people to be only "horror stories," isolated episodes or simple exaggerations. Yet experienced professionals will often relate that these illustrations are more common than many of us would like to believe. This sad observation may partly be due to a breakdown in the communication process between parents and professionals. More likely, however, it can be attributed to a reciprocal absence of trust and respect and to the attitudes that professionals have about parents and parents about professionals, be they teachers, doctors, social workers, administrators, psychologists, or any other individual who interacts with and helps a handicapped child and his or her family. One mother, describing herself as a member of a lost generation of parents (Gorham, 1975), suggests that parents are either intimidated by professionals or angry with them, or both. Some parents are unreasonably awed by them, and still others persistently assume that professionals know best. Another parent, a former president of the National Society for Autistic Children, portrays herself as a hungry vulture, a mother who has run out of patience (Akerley, 1978). She characterizes her views of parent-professional relationships as follows:

We don't begin in anger. We start out the way all parents of all children do: with respect, reverence really, for the professional and his skills. The pediatrician, the teacher, the writer of books and articles on child development, they are the sources of wisdom from which we must draw in order to be good parents. We believe, we consult, we do as we are told, and all goes well unless . . . one of our kids has a handicap.

We parents are almost always the first to notice that something is amiss, and one of our early consolations is often our pediatrician's assurance that "it's nothing—he'll outgrow it." That, of course, is exactly what we want to hear because it corresponds perfectly to the dwindling hope in our hearts, so we defer to the expert and our child loses another year. Finally the time comes when not even the most conservative professional can deny the existence of a problem. The difficulty now is to define it and plan accordingly. With luck, our pediatrician refers us to an appropriate specialist and we are (or should be) on our way.

We transfer our trust to the new god and wait expectantly for the oracle to speak. Instead of the strong, authoritative voice of wisdom, we more often hear an evasive stammer: "Can't give you a definite diagnosis . . . uh, mumble, mumble . . . virtually untestable . . . Let us see him . . . cough, cough . . . again in a year." Ironically, when the oracle *is* loud and clear, it is often wrong. (p. 40)

Parent-professional interactions do not have to be adversarial. Two elements critical to producing a meaningful relationship are communication and respect (Schulz, 1978). Communication skills can be learned and promoted; respect, on the other hand, has to grow. Perhaps the most crucial dimension of the helping exchange is that of sensitivity—to the parents and the needs of the child. Sensitivity is a prerequisite to establishing a meaningful helping relationship. What parents often remember most of their initial encounter with professionals is the quality of the helping relationship (Paul & Beckman-Bell, 1981). A sound parent-professional interaction complete with good communication, respect, and sensitivity entails professionals acknowledging their own fears and prejudices about exceptionalities, as well as divorcing themselves from the traditional superiority (professional)—inferiority (parent) role models to which many have become accustomed. Professionals need to move away from the age-old adage that only they know best; no longer can they subscribe to the theory of professional omniscience and omnipotence (Roos, 1978), the myth that they are the source of all knowledge and consequently are qualified to render decisions affecting the lives of other people. In reality, whenever a parent and professional interact, there are two specialists involved (Webster, 1977). Mesibov and La Greca (1981) believe that professionals can best serve the needs of parents by assuming the subsidiary role of facilitator, allowing parents to be the decision makers, which is both their right and responsibility. Indeed, the greater the parent involvement, the greater the effectiveness of the relationship, for parent participation is the cornerstone of success. Accordingly, when strategies and plans are jointly generated, optimal benefits and services are more likely to be achieved.

Suggestions for improving parent-professional interactions

1. Involve parents in all aspects of planning and decision making. They are the spokespersons for the child and are able to make valuable contributions when considered as legitimate, full-fledged team members.

2. Information should be openly shared with the parents. Test results, reports, and other information should be presented to the parents in a jargon-free fashion. If at all possible, avoid emotionally laden labels. Encourage parents to ask questions about and seek explanations for materials they find confusing. Parents should be furnished with copies of their child's record; in turn, parents need to maintain their own accurate documentation.

3. Be realistic and flexible about plans, goals, and objectives for the exceptional person, acknowledging not only the priorities and needs of the family but also financial realities and service limitations.

4. Professionals need to be knowledgeable about local parent and professional organizations as well as available community resources and services.

5. Professionals should be sensitive to and honest about the limitations of their own knowledge and abilities.

6. Professionals should recognize the abilities of the person as well as his or her disabilities. What the individual can do is as important as what he or she cannot do.

> *We are made wise not by the recollections of our past, but by the responsibility for our future.*
>
> —George Bernard Shaw

References

Akerley, M. (1978). False gods and angry prophets. In A. Turnbull & H. Turnbull (Eds.), *Parents speak out* (pp. 38–48). Columbus, OH: Charles Merrill.

Gorham, K. (1975). A lost generation of parents. *Exceptional Children, 41,* 521–525.

Mesibov, G., & La Greca, A. (1981). Ethical issues in parent-professional service interactions. In J. Paul (Ed.), *Understanding and working with parents of children with special needs* (pp. 154–179). New York: Holt, Rinehart and Winston.

Paul, J., & Beckman-Bell, P. (1981). Parent perspectives. In J. Paul (Ed.), *Understanding and working with parents of children with special needs* (pp. 119–153). New York: Holt, Rinehart and Winston.

Roos, P. (1978). Parents of mentally retarded children—Misunderstood and mistreated. In A. Turnbull & H. Turnbull (Eds.), *Parents speak out* (pp. 12–27). Columbus, OH: Charles Merrill.

Schulz, J. (1978). The parent-professional conflict. In A. Turnbull & H. Turnbull (Eds.), *Parents speak out* (pp. 28–36). Columbus, OH: Charles Merrill.

Webster, E. (1977). *Counseling with parents of handicapped children.* New York: Grune & Stratton.

Part two: Helping and helpers

Chapter 5:
Understanding helping

Chapter 6:
Helping skills

Chapter 7:
The helping relationship

Chapter 8:
Helping approaches

Chapter 5:
Understanding helping

To be what we are, and to become what we are capable of becoming, is the only end of life.

—Robert Louis Stevenson

Helping is a universal activity common to all concerned individuals, not necessarily just professionals. This is not to suggest that everyone can be an effective helper, but rather that helping is a basic human quality, an ability possessed in greater or lesser degrees by most people.

With this idea in mind, the purpose of this chapter is to investigate both the concept and process of helping, to examine how helping is perceived both by the person seeking help (the helpee) and the person providing help (the helper), and to explore helper attitudes and characteristics.

A definition of helping

Helping is a difficult term to define. Like art, it has different meanings for different people, and generally no two people understand it in the same way. Equally difficult is the task of distinguishing between helping and counseling. These two terms are often used interchangeably and seem to involve similar concepts. Counseling may be defined as:

— "a relationship in which one person endeavors to help another understand and solve his adjustment problem." (English & English, 1958, p. 127)

— "helping an individual become aware of himself and the ways in which he reacts to the behavioral influences of his environment. It further helps him to establish some personal meaning for his behavior and to develop and clarify a set of goals and values for future behavior." (Blocher, 1966, p. 5)

— "helping individuals learn new ways of dealing with and adjusting to life situations. . . . This, in turn, will enable them to make the fullest possible use of their inherent potential to become fully functioning individuals." (Hansen, Stevic, & Warner, 1972, p. 15)

— "an interaction process that facilitates meaningful understanding of self and environment and results in the establishment and/or clarification of goals and values for future behavior." (Shertzer & Stone, 1980, pp. 19–20)

Patterson (1967) has chosen to define counseling by describing what counseling is not. Patterson says that counseling is not the giving of information, though information may be provided in counseling; nor is counseling the giving of advice, suggestions, and recommendations. Counseling does not involve influencing attitudes, beliefs, or behavior by means of persuading, leading, or convincing. Furthermore, counseling is not the changing of behavior by admonishing, warning, threatening, or compelling. Finally, Patterson believes that counseling is not interviewing.

Counseling has, however, slowly evolved into a catchall term denoting a wide variety of practices. The concept of counseling, according to Shertzer and Stone (1980), ranges from the historical notion of advice giving, to test interpretation, to the traditional idea of a psychotherapeutic relationship. Today one can find financial and investment counselors, camp counselors, legal counselors, travel counselors, and even automotive counselors. As a result of the various meanings and misinterpretations associated with the term *counseling*, the more general concept of helping is preferred. Brammer (1979) conceives of helping as a means of assisting other people to reach goals that are important to them. Likewise, Benjamin (1981) considers helping to be an enabling act, while Fiedler (1950) concludes that a helping (therapeutic) relationship is but a variation of a good interpersonal relationship. Helping, therefore, can be concisely defined as an interactive, facilitative, growth process by which the helper assists the helpee to voluntarily change his or her behavior. It is not something that one person does *to* another, but rather, according to Webster (1977), an activity that one individual does *with* another.

Brammer (1977) cautions that two views of helping currently exist in America. The first perspective defines helping as a very specialized enterprise practiced by a few professionals with a firm foundation in medical and behavioral science. A professional guild with restricted membership is characteristic of this perspective. The second belief considers helping to be a broad human function involving basic human relations. For example, many parents of handicapped children will discover that other mothers and fathers of special needs children are an excellent source of help. Whether they are aware of it or not, most of these parents possess good helping skills and can greatly benefit those who seek their assistance. It is the premise of this text that helping is a basic human ability—that it should be viewed as a generic, nonrestrictive process, not limited to professionals, such as psychiatrists and psychologists.

Helping—art or science?

There is some question as to whether helping ought to be called an art or a science. Just as no universal agreement exists as to what constitutes helping, the issue of helping as an art or science is equally controversial. Helping would seem to involve the *what* of helping (science) in combination with the *how* of helping (art). The science of helping is based on theories of helping, generalizations about human behavior, and skills training. The art of helping is concerned with the person, the individual affective qualities of the helper, and how the individual operates in the helping relationship. Helping cannot be polarized as an either/or concept, but rather should be viewed as a marriage of art and science, a joining of theory and skills with the traits and attitudes of the helper. In support of this thesis, Laborde and Seligman (1983) assert that effective parent counseling requires that the helper's attitudes, characteristics, and biases be acknowledged, and in addition he or she must be trained in the rudiments of helping. The formula for an effective helping relationship requires both components.

The helping process

Since helping can be viewed as both an art and a science, Brammer (1979) has provided an equation illustrating this relationship. He argues that the affective qualities of the helper in conjunction with specific helping skills can produce growth conditions that lead to specific outcomes important to the helpee. Brammer's formula incorporates the basic ingredients of helper personality and skill. Figure 5.1 illustrates his formula for the helping process. This union not only helps the individual learn to meet current needs effectively, but also provides a strategy for successfully coping with future concerns. As Brammer states, helping is a process of enabling a person to learn how to learn.

Phases in the helping process

The process of helping can sometimes appear to be very mysterious. There is, however, an internal structure to most helping relationships. The helpee learns about the process by being involved in and becoming part of it. Various authorities have formulated lists of stages or phases incorporated in helping. These models should only be considered as guides, for the sequences are both arbitrary and fluid; all stages do not necessarily exist in each help-

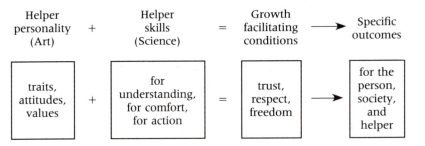

Figure 5.1 A formula for the helping process. Adapted from Lawrence M. Brammer, *The Helping Relationship: Process and Skills,* 2nd ed., © 1979, p. 4. Reprinted by permission of Prentice-Hall, Inc., Englewood Cliffs, N.J.

ing relationship. Benjamin (1981) observes that the various divisions are not always clearly visible and sometimes they fuse into each other to such an extent that it is difficult to tell them apart. Hansen and his co-workers (Hansen, Stevic, & Warner, 1982) also remind us that the phases are not separate and discrete and that a timeline cannot be provided.

Stewart (1978, pp. 43–45) proposes the following six phases:

1. Initiation or establishment of purpose: the helpee indicates the purpose for seeking help.

2. Defining the counseling process: the helper and the helpee attempt to reach a mutual agreement as to the purpose and direction of their relationship.

3. Understanding of client's needs: the helper is concerned with the helpee's perception of the difficulties and his or her feelings about them.

4. Exploring the possible alternatives: the helper presents the many possible solutions and alternatives available with the helpee deciding which course of action is best.

5. Planning a course of action: the helpee begins to move steadily toward his or her counseling objectives.

6. Terminating the session: conducted by mutual agreement with the helpee leaving with the opinion that something constructive has occurred.

Benjamin (1981) succinctly lists three phases of the helping process: initiation or statement of the matter, development or explanation, and closing. Hansen and his colleagues (1982) synthesize from the helping literature the phases of initiating and establishing the relationship, exploration of self, deeper exploration and working through, and termination of the helping relationship. Brammer (1979) enumerates eight stages that he considers to be typical and representative of a natural helping process. Brammer's stages are as follows:

1. Entry: Preparing the helpee and opening the relationship

2. Clarification: stating the problem or concern and reasons for seeking help

3. Structure: formulating the contract and structure

4. Relationship: building the helping relationship

5. Exploration: exploring problems, formulating goals, planning strategies, gathering facts, expressing deeper feelings, learning new skills

6. Consolidation: exploring alternatives, working through feelings, practicing new skills

7. Planning: developing a plan of action using strategies to resolve conflicts, reducing painful feelings, and consolidating and generalizing new skills or behaviors to continue self-directed activities

8. Termination: evaluating outcomes and terminating the relationship (p. 52)

The stages that one experiences while moving forward in the helping process will depend both on the type of help sought and on the background of the helper. Much more will be said in future chapters about the components of each phase and the various strategies for helping.

The helping process viewed by helpee and helper

It may prove useful to examine the helping process through the eyes of the helpee and helper. An individual will usually seek help due to some problem or concern. It does not matter whether the helper considers the situation to be a problem—the important thing is that the one seeking help perceives a need. As an illustration, a mother of a child recommended for placement in a learning disabilities program confronts the teacher as to the appropriateness of the suggestion. The teacher, possessing his evaluations, fully believes in his recommendations, yet he must still empathize with the mother and address her reluctance and concerns. Note that the helper need not have personally experienced the event, problem, or concern expressed by the helpee—the teacher need not have had his son or daughter recommended for special class placement. What is important is for the helpee to perceive the helper as being genuinely interested in the problem(s) at hand. People generally enter a helping relationship with an attitude of optimism and an expectation that their concerns will be successfully resolved. At the same time the helper often wonders, "What is this person's expectation of helping?" "What does he or she think will happen?" and finally, "What does he or she expect to get out of it?" (Tyler, 1969).

Brammer (1979) has articulated a general model of the helping process from the dual vantage point of the helpee and helper. His road map is typical of the experiences of both parties as together they progress from the initial contact to the final outcome. The sequence shown in Table 5.1 illustrates his model of the helping process.

Concepts held by good helpers

A vital ingredient in the helping process is how the helper perceives other people and their behavior. Combs and his colleagues were able to identify how the good helper views people and how to distinguish good helpers from poor helpers on this basis. Good helpers are generally characterized by a positive view of people; they see people as dependable, friendly, and worthy. Furthermore, effective helpers do not simply ascribe to these qualities, they behave in these terms (Combs, 1969). According to Combs, good helpers see people as:

—   *Able-Unable.* Helpers perceive others as having the capacity to deal with their problems. They believe that people can find

Table 5.1 The helping process

Helpee behavior	Helper behavior
1. Initially states problem or concern.	1. Experiences initial questions and reactions.
How do I state my desire for help? "I need help . . ." "I have a problem . . ." "I'm unhappy . . ." "Something is wrong . . ." "I can't perform . . ." "I can't decide . . ." Can I trust this other person? What am I getting myself into?	Why is this person here? How does the helpee see his or her present situation? What is the helpee feeling and thinking? How am I and how is this relationship perceived? What is the helpee's world like? What does the helpee want of me?
2. Translates initial statement into a basic message.	2. Formulates inferences, hunches, and hypotheses.
I can't cope with the demands of myself, of others, of the situation. I need more information, more skill, more love, more understanding . . .	What message is the helpee trying to convey? I see the basic problem as . . . Is this valid? Can I meet the helpee's expectations? What additional information do I need to explore?
3. Translates problem into a goal (usually in the form of "I want . . ." statements).	3. Formulates preliminary inferences and judgments about helpee need.
I want to decide . . . do . . . plan . . . I want to feel more confident . . . worthy . . . happy . . . I want others to like me . . . notice me . . . change to . . . get off my back . . .	The helpee needs a process—planning, problem solving, decision making. The helpee needs a relationship to work through feelings or obtain support. The helpee needs information. The helpee needs a referral for specialized help.
4. Experiences an awareness of process needs.	4. Makes an agreement or contract to meet helpee expectations.
I want a relationship to explore my feelings. I want specific information about . . .	I will (can)— give information give time to listen give support.

Table 5.1   continued

Helpee behavior	Helper behavior
I want to talk over my various choices . . . I want more choices to consider . . .	I will not (cannot)— relate to this person. meet his or her expectations. I expect the helpee to— do his or her agreed part. take responsibility for any decisions or plans.
5. Experiences helper's strategy and methods for reaching goal. I meet with the helper for the agreed purposes. I experience what we are doing as helpful (or not helpful) as evidenced by . . .	5. Chooses a strategy of helping. I choose specific interviewing methods to meet helpee needs. I look for feedback from the helpee on the effectiveness of my help.
6. Experiences the outcomes. I feel better about myself. I feel better about others. My skills have improved . . . I feel better about my situation . . . I enrolled in . . . I obtained a job as . . . I experienced myself as competent in . . .	6. Experiences movement toward the outcomes. I experience myself as helpful to this person. I see specific behaviors the helpee has learned, courses of action he or she has chosen, or plans he or she has made. I hear stated feelings he or she has experienced.

Source: Adapted from *The Helping Relationship: Process and Skills,* 2nd ed. (pp. 50–51) by L. Brammer, 1979, Englewood Cliffs, N.J.: Prentice-Hall. Copyright 1979 by Prentice-Hall, Inc. Adapted by permission.

adequate solutions to events, as opposed to doubting the capacity of people to handle themselves and their lives.

— *Friendly-Unfriendly.* Helpers see others as being friendly and enhancing. They do not regard them as threatening to themselves, but see people as essentially well-intentioned rather than evil-intentioned.

— *Worthy-Unworthy.* Helpers see other people as being of worth rather than unworthy. They see them as possessing a dignity and integrity which must be respected and maintained; they do not see people as unimportant beings whose integrity may be violated or treated as of little account.

— *Internally–Externally Motivated.* Helpers see people and their behavior as essentially developing from within rather than as a product of external events to be molded and directed; they see people as creative and dynamic rather than passive or inert.

— *Dependable-Undependable.* Helpers see people as essentially trustworthy and dependable in the sense of behaving in lawful ways. They regard the behavior of people as understandable rather than capricious, unpredictable, or negative.

— *Helpful-Hindering.* Helpers see people as being potentially fulfilling and enhancing to self rather than impeding or threatening. They regard people as important sources of satisfaction rather than as sources of frustration and suspicion. (Combs, Avila, & Purkey, 1971, pp. 12–13)

Helping—for whose benefit?

No one can be helped unless he or she wants to be helped. Luckily, most human beings have the basic need to strive toward personal fulfillment and self-enhancement (Wittmer & Myrick, 1974). Yet helping is a voluntary act; a person cannot be forced to accept help, nor can an individual be coerced into the role of willingly providing help. The question then arises, "For whose benefit does the helping process exist?" Brammer (1979) observes that, seemingly, the helping process is for the development and aid of the helpee, but one also must be conscious of the helper's own need for growth and development. Many people choose to help in order to meet their own unrecognized needs (for example, increased self-worth and status); some provide help out of a deep sense of obligation to their fellow man; still others believe that each individual is responsible for his or her own experiences and need fulfillment.

In his article "Who Can Be a Helper?" Brammer (1977, p. 304) cautions that a key question helpers must ask themselves is, "To what extent am I meeting my needs for self-enhancement or for satisfying my emotional hungers through this helping act?" No doubt, some helping motivation is based on a genuine concern for what happens to others; however, much helper behavior appears to be motivated by needs to dominate or overpower others, to keep them dependent, or to make them conform to the helper's conception of desirable social behavior. Helpers need to scrutinize their own behavior to be sure they are not inappropriately seeking to satisfy personal needs. They should ask themselves, "For what reason(s) do I want to help?"

The helper as a person

An effective helping relationship dictates that helpers must understand not only the helpee and the process involved, but also themselves. As Tyler (1969) observes, successful helping seems to depend as much upon who the helper is as what he or she says or does. The primary tool, according to Combs (1969), that helpers have to work with is themselves.

Benjamin (1981) asks, just what do helpers bring to the helping interview? His response appears to support the view of helping as an art and a science. According to Benjamin, helpers bring knowledge, experience, professional skills, and the information and resources at their disposal. Beyond this, and perhaps more importantly, helpers bring themselves, their desire to be of use, their liking and warm regard for other people, their prejudices and shortcomings, and their own life space and internal frame of reference. Similarly, Webster (1977) believes that helpers bring all aspects of their selves to the helping relationship—their ideas, goals, and expectations as well as their intelligence, trust and self-concept. In short, the helper brings his or her total self.

It would be nice to be able to capsulize the essential qualities of an effective helper, but, obviously, this is not possible. Part of the difficulty rests in the fact that the necessary ingredients are attitudes and beliefs and not skills that can be taught to and digested by an individual. The qualities of an effective helper are part of his or her basic personality.

Although a person cannot be trained to be genuine, sincere, or empathetic, a helper can be taught how to use himself or herself more effectively. Combs and his associates (Combs, Blume, Newman,

& Wass, 1974) believe that training a helper is not a mysterious "laying-on-of-the-hands" procedure, but rather involves helping individuals to make the most effective use of themselves. Helping is not just a matter of learning a few new skills; it requires setting one's own psychological house in order, knowing who one is and where one is going (Tyler, 1969). Benjamin (1981) suggests that the internal conditions of knowing, liking, and being comfortable with oneself are important prerequisites for a good helper. The basic attitudes that helpers possess about other people, however, are not a consequence of university training programs, inservice experiences, or special readings, but rather are developed from life's experiences. A person learns that he or she is liked, wanted, and accepted by having been treated this way and by treating others in similar fashion.

How effective helpers view themselves

According to Combs (1969), helping is a question of the use of the helper's self—"the peculiar way he [the helper] is able to combine his knowledge and understanding with his own unique ways of putting it into operation in such a fashion as to be helpful to others" (p. 11). The concept of the self as an instrument in the helping process led Combs to conclude that it is not knowledge or methods that distinguish good helpers from poor ones, but rather how the helper sees himself or herself.

An effective helping relationship requires that helpers be somebody. Equally important is that the helper be perceived as a person of some consequence. Rogers (1961) has also noted the significance of the helpee's perception of the helper's attitudes and beliefs. Not only is the helpee's perception important, but Combs (1969) believes that the helper's behavior is a reflection or expression of his or her beliefs. Thus how helpers see themselves influences their interactions with others. Combs was able to identify the following desirable perceptions that effective helpers have of themselves:

— *Identified-Apart.* Helpers feel identified with rather than apart from others. The helper tends to see himself as part of all mankind; he sees himself as identified with people rather than as withdrawn, removed, apart, or alienated from others.

— *Adequate-Inadequate.* Helpers feel basically adequate rather than inadequate. The good helper generally sees himself as enough, as having what is needed to deal with his problems.

— *Trustworthy-Untrustworthy.* Helpers feel trustworthy rather than untrustworthy. The good helper has trust in his organization. He sees himself as essentially dependable or reliable and as having the potentiality for coping with events. This is opposed to seeing self in a tentative fashion with doubts about the potentiality and reliability of the organism.

— *Wanted-Unwanted.* Helpers see themselves as wanted rather than unwanted. The good helper sees himself as essentially likable, attractive (in a personal sense, not necessarily in physical appearance), wanted, and in general capable of bringing forth a warm response in those people important to him. This is opposed to feeling ignored, unwanted, or rejected by others.

— *Worthy-Unworthy.* Helpers see themselves as worthy rather than unworthy. A good helper sees himself as a person of consequence, dignity, integrity, and worthy of respect, as opposed to being a person of little consequence who can be overlooked, discounted, and whose dignity and integrity do not matter. (Combs, Avila, & Purkey, 1971, p. 14)

Characteristics of an effective helper

Helper characteristics are an integral part of the helping process. The outcome of any helping relationship is influenced to a large degree by the characteristics and traits exhibited by the helper (Stewart, 1978). The helper's attitudes are of particular importance when interacting with parents of exceptional children. There have been numerous attempts to list those traits and attitudes deemed important in an effective helping relationship. Hansen et al. (1972) believe an effective helper should be, among other things, sincere, sensitive, sympathetic, understanding, and emotionally stable, should possess common sense, and should demonstrate good judgment. Tyler (1969) lists acceptance, understanding, and sincerity as the three essential qualities that a helper must communicate to the helpee. Many years ago, Rogers (1957) hypothesized that, in order to promote positive change in a client, the therapist must not only be a congruent, genuine, and integrated individual but also evidence empathetic understanding of the client's problem and unconditional positive regard for the person.

An investigation conducted by Wittmer and Myrick (1974) of effective and ineffective educators found that "turn on" teachers were consistently described as good listeners, empathetic, caring, concerned, genuine, warm, interested, knowledgeable, trusting, friendly, dynamic, possessing a sense of humor, and able to communicate. Ineffective or "turn off" instructors were typically described as insensitive, cold, disinterested, authoritarian, ridiculing, arbitrary, sarcastic, demanding, and punitive. The much-quoted Fiedler (1950) study comparing expert therapists with nonexperts found that the experts formed similar relationships with their clients regardless of their background. The factors that distinguished the experts' relationships from those of the nonexperts were the ability of the experienced therapists to understand the client's meanings and feelings, a sensitivity to the client's attitudes, and a warm interest without emotional overinvolvement. More recently, Brammer (1977) mentions empathy, congruence or realness, warmth and caring, self-disclosure, concreteness of expression, and positive regard or respect as qualities of an effective helper. Finally, Stewart (1978) suggests that helpers have an interest in people and also demonstrate acceptance, respect, trust, empathy, rapport, genuineness, and honesty.

Although the list of characteristics seems endless, and no single ideal helper personality appears to emerge, the preceding traits can be considered expansions of ordinary human qualities. Although the following list of desirable characteristics may not attract universal agreement, it does represent those traits most frequently associated with effective helpers and possessed in varying degrees by most people.

Genuine liking

One of the basic characteristics of an effective helper is a sincere interest in people (Stewart, 1978). Benjamin (1981) considers this trait to be a gift from heaven, an essential attribute of those involved in a helping profession. It provides a strong foundation from which the helper can learn how to use himself or herself more effectively.

Helpers must not only like other people and genuinely care about them, they must also like themselves. Helpers need to be warm and caring individuals. Liking another human being is not a role that can be acted out. Professionals who demonstrate a genuine liking of people and manifest a psychological closeness with others also see themselves as involved with and part of humankind.

Acceptance

Although acceptance means different things to different individuals, it is a concept essential to a helping relationship. Basically, acceptance involves respecting the helpee as a person in his or her own right. It originates from the helper's basic attitudes about people in general and the helpee in particular.

Rogers (1961) defines acceptance as:

a warm regard for him as a person of unconditional self-worth—of value no matter what his conditions, his behavior or his feelings. It means a respect and liking for him as a separate person, a willingness for him to possess his own feelings in his own way. It means an acceptance or a regard for his attitudes of the moment, no matter how negative or positive, no matter how much they may contradict other attitudes he has held in the past. (p. 34)

Acceptance, to Benjamin (1981), means treating the helpee as an equal and considering his or her thoughts and feelings with sincere respect. In other words, it is an attitude that the helpee has just as much right to his or her ideas and feelings as the helper does to his. The helper does not approve or disapprove, but rather attempts to understand the helpee in a nonjudgmental fashion. As Tyler (1969) points out, there are no yardsticks a helper uses to gauge or measure the helpee. There are also no preconditions established before offering help.

A helper cannot help someone without first accepting him or her. Acceptance reflects a desire to help rather than a need to control (Shertzer & Stone, 1980). An effective helping relationship requires not only that the helpee perceive acceptance but also that the helper understand and accept himself or herself.

In addition, it is particularly important that individuals who help parents of exceptional children examine and acknowledge their feelings and attitudes toward the handicapped. At one hospital a nurse experienced difficulties in communicating with some of the residents' parents. She mentioned that she had to accompany some of the handicapped children to the circus. She failed, however, to see the purpose of this experience and considered it extravagant and a poor use of limited fiscal resources. Further discussion revealed a lack of acceptance of the children as whole, productive, and responsive beings. As a consequence, her feelings toward these children apparently hindered her ability to effectively communicate with their parents. Her attitudes diminished the parent-professional relationship and detracted from the services she could offer.

Empathy

Empathy, according to Rogers (1961), is a necessary condition of helping. The word *empathy* is derived from the German *einfühlung*, meaning "feeling into." Simply stated, empathy means putting oneself in the other person's place, seeing the world through the eyes of another. "It means feeling yourself into, or participating in, the inner world of another while remaining yourself" (Benjamin, 1981, p. 49). Empathy can also be regarded as a vehicle toward understanding a person and allowing that person to feel understood. The helper, while retaining his or her own identity, attempts to understand the thoughts and feelings of the helpee and to perceive that individual's world as he or she views it. Empathy, however, is not synonymous with sympathy. Empathy says, "I understand," whereas sympathy implies, "I feel sorry for you."

This empathetic understanding, thinking with rather than for the helpee, is accomplished, according to Brammer (1979), by actively listening and asking the following questions: (1) "What is the helpee feeling at the moment?" (2) "How does the helpee see the problem?" and (3) "What does the helpee see in his or her world?" As a result of exploring the helpee's internal frame of reference, the helper can communicate and share the helpee's thoughts and feelings because he or she has seen with the person's eyes and heard with the person's ears. In other words, the helper becomes an emotional mirror for the helpee, enabling him or her to feel understood.

Understanding

No one ever feels totally understood. Yet understanding is an important component of both the helper's personality and the helping relationship. It is through understanding that help can be provided. Understanding, which is closely aligned with empathy, is defined as clearly and completely comprehending the meaning a person is attempting to communicate (Tyler, 1969). It is not a magical process, but rather a result of being able to carefully attend.

Understanding can occur at several levels. Benjamin (1981) identifies three ways. The first way is to understand *about* the helpee—that is, to understand the helpee through the eyes of others, not the helper's own. This may be accomplished through reports or the evaluations and opinions of others. The second way of understanding an individual is based on the helper's experience, skills, background, and perceptions. The helpee is thus understood in terms of the helper's internal frame of reference. The final way of understanding is understanding *with* the person. This is the most useful type of understanding and is closely aligned with the concept of empathy. It is understanding based on the helpee's internal frame of reference and represents an attempt to enter into the perceptual world of the helpee.

Genuineness

Helpers should always endeavor to be themselves in a helping relationship. This attempt has been referred to in the helping literature as genuineness, sincerity, and authenticity. It is the opposite of being phony. A helper is and behaves as a genuine person. The helper does not pretend or act out a role, but is unafraid of being himself or herself. An effective helper acts as a human being and does not hide behind a disguise or façade. Helpers cannot expect the helpee to be open and honest if they themselves do not exhibit these qualities.

Rogers (1961) also talks about congruence or the harmony between the helper's words, actions, and attitudes. In other words, when the parents tell the physical therapist that they have been unable to follow through with Jerome's daily and time-consuming exercise regimen, she should not say, "It's okay, I understand," when her facial expressions and physical demeanor show her anger and frustration at the parents' lack of compliance. The actions of the helper must be consistent with his or her innermost feelings. A discrepancy cannot exist between what the helper says and does—otherwise, helpees will quickly discover when the helper's words contradict what he or she feels or believes.

Rapport

Rapport is another condition that is basic to the success of the helping relationship. Essentially, rapport means that an appropriate working relationship has been established and maintained between the helper and helpee. Rapport is more than just a pleasant welcome and making a person feel comfortable and at ease; it is a sensitivity to the helpee's needs, moods, and conflicts throughout the relationship. It is an intangible entity characterized by pleasantness, cooperation, respect, sincerity, and a genuine interest in and acceptance of the helpee (Shertzer & Stone, 1980). Stewart (1978) notes that rapport is symbolized by harmony, trust, and confidence. Hence rapport is neither artificial nor superficial.

Unconditional positive regard

The final helper characteristic, one frequently associated with the writings of Carl Rogers (1961), is unconditional positive regard, or the absolute and unqualified acceptance of the helpee in his or her present condition. That is, the helpee is allowed to be himself or herself; helpers accept and respect this individual without any prerequisites. While most helpers recognize the importance of positive regard, few suppose that it must always be unconditional.

Brammer (1979) believes that unconditional acceptance is related to the stages involved in the helping process. In the initial stages, positive regard is significant; the helper must communicate to the helpee that

I neither approve nor disapprove of what you are saying. I want you to express yourself freely, and I will respect your right to feel as you please and to act as you feel within the limits of our mutual welfare. I want you to become your most real and effective self. Furthermore, I want to like you and respect you as a person. (p. 40)

Yet as the helping relationship matures and the helpee becomes more receptive to feedback from the helper, regard becomes more conditional. The helpee experiences positive regard when the helper's words are congruent with nonverbal expressions of warmth, empathy, and acceptance.

A final word

Regardless of whether the reader conceives of the helping process as an art, a science, or, as suggested, the union of both, he or she should by now have begun to develop an understanding and appreciation for the helping scheme and undertaken a careful self-examination, including the attitudes he or she possesses toward and about other people, while also being aware of the reasons why he or she wants to help others.

The examination of the first half of the helping equation, the helper as a person, is now complete. As noted earlier, no single, overall ideal helper personality exists. However, the preceding list of characteristics, although few in number and deceivingly simple, represents those traits most frequently identified as necessary for facilitating a helping relationship and, hence, helpee growth. The following chapter surveys helping skills that promote growth conditions.

Nothing great was ever achieved without enthusiasm.

—Ralph Waldo Emerson

References

Benjamin, A. (1981). *The helping interview* (3rd ed.). Boston: Houghton Mifflin.

Blocher, D. (1966). *Developmental counseling.* New York: Ronald Press.

Brammer, L. (1977). Who can be a helper? *Personnel and Guidance Journal, 55,* 303–308.

Brammer, L. (1979). *The helping relationship: Process and skills* (2nd ed.). Englewood Cliffs, NJ: Prentice-Hall.

Combs, A. (1969). *Florida studies in the helping professions.* Gainesville, FL: University of Florida Press. (Monograph 37).

Combs, A., Avila, D., & Purkey, W. (1971). *Helping relationships: Basic concepts for the helping professions.* Boston: Allyn & Bacon.

Combs, A., Blume, R., Newman, A., & Wass, H. (1974). *The professional education of teachers* (2nd ed.). Boston: Allyn & Bacon.

English, H., & English, A. (1958). *A comprehensive dictionary of psychological and psychoanalytic terms.* New York: David McKay.

Fiedler, F. (1950). The concept of an ideal therapeutic relationship. *Journal of Consulting Psychology, 14,* 239–245.

Hansen, J., Stevic, R., & Warner, R. (1972). *Counseling: theory and process.* Boston: Allyn & Bacon.

Hansen, J., Stevic, R., & Warner, R. (1982). *Counseling: Theory and process* (3rd ed.). Boston: Allyn & Bacon.

Laborde, P., & Seligman, M. (1983). Individual counseling with parents of handicapped children: Rationale and strategies. In M. Seligman (Ed.), *The family with a handicapped child* (pp. 261–284). New York: Grune & Stratton.

Patterson, C. (1967). *The counselor in the school.* New York: McGraw-Hill.

Rogers, C. (1957). The necessary and sufficient conditions of therapeutic personality change. *Journal of Consulting Psychology, 21,* 95–103.

Rogers, C. (1961). *On becoming a person.* Boston: Houghton Mifflin.

Shertzer, B., & Stone, S. (1980). *Fundamentals of counseling* (3rd ed.). Boston: Houghton Mifflin.

Stewart, J. (1978). *Counseling parents of exceptional children.* Columbus, OH: Charles Merrill.

Tyler, L. (1969). *The work of the counselor* (3rd ed.). Englewood Cliffs, NJ: Prentice-Hall.

Webster, E. (1977). *Counseling with parents of handicapped children.* New York: Grune & Stratton.

Wittmer, J., & Myrick, R. (1974). *Facilitative teaching: Theory and practice.* Santa Monica, CA: Goodyear.

Chapter 6:
Helping skills

A word is worth one coin; silence is worth two.

—The Talmud

Helping skills are an important part of the professional's repertoire. As the model of an effective helping relationship suggests, helping involves both the helper's affective characteristics and learned helping skills. Unlike such attributes as genuineness and warmth, which develop from life's experiences, helping skills can be taught and practiced. These skills, although more easily enumerated than acquired, do not develop in a vacuum; they too must become part of the helper's total, natural helping style. They cannot exist separate from the feelings and attitudes shared in a helping relationship.

The issue of helping skills, however, has met with some controversy, centering around the development of these skills. Rogers (1957) believes that helping skills evolve naturally from helping attitudes such as positive regard and empathy. The opposing philosophy, as evidenced by the work of Ivey, Carkhuff, and others, is that although such characteristics are important, they cannot guarantee appropriate helper behavior. The helper must be instructed in specific helping skills, which will then complement his or her affective qualities (Brammer, 1977). This latter approach is the one most in accord with the model of helping in this book.

This chapter will focus on those fundamental skills most frequently cited in the helping literature as basic to promoting and maintaining a helping relationship—for example, listening, leading, and questioning, to name a few. Webster (1977) observes that because each helper is unique, learning to constructively interact with parents cannot be reduced to a simple recipe. Consequently, it is not the purpose of this discussion to suggest specific training techniques for developing these skills, but rather to illustrate their importance. In addition to these skills, roadblocks or barriers to effective helping will also be addressed.

Listening

Many problems are the result of poor communication. The basis for most of these difficulties lies in the inability of individuals to listen effectively. Listening is the most essential element of any helping relationship, the foundation upon which the entire relationship is established. Without listening, one does not have a helping relationship.

Listening has tremendous therapeutic value. Genuine listening, however, is a difficult skill to acquire; it is hard work and requires much practice. Effective listening demands both effort and skill, yet the ability to listen is often taken for granted. Most people really do not listen or know how to listen, as evidenced by an examination of everyday adult conversation. Conversations with colleagues at lunch, in the teachers' lounge, or when car-pooling suggest that most individuals are only waiting for the speaker to stop so they can present their own thoughts and ideas. After the first few words are spoken, most people are already planning their response without hearing the speaker's entire message or trying to understand its meaning. Wittmer and Myrick (1974) observe that the listener's silence, as he or she awaits a turn to speak, is more often a period of toleration rather than evidence of true listening. "Hence the purpose of much conversation is not to hear what the other person has to say, but to enjoy the opportunity to express oneself" (Combs, Avila, & Purkey, 1971, p. 194).

Finding a good listener is a difficult task. In fact, good listeners are often described as terrific conversationalists. Their secret lies in their ability to concentrate on the person and the meaning of his or her message. Some professional helpers maintain their livelihood by being good listeners; they realize that most helpers talk too much!

Listening is not a mechanical act. According to Benjamin (1981), it requires that helpers be not preoccupied but capable of fully attending to the helpee. The listener must also be aware of the manner in which things are said, that is, the expressions and gestures employed. In addition, he or she needs to be perceptive to what is not being said, what lies just beyond the surface or is only hinted at. This skill is sometimes referred to by psychologists as listening with a third ear (Reik, 1972).

The listening required in a helping relationship is unlike the superficial listening found in a social situation or college classroom. Helping demands that the helper fully attend to both the verbal and nonverbal messages of the helpee. Selective listening, which so many individuals are guilty of, does not belong in a helping environment; rather, helpers must listen with understanding. Effective listeners want to know what the other person is thinking and feeling. These listeners focus in on the feelings and attitudes underscoring the content of the words (Wittmer & Myrick, 1974). Listening, therefore, is an active process of responding to a total message, an awareness of what is being said and felt (Brammer, 1979; Stewart, 1978). This notion was expanded by Lichter (1976), who describes listening as occurring in two ways, either passive or active. Passive listening occurs when a person listens in relative silence. This silence is seen as an indication of openness and acceptance. Listening, however, can also be an active process wherein the listener puts his or her understanding of the speaker's verbal message and accompanying feeling into his or her own words and presents this to the speaker for verification and clarification. This process provides the listener with an opportunity to test his or her understanding of what the other person is attempting to communicate, and also serves as a means of allowing the speaker to see that the listener is truly trying to understand. For instance:

Parent:	I wish Jennifer was making as much progress as some of the other kids in her class.
Teacher:	You're feeling a little envious of others.
Parent:	Yes. They all seem to be moving so much more quickly than Jennifer.
Teacher:	You wish she would make faster progress.
Parent:	Yes, I do. It's so frustrating to see everybody—you, me, and Jennifer—work so hard and yet make such slow progress.
Teacher:	You really get frustrated when you do so much and you don't see results.
Parent:	Sometimes I begin to think, "What's the use?"
Teacher:	It's more than being frustrated; sometimes you think all our work is useless.
Parent:	Yes. Somedays I think she never learned anything.
Teacher:	You feel she can't learn.
Parent:	Well, no, not that she *can't* learn—but that it's so much harder for her than others.
Teacher:	Learning for her is very difficult.
Parent:	Yes it is. And I guess I feel sorry for her because she has to work so hard. But I also know it's not good to pity her.
Teacher:	It sounds like you're really struggling with two conflicting emotions.
Parent:	I guess I am. But just talking about this with you makes me feel better. (Lichter, 1976, p. 71)

This concept of active listening is very similar to Benjamin's (1981) goal of listening with understanding. Benjamin suggests the following strategy as a test to see if one is able to listen with understanding.

If during the interview you can state in your own words what the interviewee has said and also convey to him in your own words the feelings he has expressed and he then accepts all of this as emanating from him, there is an excellent chance that you have listened and understood him. (p. 47)

A note of caution must be sounded: as helpers attempt to listen with understanding, they need to guard against losing their internal frame of reference (Benjamin, 1981). The effectiveness of the helping relationship requires that helpers, although very much involved, retain their personal sense of identity. The helper is part of the relationship, yet is not captured by it. Also, active listening should not develop into a highly stylized way of responding that could be interpreted as phony and an indication of a lack of genuine concern.

Lichter (1976) has stated the following guidelines for active listening:

1. Listen for the basic message of the speaker.

2. Restate to the speaker a simple and concise summary of the basic content and/or feeling of the message.

3. Observe a cue or ask for a response from the speaker to confirm the accuracy and helpfulness of the reflection.

4. Allow the speaker to correct your perception if it was inaccurate. (p. 70)

Roger Kroth (1975) proposes a model of listening based on whether an individual is a listener or nonlistener and is actively or passively engaged in this activity.* This model is shown in Figure 6.1.

Although helpers cannot always be neatly categorized as particular types of listeners, and no individual is in any one quadrant all of the time, each person has a tendency to exhibit the charac-

---

* The terms active and passive listening as used here are not synonymous with those developed by Lichter (1976).

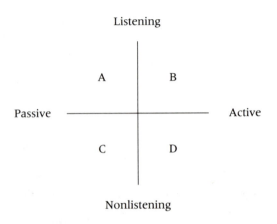

Figure 6.1   A listening paradigm. R. Kroth, *Communicating with Parents of Exceptional Children,* © 1975, p. 29. Reprinted by permission of Love Publishing Company, Denver, Colo.

teristics of a particular type of listener more frequently than others. These characteristics are as follows:

Quadrant A: passive listening   According to Kroth, a passive listener, sometimes referred to as a supportive listener, is "there"; he or she is "with it." The helper can think out loud with the helpee, who feels comfortable due to the presence of nonverbal signs of acceptance such as a nod of the head or a smile. The helpee thus feels understood and is encouraged to continue talking. Many helpers are at first uneasy with this listening style, but practice often relieves this feeling.

Quadrant B: active listening   "The active listener is actively involved in helping another person identify and clarify his problems, his beliefs, and his value system" (Kroth, 1975, p. 29). Kroth considers an active listener to be like a fine dancing partner who seems able to feel the rhythm of the conversation and to move in step with its flow. Statements are reflected back to the helpee as a means of allowing the helper to verify his or her perceptions. A major asset of active listening is that it keeps the ownership of the problem where it belongs—with the one seeking help. The purpose of the helper is to clarify the problem and assist the helpee in establishing a proper perspective.

Quadrant C: passive nonlistening   The third quadrant exemplifies the individual who "hears" what is being said but does not listen. This posture can be extremely frustrating to the speaker. Although capable of accurately repeating the content, passive non-listeners, often preoccupied with their own thoughts, are unable to capture the underlying emotions that accompany the verbal message. Teachers are very vulnerable to this style of listening, especially when conducting several parent conferences in a single day.

Quadrant D: active nonlistening   Two kinds of active nonlistening are identified by Kroth: the "Cocktail Party Type" and the "Wipe-out Artist." Most people have had experiences at social functions where a great deal of conversation occurs but little listening is evident. People are observed talking *to* each other but seldom *with* each other. Neither party is really concerned with what the other person has to say. Each individual politely listens and then talks about whatever he or she feels is important, which often results in fragmented conversations. As an example:

Mrs. Smith:	We're so glad you could come. I heard you were out of town.
Mrs. Jones:	We just got back. We were attending my aunt's funeral in California.
Mrs. Smith:	California is so pretty this time of the year. We were at Disneyland last spring, I enjoyed it so much.
Mrs. Jones:	We were in Albuquerque last spring. Oh, there's Ruby. I must tell her about the Squash Blossom necklace I found. (Kroth, 1975, p. 32)

Cocktail party listening is not limited to social surroundings. If allowed, it can easily occur in a helping situation. The following dialogue between a teacher and parent characterizes this listening style.

Teacher:	I'm so glad you could come. I've been wanting to talk with you about Billy.
Parent:	I'm having trouble getting Billy to do his homework. He always wants to put it off, and we have frightful arguments around the home.
Teacher:	He's been fighting on the playground. I've had to keep him in from recess twice this week.
Parent:	I don't think he understands the new math. That's probably why he doesn't do his homework. I wish you could do something about it.
Teacher:	Do you have any idea why he's started fighting so much? Does he ever talk about it at home? We just don't know what to do with him. It's getting to be a real problem.
Parent:	We're having a real problem, too. We're open for any suggestions. This arguing is getting both his Dad and me upset.
Teacher:	We at school want to cooperate in any way that we can. If you have any ideas about his fighting, call me, will you? It's sure been nice talking to you, and I'm glad you could come. You're always welcome at school.
Parent:	I'm happy to have met you. If you have any ideas how we can help at home, just call. We want to work closely with the school. (Kroth, 1975, pp. 32–33)

Kroth believes that this type of listening happens much more frequently than most of us realize. At best, the teacher and parent were able to talk about their concerns, yet little was accomplished.

"The Wipe-out Artist is probably the most exasperating type of active nonlistener" (Kroth, 1975, p. 34). In this form of nonlistening, the person appears to be actively listening but responds to superficial issues. Consequently, the conversation lacks a clear focal point, which leads to frustration and lack of communication. For instance:

Parent:	Billy had the neatest thing happen to him on his way home from school.
Teacher:	How does he go home from school?
Parent:	Down Center Street and—
Teacher:	Isn't that past the fire station?
Parent:	Yes, and—
Teacher:	Last year five of our boys said they wanted to be firemen when they grow up. What does Billy want to be?
Parent:	A nuclear physicist.
Teacher:	Isn't that cute? And to think he can't even spell it. What happened to him on the way home?
Parent:	Well, he ran into this man who—
Teacher:	I hope he said "Excuse me." We stress good manners in our room. We have a unit on the magic words—*Please* and *Thank you.* I hope you notice the improvement at home. (Kroth, 1975, p. 34)

The importance of listening in the helping relationship cannot be stressed enough. Professionals need to be constantly aware of the helpee's verbal messages and their emotional significance. Listening demands the use of both the head and the heart.

Attentiveness

Related to listening and just as basic is the skill of attentiveness. *Attentiveness* refers to a person's complete involvement with another's verbal and nonverbal messages (Stewart, 1978). Shertzer and Stone (1980) state that attending "requires skill in listening and observing through which the counselor comes to know and understand the core of content and feeling presented by the counselee" (p. 266). Attending allows a person to participate in another's communication and also demonstrates interest in what he or she has to say. Attentiveness encourages the speaker to continue freely verbalizing his or her thoughts and feelings. It also allows the speaker to explore in his or her own fashion and tends to create within the speaker a sense of responsibility for the relationship (Brammer, 1979).

Just how does one attend to another human being? Ivey (1971) and Brammer (1979) have both identified several subskills that contribute to attentiveness. Varied use of eye contact is one way of demonstrating attentiveness. Eye contact does not mean staring, but naturally gazing at the person while he or she is talking. The eyes, as the saying goes, are the windows of the soul and a key vehicle for communicating caring and understanding as well as for maintaining attention.

Attending also requires that the listener be physically relaxed and seated comfortably with a natural posture. Ivey (1971) believes that when a helper is comfortable he or she is better able to listen to the helpee. If the helper is relaxed and comfortable, this is transmitted to the helpee, who also tends to be more at ease. The use of natural body movements and gestures also denotes attentiveness. But certain motions or postures—such as arms crossed over the chest—although natural, can be interpreted as disinterest or a lack of agreement.

The final element of effective attending is the helper's verbal behavior. The purpose of the helper's verbal comments, which are based upon what the helpee has said, is not to guide the discussion in a new direction, but rather to clarify and develop the topic and to assure that the helper is indeed listening.

In summary, attending requires that the helper be physically comfortable, maintain a natural gaze, and be capable of verbal feedback that indicates an understanding of what the helpee is communicating.

Leading

A professional must not only be able to receive messages but must also be capable of eliciting information from the helpee. The helper needs to be skillful in verbally inviting and encouraging the helpee to respond to open communication (Brammer, 1979). This ability is referred to as leading. *Leading* has been defined by Robinson (1950) as "a teamlike working together in which the counselor's remarks seem to the client to state the next point he is ready to accept" (p. 66). It is analogous to the relationship between a quarterback and his receiver. That is, a successful forward pass requires that both the ball and receiver arrive at the same spot at the same time. This is accomplished only as a result of many hours of combined practice. Likewise, leading is characterized by teamwork as both helper and helpee work toward a common goal. In essence, a lead should assist the helpee toward the next stage in his or her thinking. It says, "I want to know more about this subject." For instance:

"Tell me more about Joan's teacher."

"I'd like to hear what you think about your son's placement in the remedial reading program."

"I was wondering how you feel about Elizabeth's new bus schedule."

Brammer (1979) identifies the following three specific objectives of leading:

1. To encourage helpees to explore feelings and to elaborate on those feelings already discussed.

2. To allow helpees freedom to explore in a variety of directions and to respond freely to what is going on.

3. To encourage helpees to be active in the process and to retain primary responsibility for the direction of the interview. (p. 75)

Benjamin (1981) cautions that a helper can never be certain of the impact of his or her leads on the helpee. While leading is designed to be a helpful skill, it can be interpreted in a negative and defensive manner by the one being led. Even when helpers are sincere in their intentions, it is the manner in which the lead is perceived by the helpee that is important.

Varying degrees of leading occur in a helping relationship. A helper may lead too little or too much. Leads may be beneficial or detrimental. And there is not always a clear distinction between a lead and a response: a lead could be interpreted as a response and a helper's response may change into a lead.

A variety of schemes exists for classifying the many leads available to the helper. For example, Buchheimer and Balogh (1961) describe leads according to whether they are designed to elicit feelings, increase self-understanding, or promote action. Brammer (1979) suggests two types of leading: indirect or direct. Benjamin (1981), based on the early writings of Francis Robinson (1950), addresses the question of whether leads are helper- or helpee-centered. The following select leads have been organized according to the extent of helper involvement and participation with the helpee's verbal message. These leads or responses, depending on one's perspective, evidence a concern for the way things appear to the helpee rather than how things seem to the helper. The unwritten assumption of this position is that the helpee is capable of finding his or her own solutions. The type of lead employed by the helper, however, should reflect the background of the helpee and the amount of resistance or defensiveness the lead will likely arouse. The degree of leading will also vary from topic to topic and from moment to moment within the relationship (Robinson, 1950). Following are illustrations and explanations of various types of leading.

Silence

Silence is a natural occurrence in a helping relationship. Still, many helpers are initially uncomfortable with silence even though silence communicates a great deal. As a nonverbal lead (response), silence expresses understanding and respect and provides an opportunity for the helpee to gather his or her thoughts or to find a way of expressing deeper feelings. As a deliberate lead, silence leaves the responsibility for maintaining the relationship squarely on the shoulders of the helpee. Unfortunately, there are no standards by which the helper can gauge the appropriateness of his or her silence; it is a matter of sensitivity and judgment. Benjamin (1981) contends that silence is an important aspect of the helping experience. The helpee should leave feeling, "Here I was listened to."

Most helpers do not realize the value or importance of silence. Often, as the result of a seemingly endless pause, a beginning helper or even an experienced one will encounter the urge to speak or ask questions, thus invading the helpee's thoughts. This action is probably precipitated by a sense of wasting time and/or a belief that the helper has failed and is not doing a good job (Seligman, 1979). More often than not, when silence does occur, it is the helper who is embarrassed or feels uncomfortable, not the helpee. This may be the result of a cultural expectation: our society tends to discourage silence, and to some helpers silence is synonymous with rejection, hostility, and defensiveness. Silence, therefore, needs to be examined in the context in which it occurs. A pause may indicate a natural conclusion to a line of thinking or could be the result of confusion about something that was said. Silence could reflect the helpee's perception of his or her role in the helping relationship. It may even signal defensiveness, as if the helpee were fending off probing comments and questions. Regardless of the reasons for silence, an effective helper, needs to understand silence, be able to tolerate it, and remember that silence can benefit both helpee and helper.

Acceptance

In many instances a helper's verbal comments can destroy the flow or momentum established by the helpee. Yet the helper feels the need to communicate or express acceptance of the helpee's remarks. A response such as "Mm-hm," "Yes," or "I see" connotes this acceptance and also implies permission for the helpee to continue. This strategy stimulates further discussion and elaboration and allows the helpee to continue without threat (Shertzer & Stone, 1980). Although the utterance of "mm-hm" may appear to be noncommittal, it is usually a powerful reinforcer. However, it could also be interpreted as suggesting criticism or disapproval of the helpee's verbalization. Thus the many variations of this simple sound can greatly affect the direction of the helping interview.

Paraphrasing

Paraphrasing, or restatement, is a technique by which the helper translates or feeds back to the helpee the essence of his or her basic message but in a simpler, more precise manner. This tactic allows the helper to demonstrate understanding of what was said without adding ideas or filtering the message through his or her own frame of reference. No attempt is made to clarify or interpret the helpee's statement. Restatement provides the helper with an opportunity to double-check his or her perceptions of what the helpee is describing. The focus is more on the objective, cognitive components of the message than the affective aspects, although feelings are not totally ignored. Poor paraphrasing represents mere repetition of what was said, whereas an effective restatement causes the helpee to feel understood and encouraged to move forward with a clearer sense of direction. An example of a paraphrase would be:

Parent:	Every day seems to present a new crisis. Mark is constantly on the go. I just can't seem to settle him down. No sooner do I get the house picked up than he destroys it.
Teacher:	You're really having difficulty keeping up with Mark.
Parent:	Yeah, and with school almost over, I'm not sure if I can survive the summer.

If one is not careful, however, paraphrasing can become artificial and develop into a stylized way of responding to and interacting with the helpee. The helper should practice until paraphrasing becomes comfortable and appears more natural.

Clarification

Sometimes a person's statements are vague and lack direction or a clear focal point. In such cases the helper may need to elucidate and more precisely state what the helpee has said. In other words, the helper attempts to clarify the content and feelings of the helpee's statement without interpreting it. The helpee then has to decide whether or not the helper's efforts at clarification were successful. For instance, the helper might use statements such as:

"Let me see, in other words you are . . ."

"Unless I'm mistaken, you think that . . ."

"You seem to be saying . . ."

Clarification has a dual role. Not only does it refer to efforts to assist the helpee, but it can also be for the benefit of the helper. That is, the helper may need assistance in understanding what the helpee is attempting to communicate. Professionals are not infallible; they too can become confused or guilty of inattention and require the use of a clarifying statement. For example, a helper might say, "Excuse me, I really don't understand what you mean. Could you please explain?" In this instance, it is the helpee who is assisting the helper. Regardless of who is helping whom, the outcome should be better understanding and clearer communication.

Reflection

Reflection is a difficult skill to master, yet it is vitally important for a helper to be sensitive to the helpee's feelings. Reflection demands empathetic listening and an appreciation of the helpee's internal frame of reference. Reflecting involves the helper's verbalizing the feelings and attitudes that he or she perceives to lie behind the helpee's verbal message. Reflection goes beyond mere words to the underlying feelings, which may or may not have been clearly articulated by the helpee. The helper senses these feelings and, like a mirror or echo, feeds back to the helpee the feelings perceived. Nothing new is offered. The helper responds in terms of the helpee's perspective, not his or her own. The goal of reflection is to communicate to the helpee, "I am with you and trying to perceive your world as you see it." The following examples represent reflective statements:

— *Positive feelings:*
  "Norman makes you feel loved and needed."
  "You seem to be very pleased with your accomplishments."

— *Negative feelings:*
"You're deeply worried about being able to pay your bills."
"Martha really irritates you when she acts that way."

— *Ambivalent feelings:*
"The challenge of your new job excites you. Yet you're afraid of the new responsibilities."
"Sara provides a lot of support and encouragement but you're suspicious of her motives."

Reflection demonstrates a concern for the feeling behind the words rather than the content of the conversation. The helper must be aware not only of *what* the helpee is stating but of *how* it is being expressed. For example, the nonverbal expressions of a clenched fist or a change in breathing can provide the helper with clues to underlying feelings.

One of the purposes of reflection is to assist the helpee in identifying feelings and also in assuming ownership of them; that is, to view feelings as part of oneself rather than as outside elements. However, as Wittmer and Myrick (1974) note, society has not always fostered such ownership of feelings. Until recently, emotions were considered too private to be shared openly with another person. The proper thing to do was to deny, disown, or distort feelings for fear they may reveal an internal flaw or character deficiency. As a consequence, a great many relationships are distant, formal, and lacking in personal understanding. Before helpers can perceive the feelings of another person, they must recognize and own their own feelings. Individuals who are unable to express their feelings are often unable to recognize feelings in others. In order to be effective in a helping relationship, the helper must acknowledge his or her own emotions.

Sometimes reflective statements may be rejected by the helpee, thereby indicating that the helper missed the mark. This may be due to inaccuracies or distortions in the helper's perceptions. As an illustration, during a parent-teacher conference focusing on Leslie's improved grades:

Parent: Leslie's father was pleased to see her latest report card.

| **Teacher:** | I bet he was really proud of her big improvement. |
| **Parent:** | Oh, no, not really. He still believes that she's not trying hard enough and can do better. |

In other instances, the helpee may be unable, at that moment, to admit to the validity of the reflection, or possibly the reflective statement was threatening or viewed as too deep or too close for comfort. At a later point in time, reflection may be effective and will allow the helpee an opportunity to acknowledge his or her feelings.

Because reflection is a difficult skill to develop, errors are sometimes frequent. One of the more common mistakes is a stylized or stereotyped way of responding to the helpee's statements; for example, "You feel . . ." or "You seem to . . ." Such responses may cause the helpee to interpret the helper's actions as phony or insincere. In the same vein, helpers should not pretend to understand a person's feelings. Also, some helpers feel compelled to reflect and identify feelings after every phrase or, at the other extreme, at the conclusion of a lengthy statement. Reflection should only be used when it appears appropriate and the interview allows for it to occur naturally. Overly frequent interruption can slow down the progress of the interview. Additionally, the language that the helper uses should be appropriate to the experiences and education of the helpee as well as natural for the helper. Although many pitfalls exist in the use of reflection, they can be overcome with practice (and more practice) and experience in attending to the feelings of another.

In summary, reflective statements should not only heighten in a nonthreatening way the helpee's awareness of his or her feelings but also assist the individual in realizing ownership of feelings. The helper's purpose is to understand the helpee's experience and to communicate to that person, "I am with you." Reflection may effectively enhance the helpee's understanding of self and others.

Summarization

During the helping interview, the helpee may sometimes wander and ramble along many diverse paths. The helper will need to bring these thoughts into focus by using the skill of summarization. Briefly, *summarization* brings together the several ideas expressed by the helpee. The goal of summarization is to integrate and present to the helpee a meaningful review of his or her comments. The helper needs to be aware of both the feeling and content of the helpee's message. Summarization differs from both reflection and paraphrasing in that it covers a broader time period. Summarization is concerned with the overriding emotional aspects of the conversation and/or the cognitive themes expressed by the helpee. From the helper's perspective, summarization provides an opportunity to confirm the accuracy of his or her perceptions of the helpee's message. It also demonstrates to the helpee that the listener has been "tuned in" to what he or she has said. As an example:

Therapist:	Our time today is almost up. Let's see, we've talked a lot about your worries over Barbara's behavior toward Billy and the effect that his cerebral palsy has on her social life. I think you realize now how important it is to keep the lines of communication open between Barbara and you.
Mother:	Yeah, you're right. I guess I've never given Barbara the chance to talk about how she feels about her younger brother.

Some helpers may, however, want the helpee to summarize as a test of their understanding.

Procedurally, summarization allows the dialogue to end on a natural note. It can be used as a way of emphasizing the accomplishments of a helping interview. A person could also structure ensuing interviews by reviewing, at the beginning, the highlights of the previous session (Ivey, 1971). Summarization is a shared responsibility of both helper and helpee.

Questioning

One of the more commonly used strategies in a helping relationship is the question. Many helpers could not conduct a helping interview without using questions—in fact, most helpers ask too many questions. Although the ability to skillfully pose questions is a valuable tool, questioning can be a two-edged sword. If misused, it can destroy a helping relationship. Questioning should be used primarily for fostering understanding and assisting the helpee. The goal should be to stimulate the helpee into further developing and exploring an issue as well as providing the helper with needed information. However, the primary beneficiary of questioning should be the helpee. Benjamin (1981) suggests that before querying the helpee, helpers should quiz themselves and determine if their questions will benefit or inhibit the helping interview.

Some helpers feel very comfortable in asking a lot of questions. But those who freely adopt this style may fail to realize that a pattern of helper-helpee behavior is being generated. Questions beget more questions, and soon the helpee learns what is expected of him or her. Spontaneous and free discussion fall by the wayside. The helpee becomes conditioned to waiting for the next question and then responding to that specific inquiry. Hence a stifling question-answer-question-answer format develops that is nonproductive and does not promote helpee growth. Also, the helper may be spending so much time thinking about the next question that he or she is unable to effectively attend to the helpee. However, as both Wittmer and Myrick (1974) and Benjamin (1981) have observed, an even greater danger exists. What this question-and-answer format communicates to the helpee is that the helper is the expert, the authority, and knows what is relevant and important. The helper is seen as superior, whereas the helpee is considered subordinate. As a result of this pattern of interrogation, the helpee expects the helper to present the solution to his or her problem. The pattern of thinking may be: "You asked all the questions and have all the answers; now, what is the verdict, what should I do, how should I proceed? If you don't have *the* answer or solution, why did you ask all those questions?" Obviously, this is not a desirable situation. It is, however, a predicament that could easily evolve from an overreliance on the question as a helping tool. Even so, properly used questions can be effective in the helping relationship.

There are many different types of questions and strategies for asking them. Some are more effective than others. The following categories of questions are organized according to what Wittmer and Myrick (1974) refer to as most person-centered and least person-centered questions. Most person-centered questions focus on the helpee and his or her ideas and feelings; least person-centered questions hinder personal reflection and growth and/or are offered from the helper's perspective.

Most person-centered questions

Open vs. closed questions   In terms of questioning style, this division is probably the most basic. Simply stated, open questions are broad and provide the helpee with an opportunity to explore his or her thoughts and feelings. Open questions allow the helpee freedom of expression without any artificial barriers established by the helper. In contrast, a closed question is constraining and narrow. A closed question forces the helpee to answer a question from the helper's perspective. Whereas open questions focus on feelings, closed ones generally concentrate on factual information. In its extreme form, the closed question can be answered simply yes or no, or in very few words, thereby limiting the helpee's opportunity for elaboration and exploration. Closed questions are generally designed to promote helper understanding rather than helpee understanding. They can also give the helpee the feeling that he or she is being cross-examined. The following examples demonstrate an open vs. closed questioning format:

Open:	"How do you feel about having a boss younger than you?"
	"What do you dislike about Christina?"
	"How do you feel when you are ignored?"
Closed:	"Do you like your new neighbors?"
	"Are you married?"
	"Are you happy with your grade?"

Questions that begin with "what" or "how" usually evoke elaborated responses; those starting with "do" or "are" generally require only a yes or no answer. Although open questions are more effective, closed ones do have their place in the helping interview—for example, to gather specific information that may help to clarify a situation. It is suggested, therefore, that a balance be struck between the use of open and closed questioning styles, depending upon the needs of the interview.

Least person-centered questions

Binding questions   Sometimes a question is asked for which an answer is not desired. This is the case with a binding question, where the answer is already contained within the question or at least strongly implied. Thus the helpee does not have an opportunity to provide an alternative response. It is an easy way for the helper to make a statement. As an example, "Everybody knows that Ellen is prejudiced against blacks; isn't that so?"

Soliciting agreement questions   A soliciting agreement question is a variation of the binding question. Although an answer is expected, the question is asked in such a way that the respondent is expected to agree with the questioner. To disagree would only invite confrontation or helper displeasure. For instance, "You really don't think you did a good job, do you?" or, "You didn't mean to hurt Cara, did you? It was an accident, wasn't it?"

Forced choice questions   This questioning strategy is sometimes referred to as the either-or question due to the restrictions it imposes on the response. The helper forces the helpee to choose from the possibilities offered, even though the helpee may prefer none of the options. For example, "Do you want milk or a diet soft drink?" or, "Do you want your next appointment in the early morning or late afternoon?" This is generally viewed as a poor questioning technique. No opportunity is provided for helpee input. The sole exception would be when only two choices are legitimately available.

Double-bind questions   On occasion a helpee may be trapped regardless of how he or she answers the query. The helpee is forced into a no-win situation in which he or she will be judged irrespective of the response given. The following examples illustrate the double-bind question: "Are you still beating your wife?" and, "Have you stopped stealing from your boss?"

The why question   The use of *why* is a notoriously poor questioning strategy. It is also potentially dangerous to the helping interview. Rather than benefiting a relationship and building trust, asking *why* hints at criticism or advice. The implication of the word *why* is that the person needs to modify his or her behavior. To many individuals the word historically signifies displeasure or disapproval. For example, "Why didn't you take Billy to the doctor's?" "Why don't you shave?" "Why can't you behave?" "Why are you late?" Thus people may feel threatened, judged, pushed, or prodded. As a consequence, they may withdraw, or feel the need to rationalize and defend themselves and, if possible, explain the reasons for their behavior. Too frequently, however, the helpee is unaware or uncertain of the reason or reasons behind his or her behavior. Therefore, he or she is likely to respond in a vague manner, which is probably unacceptable or unsatisfactory to the helper. Rather than focusing on the rational aspects of a person's actions, it may be better for the helper to initially explore the feelings behind the helpee's behavior. As Wittmer and Myrick (1974) observe, if one is truly interested in knowing the causes and motivation of a person's conduct, it is probably more appropriate to focus on the what, where, when, and how dimensions of that behavior. This perspective increases the possibility that the helpee will reveal more, gain additional insights, and maybe clarify those forces which might be contributing to his or her decision-making process. As an illustration, the helper might ask, "What is it about Mrs. Jones that you dislike?" instead of, "Why don't you like your supervisor?"

Helpee inquiries

Invariably the helpee will put the shoe on the other foot and direct questions to the helper. How should the helper handle such queries? There is no rule of thumb. However, helpers generally react to questions in a manner similar to that of the helpee—they feel threatened and often act defensively. Helpers are usually very good at asking questions, but quite poor at receiving them. First, the helper needs to guard against communicating an attitude of, "I do the asking and you do the answering." A helpee's inquiry should be treated with respect and should command the usual attentive listening. After all, it is a communication from the helpee and should be viewed as a means of expression. Benjamin (1981) also suggests that professionals should listen with the "third ear," being aware of the possibility that something may be concealed behind the helpee's request.

The manner in which the helper replies to the helpee's question could very well serve as a model for the helpee to emulate. The professional who treats the helpee's question in a sensitive, straightforward fashion and honestly responds in a helpful manner may bring the helpee to see the use of questions in a better light. Yet helper response is an individual choice. It depends on the status of the helping relationship, the nature of the helpee's inquiry, and whether a response is ethically appropriate and contributes to the helpee's growth and understanding.

The ability to ask questions effectively is not an easy task, and not all helpers will be able to meet the challenge of the question. Yet, as a basic tool, this instrument of helping is important to acquire. Too many helpers ask questions indiscriminately. An effective question should be helpful and provide the helpee with an opportunity to explore and enhance his or her understanding. Questions should generally be asked for the benefit of the helpee rather than the helper. Once the helper has asked a question, however, he or she must be prepared to stop and listen to the answer. As the proverb states, "He who asks questions cannot avoid the answers."

Barriers to effective helping

The preceding discussion of various types of leads was based on the helpee's internal frame of reference—that is, how things appeared to the helpee rather than the helper. This viewpoint was also seen as being most effective. Some helpers, however, rely on strategies that are very directive and focus more on the helper's perspective than the helpee's. The helper now becomes the central figure in the relationship rather than the helpee; he or she assumes an authority role. The helpee reacts to what the helper puts forth, as opposed to the helper's responding to the helpee's communication. This focus demands greater involvement and, in comparison to the skills discussed earlier, is generally considered less effective and even detrimental to the helping relationship.

The directive helper believes that the helpee requires his or her guidance in order to find solutions to concerns. In essence, the helper assumes, at least on a temporary basis, the responsibility for the helpee's concerns. Rather than benefiting the helpee, such a position fosters dependency and is an obstacle to helpee growth. The role of the helper also shifts. Before, the helper was content to restate what was said or reflect on the helpee's feelings; now, however, the helper assumes a role of guiding and instructing. The helper knows what is best for the helpee—and tells him so.

The following representative helper-centered strategies progress from those which minimally block helpee growth to those which can be considered major barriers or roadblocks.

Reassurance

When a helper reassures a helpee (for example, "Don't be afraid, I know that if you really try you can do it," or, "Don't worry, I'm sure everything will work out"), he or she is confirming a belief in the helpee's ability and potential to act and meet the challenge at hand. It is sort of a pat on the back, a vote of confidence. Yet supportive and reassuring statements also depreciate the helpee's view of the situation, belittle his or her judgment, and imply that the helpee's worries are unnecessary. The helpee's feelings are sometimes dismissed as ordinary—he or she really has nothing to worry about; the concerns are either unimportant or invalid. In this manner, the helper denies the helpee's feelings and perceptions, and as a result understanding is hindered. Besides, unless the helper could see into the future, he or she would really have no way of knowing how valid the helpee's concerns might be.

Interpretation

Interpretation is somewhat like a paraphrase or reflective statement in that it focuses on both the cognitive and affective elements of the helpee's statements. Yet, unlike these two facilitative skills, which concentrate on the helpee's frame of reference, interpretation adds a new dimension and is presented from the helper's viewpoint. For example:

| **Husband:** | I don't know if I like Lynn's new job. She works evenings and that leaves me to feed, bathe, and take care of Lonnie. I can't even bowl anymore. |
| **Therapist:** | The way I see it, you find it hard to accept your responsibilities as a father and a husband. |

Interpretation considers how things appear to the helper rather than the helpee, and thus shifts the responsibility for the interaction to the helper. Meanings or causes are attached to the helpee's messages, but they are filtered by the attitudes, feelings, and value system of the helper. An attempt is made to provide the helpee with a potentially effective way of viewing himself or herself or problems and concerns. The helper thinks diagnostically and tries to analyze or explain and make sense out of what the helpee is communicating, usually within the framework of a particular theoretical orientation. But Brammer (1979) considers interpretation to be an ineffective strategy and a hindrance to the helping process. The helper could easily get caught in thinking *about* or *ahead* of the helpee rather than *with* the helpee.

Often the helper's interpretive remarks meet with resistance or defensiveness because they are presented too early in the interview, lead too much, are too deep, or have negative implications for the helpee. Rather than benefiting the helpee and promoting growth, interpretation can become detrimental to the helping relationship. The final determination, however, of an interpretation's usefulness is if it assists the helpee in better understanding himself or herself and has application to new areas of the helpee's life.

Advice giving

Advice giving is a common, popular strategy considered by some to be the traditional role of helpers. It is not unusual to find advice columns in newspapers and magazines. A person can also obtain advice from religious leaders, uncles, automobile mechanics, neighbors, teachers, beauticians, parents, and sometimes even from perfect strangers. As a society, we seem programmed to both give and accept advice. Many individuals are quick to give advice or offer solutions, probably much more frequently than they realize. Frequently heard phrases include: "If I were you . . . ," "The best thing to do . . . ," "I think . . . ," or "One good way . . . " However, advice is often indiscriminately provided, generally ineffective, rarely accepted, and, in the context of a helping relationship, is a poor promoter of helpee growth and understanding.

Advice can be succinctly defined as telling someone else what to do or how to behave. An attempt is made to influence a person's actions and thinkings. A helper's pronouncements are based on his or her value system and frame of reference—the advice is given from the helper's perspective, not the helpee's. Advice giving provides the helper with expert status and maybe even a "father-knows-best" attitude. It also shifts the responsibility for the problem or concern from the helpee's shoulders to those of the helper. The helper now accepts ownership of the helpee's problem.

A basic question that the helper needs to answer is whether ethically or morally he or she has the right to determine a course of action for another human being. Equally reflective is the question of who will benefit from the advice given. Some helpers need to dominate and control, others need to give advice, and still others may have a vested interest in the advice they provide.

The helper who carefully analyzes the helpee's request ("What should I do?") will see that often what the helpee is really asking for is not advice but rather an empathetic ear and confirmation of what he or she believes should be done. It is not unusual to find that the helpee already has a solution formulated and only seeks outside approval for that course of action. Therefore, before offering advice, the helper should determine the helpee's views concerning the problem or situation, making certain that advice is being sought. If advice is truly required, the helper needs to elicit as much information as possible from the helpee. Many times this process of determining the helpee's perspective will serve as a catalyst and allow the helpee to discover his or her own solutions.

When a helper provides advice he or she runs the risk of having the advice rejected. If it is accepted, the helper could be blamed if the advice later appeared to be invalid or unprofitable.

If, however, the advice is perceived as beneficial, it is not uncommon to find the helpee returning again and again for additional wisdoms. The helper has established a dependency rather than provided the helpee with strategies for seeking his or her own solutions. This is a drawback to advice giving. It occurs because it is easier to provide advice than to become deeply involved and assist the helpee in successfully resolving dilemmas.

Circumstances do dictate that occasionally advice be given. If it is timely and relevant to the helpee, the advice may be useful. It is recommended, however, that rather than offering the traditional take-it-or-leave-it ultimatum, the helper might present a suggestion, a milder form of advice. Unlike advice that can generate defensiveness and is sometimes threateningly received, a genuine suggestion is couched in terms of hunches, tentative ideas, or possible avenues of action that the helpee can easily accept, reject, or modify. Compliance is not required and the helpee still remains at the controls and makes the final decision.

Mother:	I really can't decide whether to send Marvin to summer camp. We really can't afford it. He's never been away from home before and I wonder if the camp counselors can deal with his blindness. On the other hand, it really would be good for the entire family if Marvin was able to go for the two weeks. I think we all need the break. What do you think is best?
Helper:	The best thing to do is to find the money and send Marvin to camp.

This conversation could be contrasted with the following helper response:

Helper:	I really can't say what's best for the family and Marvin. Do you know if there is a day camp available? How about sending him to camp for only one week? Perhaps either one of these would be helpful.

Urging

Urging is another example of an ineffective lead. Basically, it is used when the helper perceives a lack of action on the part of the helpee. Previously agreed-on strategies or courses of action are not followed up or acted on. The helper, therefore, believes it is best to push, prod, and try to spur the helpee into action. Although initially an idea may have seemed good, the helpee's lack of response or hesitation should signal the possibility that it is now viewed as inappropriate or irrelevant. Rather than pushing ahead, the effective helper reanalyzes the situation, asking, "Whose idea is being advocated? For whose benefit am I trying to persuade the helpee?" Maybe the helpee has a better strategy.

It should be obvious by now that successful resolution of a problem or conflict needs to take place within the helpee's frame of reference, not the helper's. An idea that appears sound to the helper may not be practical or meaningful to the helpee. Therefore, urging or cajoling ("You ought to . . .") the helpee into action he or she does not believe in will probably harm the helping relationship.

Moralizing

According to Benjamin (1981), moralizing is a mixture of urging and advice giving with the addition of two new potent tactics, the sacred norms of society known as morals, and the conscience—the helpee's, helper's, or society's collective opinions. An attempt is made to motivate or change the helpee's behavior, to show him or her "the light." Moralizing places the helper in a superior position of knowing what is best; this posture implies both judgment (generally disapproval) and condescension. As a result, the helpee may become defensive and may challenge, rebel, or argue. Even if the helpee "wins," the price may have been exceedingly high. A helpee may also admit defeat and become submissive. All too often, when faced with such opposition, the helpee does not reveal his or her true feelings, but only presents a façade.

Moralizing, on occasion, has been known to be productive. More often than not, however, it represents the opposite of an effective helping relationship or, for that matter, any relationship. As Benjamin (1981) observes:

Moralizing can be overwhelming. At best, it helps the interviewee see how society judges him, how others look upon his behavior. At worst, it blocks examination of self and self-motivated action and stifles further expression of feelings and attitudes. It can result in insightless submission or stubborn defiance. (p. 146)

Ridicule and sarcasm

This technique usually masks its true intent in the form of sharp and biting teasing. The goal is to demonstrate to the helpee the ridiculousness and absurdity of his or her feelings and/or perceptions. The helper mocks or makes fun of the helpee in order to influence his or her thinking or behavior and to get the helpee to behave "sensibly," as others (especially the helper) do.

Scolding and threatening

When a helper scolds or threatens a helpee, he or she admonishes that individual to do better or to remedy behavior. The helper has evaluated the actions and feelings of the helpee and decided that they are inappropriate and require correction—hence the helper administers a verbal spanking or tongue thrashing. When threats are involved, the helpee is warned that his or her present course of action will force the helper to take certain steps, usually punitive or unpleasant, if he or she persists with the current behavior.

Lichter (1976, p. 68) articulates some of the various barriers to an effective helping relationship. Using the scenario of a young mother who enrolls her handicapped child in a preschool program but fails to maintain regular attendance, he provides the following examples of ineffective strategies.

Ordering:	"You must bring Cindy to class on a more regular basis."
Admonishing:	"If you don't bring her to school you'll be sorry later on."
Exhorting:	"You shouldn't act like this."

Moralizing:	"It's your responsibility as a parent to see that Cindy gets all the help she needs."
Preaching:	"You should show more respect for education."
Advising:	"Let me suggest that you bring the child more often."
Blaming:	"You're doing Cindy a lot of harm."
Psychoanalyzing:	"You're just afraid to face the truth about Cindy's handicap."
Ridiculing:	"You're acting like a little child yourself."
Lecturing:	"Handicapped children need this kind of early intervention."
Questioning:	"Why don't you come more often?"
Humoring:	"Maybe you'll be lucky and break your leg so you won't have to come more often."
Criticizing:	"You're not behaving very rationally."
Persuading with logic:	"Don't you realize that early intervention can minimize the effects of the handicapping condition?"

A final word

A helping relationship can be either promoted or hindered, depending on how helpers employ the many skills available to them. Skills alone, however, do not produce an effective helper; they are only the tools with which the helper constructs a helping environment. Helping is a process requiring the union of the helper's affective characteristics and certain learned skills. There are no guidelines or rules to tell a helper when to paraphrase or when to keep silent. Likewise, some individuals feel very comfortable in providing advice, and others may believe that sarcasm and ridicule have a place in the helping relationship. In the final analysis, the only true criterion of whether helpers have used themselves and their skills effectively is if the helpee perceives that he or she has been understood and helped.

> *Giving advice is sometimes only showing our wisdom at the expense of another.*
>
> —Lord Anthony Shaftesbury

References

Benjamin, A. (1981). *The helping interview* (3rd ed.). Boston: Houghton Mifflin.

Brammer, L. (1977). Who can be a helper? *Personnel and Guidance Journal, 55,* 303–308.

Brammer, L. (1979). *The helping relationship: Process and skills* (2nd ed.). Englewood Cliffs, NJ: Prentice-Hall.

Buchheimer, A., & Balogh, S. (1961). *The counseling relationship.* Chicago: Science Research Associates.

Combs, A., Avila, D., & Purkey, W. (1971). *Helping relationships: Basic concepts for the helping professions.* Boston: Allyn & Bacon.

Ivey, A. (1971). *Microcounseling: Innovations in interviewing training.* Springfield, IL: Charles C Thomas.

Kroth, R. (1975). *Communicating with parents of exceptional children.* Denver: Love.

Lichter, P. (1976). Communicating with parents: It begins with listening. *Teaching Exceptional Children, 8,* 66–71.

Reik, T. (1972). *Listening with the third ear.* New York: Farrar, Straus, & Giroux.

Robinson, F. (1950). *Principles and procedures in student counseling.* New York: Harper and Brothers.

Rogers, C. (1957). The necessary and sufficient conditions of therapeutic personality change. *Journal of Consulting Psychology, 21,* 95–103.

Seligman, M. (1979). *Strategies for helping parents of exceptional children.* New York: Free Press.

Shertzer, B., & Stone, S. (1980). *Fundamentals of counseling* (3rd ed.). Boston: Houghton Mifflin.

Stewart, J. (1978). *Counseling parents of exceptional children.* Columbus, OH: Charles Merrill.

Webster, E. (1977). *Counseling with parents of handicapped children.* New York: Grune & Stratton.

Wittmer, J., & Myrick, R. (1974). *Facilitative teaching: Theory and practice.* Santa Monica, CA: Goodyear.

Chapter 7:
The helping relationship

No finer aim can man attain than to alleviate another's pain.

—Alexander Pope

Approaches or strategies for helping are frequently organized along a continuum. Some helping relationships have an authoritarian flavor to them, in which the helper is the leading character and clearly in charge. The helpee thus comes to rely on the expertise of the helper. On the other end of the continuum, helping could be categorized as a democratic relationship in which helper and helpee work together. This philosophy is characterized by understanding and mutual respect. The helper is seen as a facilitator rather than a leader. Regardless of how a person views helping, the common denominator is the helping relationship, that is, the environment or arena in which change takes place.

The real power of helping lies within the relationship. No two helping relationships are exactly alike, just as no two helpees or helpers are alike. Each helping relationship possesses its own unique characteristics. It is extremely difficult to reduce such a relationship into its various components; just by its nature, the helping relationship is greater than its individual elements. One cannot meaningfully separate the art from the science, the skills from the feelings.

Understanding the helping relationship

Defining a helping relationship is an elusive task; it is easier to speak in generalities than specifics. For example, Rogers (1961) talks about "a relationship in which at least one of the parties has the intent of promoting the growth, development, maturity, improved functioning, and improved coping with life of the other" (pp. 39–40). More recently, Brammer (1979) has concluded that a helping "relationship is the principal process vehicle for both helper and helpee to express and fulfill their needs, as well as to mesh helpee problems with helper expertise" (p. 45). Figure 7.1 shows how Brammer sees the helping relationship from the perspective of the helper and helpee.

Although the essence of a helping relationship is diminished when one attempts to discern its various features, both Rogers (1961), through a series of searching and penetrating questions, and Brammer (1979; Brammer & Shostrom, 1977) have endeavored to describe the helping process. Rogers asks (pp. 50–55):

1. Can I *be* in some way which will be perceived by the other person as trustworthy, as dependable or consistent in some deep sense?

2. Can I be expressive enough as a person that what I am will be communicated unambiguously?

3. Can I let myself experience positive attitudes toward this other person—attitudes of warmth, caring, liking, interest, respect?

4. Can I be strong enough as a person to be separate from the other?

5. Am I secure enough within myself to permit him his separateness?

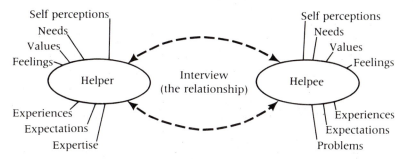

Figure 7.1   The helping relationship in the interview. Lawrence M. Brammer, *The Helping Relationship: Process and Skills,* 2nd ed., © 1979, p. 45. Reprinted by permission of Prentice-Hall, Inc., Englewood Cliffs, N.J.

6. Can I let myself enter fully into the world of his feelings and personal meaning and see these as he does?

7. Can I receive him as he is? Can I communicate this attitude?

8. Can I act with sufficient sensitivity in the relationship that my behavior will not be perceived as a threat?

9. Can I free him from the threat of external evaluation?

10. Can I meet this other individual as a person who is in the process of *becoming,* or will I be bound by his past and my past?

Following are examples of various dimensions of the helping relationship that Brammer (1979) and Brammer and Shostrom (1977) believe contribute to the overall quality of the helping experience.

1. *Uniqueness-Commonality.* Each helper-helpee interaction forms a unique human relationship that is as diverse as the individuals involved. As suggested in Chapter 5, helping relationships can be considered extensions of ordinary interpersonal associations, yet they do possess certain singular aspects. For instance, a helper is unusually accepting of the helpee and can be objective as well as emotionally involved while providing help within a structured framework. However, as Brammer and Shostrom note,

helping relationships have much in common with friendships, family interactions, and other human engagements—when reduced to their basic elements, all look very much alike.

2. *Objectivity-Subjectivity.* A helping relationship is also a paradoxical relationship. On the one hand, the helper must be deeply and warmly interested in the helpee, but on the other hand a certain psychological distance needs to be maintained. A balance must be struck between emotional involvement and helper objectivity. Helpers need to communicate that they care and understand, yet they must also be able to rationally examine the helpee's situation while maintaining control of their own feelings.

3. *Ambiguity-Clarity.* A further dimension of helping relationships is whether they are perceived by helpees as being either vague or structured. The dilemma presented here is that if the relationship is too ambiguous, the helpee may become anxious or drift into social conversation instead of exploring his or her true feelings or concerns. Conversely, a highly structured relationship requires the helpee to respond within a narrowly perceived framework, thus extinguishing possible avenues of significance and interest. To resolve this problem, helper and helpee must jointly decide on the objective of the relationship and then establish a level of ambiguity agreeable with their purpose.

4. *Trust-Distrust.* Trust is a crucial component of helping relationships, one of the cornerstones on which relationships are constructed. Generally, people will only accept help from individuals they trust. Trust is evidenced by both verbal and nonverbal actions perceived by the helpee as being trustworthy. People are more likely to reveal themselves if they believe that the helper is being open, honest, and sincere in the relationship. Distrust is generated when offers of help, for whatever reason, are apparently rejected or resented by the helpee. The helper, sensing this resistance, increases his or her efforts, often beginning a vicious cycle of events eventually leading to the destruction of the relationship. Helpees should always be free to accept or reject

a helping relationship and the conditions under which it is offered.

The intent of this chapter is not to define the helping relationship per se, but rather to explore several aspects normally encountered when helping another human being. The position taken falls between those that argue that helping is a highly structured venture that can be precisely defined and documented and those that consider helping as an extension of a naturally evolving process between two people.

The helper's purpose

The vast majority of human behavior is purposeful. "Each of us always behaves in terms of what seems to be important and appropriate" (Combs, Avila, & Purkey, 1971, p. 15). Therefore, how helpers view their purpose affects their role in the helping relationship. Helping is, in part, a by-product of certain intentions. Combs and his colleagues (1971) identify the following purposes of effective helpers:

1. *Freeing-Controlling.* Helpers perceive their purpose as one of freeing rather than of controlling people—that is to say, the helper sees the purpose of the helping task as one of assisting, releasing, and facilitating rather than as a matter of controlling, manipulating, coercing, blocking, or inhibiting behavior.

2. *Larger issues–Smaller ones.* Helpers tend to be more concerned with larger rather than smaller issues. They tend to view events in a broad rather than a narrow perspective. They are concerned with the larger connotations of events and with more extensive implications rather than with the immediate and specific. They are not exclusively concerned with details, but can perceive beyond the immediate to the future.

3. *Self-revealing–Self-concealing.* Helpers are more likely to be self-revealing than self-concealing. They are willing to disclose the self. They can treat their feelings and shortcomings as important and significant rather than hide or cover them up. They seem willing to be themselves.

4. *Involved-Alienated.* Helpers tend to be personally involved with rather than alienated from the people they work with. The helper sees his appropriate role as one of commitment to the helping process and willingness to enter into interaction, as opposed to being inert or remaining aloof or remote from interaction.

5. *Process-oriented–Goal-oriented.* Helpers are concerned with furthering processes rather than achieving goals. They seem to see their appropriate role as one of encouraging and facilitating the process of search and discovery as opposed to promoting or working toward a personal goal or preconceived solution.

6. *Altruistic-Narcissistic.* Helpers have altruistic purposes rather than narcissistic ones. Their purposes are more oriented toward aiding and assisting other people rather than attending to their own personal or selfish goals. (pp. 15–16)

Helping goals

Broadly stated, the goal of most helpers, regardless of their background, is to bring about a change within the helpee. It is hoped that this change allows the individual to function in a more effective and personally satisfying manner. The helping relationship is the primary vehicle for accomplishing this goal. The helper's task is to establish a psychological environment in which the helpee is provided with the freedom needed for exploration and personal decision making.

When addressing goals appropriate to parents of exceptional children, Telford and Sawrey (1981) are more specific. They consider counseling goals to be essentially intellectual, emotional, and behavioral in nature. Intellectually, parents need diagnostic information, that is, information pertaining to the nature and extent of their child's disability as well as facilities and available services. Yet, as an exclusive goal of helping, this objective falls short of its mark. An intellectual approach to a highly emotional situation is notoriously inadequate. It is extremely important that parents be assisted in understanding their attitudes and feelings. These beliefs must be explored and openly dealt with prior to planning for the child and his or her family. As Telford and Sawrey observe, parents' feelings often carry more weight than their intellect. Finally, helping should result in the modified behavior of the parents with specific plans and practical suggestions for the family and the handicapped child.

Over two decades ago, Roos (1963) offered the following goal, which is still appropriate today. Roos believes that the helper's "goal should be to help the parents reach their decisions with as full an awareness as possible of their own feelings and of the reality of the situation" (p. 348). Likewise, Smith and Neisworth (1975) suggest that one aim of helping parents of exceptional children is to bring them to a realistic understanding of conditions as they are. The exceptional child can only be helped if those closest to him or her are able to recognize and accept his or her unique assets and liabilities. In a similar vein, Stewart (1978) recommends that when working with parents of exceptional children, helpers should have as their objective a better understanding of the difficulties created by the presence of a handicapped child in the family.

Although helpers are able to articulate both general and specific goals, most parents, according to Telford and Sawrey (1981), are universally dissatisfied with their contacts with professionals. One mother described her experiences with various doctors as "a masterful combination of dishonesty, condescension, misinformation, and bad manners" (Bennett, 1974, pp. 7–8). Murray (1959), a parent of a mentally retarded child, ably summed up the greatest need of parents as "constructive professional counseling at various stages in the child's life which will enable us as parents to find the answers to our own individual problems to a reasonably satisfactory degree" (p. 1087).

The following passionate plea by a mother of a young woman with multiple handicaps should guide helpers as they work with parents to formulate appropriate, meaningful goals.

The next time you are faced with a handicapped child and his or her family, don't be so ready to make judgments. If the child has only one visible handicap, don't automatically assume that that is all you have to deal with. If a parent comes across as very verbal and competent, don't assume that they have everything under control, or that they are cold and unfeeling. Listen for the little clues that tell you that the intellectualizing is their way of handling feelings that are too painful to surface easily. Don't be easily misled if the child is pretty and has a winning smile and seems very docile in your presence. Listen, really listen, to what the parents tell you about the child at home. And, perhaps most importantly of all, help parents to admit to feelings of grief, and shame, and anger, and tiredness, and despair. If you do that, you will not only help parents to seek the fulfillment of their own personal lives, but you will have helped immeasurably to make the child's personal burden much lighter. (Baxter, 1977, pp. 7–8)

The helping setting

The physical setting in which helping occurs is a matter of some importance. Helping can take place in a variety of locations. Not all helpers have private offices. Some individuals hold sessions in a vacant classroom or unoccupied conference room. Regardless of where the helping interview is conducted, some basic principles need to be observed.

First and foremost is the helpee's right to auditory and visual privacy. Very few people would wish to enter into a helping relationship in which privacy could not be assured. The dialogue between helpee and helper should never be overheard by third parties, nor should the helpee feel as though he or she is on display or being watched by others. These two conditions are important prerequisites and their absence can quickly destroy any trust or confidence the helpee may have placed in the helper.

Related to this is the expectation that a helping interview will be free from interruptions by colleagues, secretaries, or telephone calls. A helpee has the right to expect, maybe even demand, the helper's undivided attention. Interruptions should be avoided as much as possible, for they only impede the helping process. Frequent external distractions can completely sabotage a helping experience.

The question of seating arrangements repeatedly arises. There is no clear guidance to be offered; often how chairs are arranged is a matter of personal preference or is dictated by the location of the helping interview—for example, in a vacant office. Most people believe, however, that sitting behind a large desk signifies an authoritarian position and presents a barrier to effective interpersonal communication. Some helpers, especially beginning ones, feel more comfortable with a large piece of furniture between themselves and the helpee. Still, while nearly everyone has a sense of personal space, helpers need to remember that as the physical distance between people increases, so does the mental distance. If possible, helpers should experiment with various arrangements until they discover the one that is best for them. An optimal arrangement of furniture allows both helper and helpee a clear view of each other at a comfortable distance.

If, as Benjamin (1981) suggests, the helper's goal is to secure an atmosphere conducive to open communication, a helping environment must be established that is not overwhelming, noisy, or distracting. Help should be provided in a location that is comfortable, attractive, and reflects the personal taste of the helper.

The helping interview

Helping occurs within the framework of a relationship that is special and distinct from ordinary human encounters. It is here that one individual endeavors to aid or assist another. The primary tool at the helper's disposal is the interview. A helping interview is more than just ordinary conversation. It is a unique process, an active and purposeful exchange of dialogue between helpee and helper, proceeding in an orderly fashion. It may be used to transmit information, to try to change attitudes, or to provide support and reassurance. Regardless of the purpose, a helping interview is characterized by teamwork, with honesty, understanding, and mutual respect as its bench marks.

Helping interviews proceed through various phases or stages, outlined as follows:

Phase I: the initial interview

The initial interview is generally the most difficult and yet the most important. It is the first exposure of helpee to helper, both of whom may be somewhat uncertain as to what this encounter will hold for them. Each helpee has certain expectations and a variety of emotions that will affect his or her behavior in the helping relationship. Similarly, the helper's actions are influenced by his or her perceptions of the helpee and their theoretical persuasion.

People's reasons for seeking help are as varied as the individuals themselves. Yet it is axiomatic that a person cannot be helped unless he or she wishes to be helped. Some helpees possess a low motivation to change; others, even if self-referred, may be reluctant or defensive about entering into a helping relationship. One explanation for this behavior is the fear that some individuals have of confronting their feelings in an open and honest fashion. More basic than this, however, is a myth perpetuated by and strongly rooted in our culture. Specifically, this myth states that seeking help for an emotional problem or conflict is an admission of weakness and vulnerability. This runs counter to the American pioneer spirit of self-reliance, independence, "pulling oneself up by the bootstraps," and solving one's own problems. Individuals will readily seek out a physician for a medical problem and will even share such experiences at social gatherings, but very few people will admit to seeking assistance for emotional ailments. People avoid sharing this information for fear of what others will think. It is within this framework, then, that the initial interview occurs.

The primary objective of the initial interview is to secure a sound working relationship with the helpee, that is, to lay the foundation from which help can be offered. This calls for the helper not only to establish rapport with the helpee but also to create an environment where the helpee can safely explore his or her concerns and feelings.

It is not easy to ask for help, nor is it unusual for a helpee to have trouble explaining his or her reason(s) for desiring help. Some helpees have only a vague notion of discomfort or distress, whereas others are highly anxious and desire help due to specific concerns or needs. The helper must be sensitive to the helpee's feelings and expectations as the helping process begins. It is at this point that the skill of active listening comes into focus.

The helper's task in the initial interview is to be both verbally and nonverbally receptive. A forum must be provided in which the helpee can freely express himself or herself. The helper's goal should be to understand the helpee's concerns from his or her perspective—that is, how things appear to the helpee. This requires that a dialogue be established between helpee and helper. However, helpees may be reluctant or unable to verbalize their concerns. If the helpee is incapable of taking the initiative—and many will be—vague and nondirectional leads or openers will be needed. Most helpees experience a natural hesitancy, but ordinary conversation can be an effective technique for initiating the required communication. Examples of such simple and neutral openers are: "I understand you asked to see me," or, "I hope you did not find parking to be a problem. I know how difficult it is to find a parking spot at this hour." In some instances, it may be necessary to use a more specific strategy, such as, "Good morning. I'm Joan Koth, the seventh grade guidance counselor. Please feel free to discuss Margaret's class schedule with me." Helpers should avoid any reference to a problem and allow the helpee to guide or lead the direction of the initial conversation. During this early contact, the helper should also suspend judgment about the helpee and the nature of his or her difficulties. Active listening and reflection are the immediate assignments.

As part of the initial interview, or in some instances shortly after it, the helper needs to structure the helping experience for the helpee. Very few individuals approach a helping situation with a complete and accurate understanding of the nature and function of the relationship. Simply defined, *structuring* is explaining the helping process to the helpee. According to Brammer (1979), "structuring defines the nature, limits, and goals of the prospective helping relationship. During this process the roles, responsibilities, and possible commitments of both helpee and helper are outlined" (p. 58). Generally, this objective is accomplished by a few sentences rather than a detailed description or lecture about the process. By providing this framework the helper hopes to eliminate any misconceptions and affords the helpee an idea about the purpose and direction of their endeavors. Here is an illustration depicting the process:

Teacher: I think it's good that we're talking about Bob's stealing. It's become a problem at school, too. I think by working together we can accomplish a great deal. Between the two of us, we should be able to develop some strategies and good ideas. You can then decide which ones are best for you. If Monday afternoons are convenient for you, we can plan to meet for the next couple of weeks.

| **Parent:** | Sounds good. My husband and I are very concerned about this. We realize it's our problem but appreciate your willingness to help us. |

In addition, structuring can help reduce any anxiety the helpee may have about the helping process. Many individuals may be experiencing their first exposure to a helping relationship. Hence some helpees may possess, as a result of the media and popular press, inaccurate ideas about helpers and what happens when a person seeks help. For instance, certain helpees anticipate that they will be psychoanalyzed. Others may believe that the helper has magical cures or is proficient at reading minds; still others may presume that helpers know what they are really thinking and will betray these thoughts to others. Structuring often allays these fears, decreases helpee misunderstanding, and clarifies the true intent of the helping interview.

The formality of structuring the helping interview varies considerably. Some helpers believe that the relationship must be explicitly interpreted to the helpee, whereas others prefer that it emerge naturally. There is no clear evidence as to which strategy is preferable. Helpers will need to carefully examine each helping situation and make their own determinations as to the type of orientation needed. Some helpees, due to their particular circumstances, will require a formal framework from which assistance can be provided. Other situations will dictate a more casual and informal style. Likewise, the helper's theoretical and philosophical beliefs about helping will also influence his or her actions. Regardless of whether a formal or informal format is adopted by the helper, an orientation to the helping process must be communicated to the helpee.

Brammer and Shostrom (1977) recommend that certain limits be conveyed to the helpee as part of the structuring process. Time limitations should be shared with the helpee—not only how much time is available for each helping interview, but also an estimate of how much time will be required for the entire process. Also, although helpers do not inhibit verbal expression, restrictions are imposed on actions that may result in physical harm or damage to property. The third limitation addresses the helper's role. In certain circumstances the helper occupies a position of authority in the helpee's life because he or she wears two hats, for example, teacher-helper or supervisor-helper. Under these conditions it is vital that the helper's role be clearly explained to the helpee. Succinctly stated, the helpee needs to know "where the helper is coming from." Finally, procedural or process limitations need to be discussed with the helpee. If the helping interview is to be at all successful, the helpee must accept his or her share of responsibility for the interview. The helpee must also understand that open and honest expression of feelings is both legitimate and important. No topic is too sacred or taboo for discussion purposes. Furthermore, helpees need to appreciate that it is their perspective of the particular situation, not the helper's, that is crucial. These process values may evolve naturally during the course of the interview, or they may be specifically mentioned by the helper.

Another concern in the helper's early contacts with the helpee is that attention be directed toward affective considerations. Feelings of trust and respect need to be engendered. The helpee should perceive the helper as a warm, genuine, and understanding individual, someone he or she can have confidence in. What the helpee does not need, however, is pity. Helpers are empathetic rather than sympathetic. These initial helpee impressions of helper attitudes and actions can either enhance or impede the overall helping experience.

As the initial exposure to the helping interview draws to a close, helper and helpee should jointly formulate their future plans. The helpee, however, always retains the freedom to accept or reject any proposed course of action. Misconceptions about purpose and process should also be clarified before the interview is closed. Tyler (1969) eloquently phrases the significance of the initial interview:

The initial interview is the hardest part of our task—the part that demands from us the most intensive concentration. Each person constitutes for us a new adventure in understanding. Each is destined to broaden our own lives in directions as yet uncharted. Each initial interview renews our appreciation of the challenge and the fascination of the counseling task. (p. 63)

Phase II: exploration

After establishing the foundation for the helping relationship, both helpee and helper are in a position to move forward and more deeply explore the helpee's feelings and concerns. For some individuals this may be immediate; others will require additional time and exposure to the helper. Generally, helpees need to feel secure in a relationship and experience acceptance prior to commencing deeper exploration.

Feelings and concerns expressed during the initial contact with the helper are sometimes vague and poorly phrased. Thus, before beginning to explore the person's problems, the helper needs to obtain a clear understanding of those problems. Great caution must be exercised at this point. Often the helpee's initial remarks regarding his or her concerns or reasons for seeking help are far removed from the actual issues. Helpers need to guard against responding to surface messages rather than the authentic concerns of the helpee. The helpee's early comments may in fact only represent those concerns which he or she is comfortable acknowledging at that time. Helpers must be sensitive to this matter and capable of distinguishing between irrelevant themes and central or core concerns. A helper should not assume, however, that there is always a "hidden agenda." Not all people camouflage their reasons for desiring assistance. The following example illustrates an episode in which a dual meaning was evident.

A client was once bitterly complaining about the forty-five-minute bus ride her young mentally retarded, cerebral-palsied son had to endure. This mother related in detail all the difficulty she experienced in getting him fed, dressed, and ready for his daily pre-school experience. Yet, as the relationship progressed and matured, it became evident that her reason for seeking help was unrelated to what she initially described. It became apparent that underlying her concern was the absence of her spouse's assistance. Mrs. S. eventually told how her husband left for work every morning before the child awoke and returned home only after he felt certain he wouldn't have to interact with the son he was ashamed of. Her genuine problem focused on her husband's bitterness and rejection at being the father of a boy who wouldn't grow up to be the son he had always wanted and envisioned. Thus any action aimed at developing a better morning routine or rescheduling activities would have been both premature and ineffectual in assisting Mrs. S. to resolve her problem.

Such incidents highlight the importance of allowing the helpee to guide the direction of the helping interview. Helpees' concerns will emerge according to their perceptions of the situation. Hence active listening and the appropriate use of reflective and clarifying statements are necessary. These skills will not only help clarify the nature of the helpee's difficulty, but will also assist in establishing a climate where empathetic understanding and acceptance are manifested.

The exploratory phase is a working stage (Brammer, 1979). The helper's objective is to support the helpee in examining his or her feelings and problems in greater detail and depth. It is also the point of contact where earlier dialogue is initially translated into *tentative* plans of action. In this regard, Stewart (1978) states that "the counselor and client, working together, attempt to examine as many facets of the difficulty as possible so that an appropriate plan of action can be formulated" (p. 43).

According to Brammer (1979, p. 61), two key questions need to be answered at this stage: (1) "What changes in helpees' behavior are appropriate and needed to achieve their goals? and (2) What strategies for intervention will most likely produce these outcomes?" Although responses will vary with the nature of the helpee's concerns, it is recommended that affective considerations be dealt with before cognitive matters. If the helpee's difficulty is to be resolved successfully, the feelings and emotional content of the concern must be openly explored and discussed before any attempt is made at investigating appropriate behavioral alternatives. This is especially relevant for the helper working with parents of exceptional children. Being the parent of a handicapped person is an emotionally laden event (see Chapter 2). Therefore, rather than initially focusing on diagnostic information, treatment plans, management suggestions or educational opportunities, it is suggested that the helper explore with both parents their feelings and attitudes about themselves and their son or daughter. Exploring and understanding feelings are prerequisite to executing a plan of action.

Tentative plans of action emerge from joint exploration of the helpee's situation. These strategies provide the framework for further discussion. Yet, as helpee and helper move forward and possible solutions and alternatives are investigated, it is the helpee's prerogative to decide which avenues are worthy of additional examination. It is not the helper's responsibility to decide which course of action is best for the helpee. Helpers only assist in the process; the helpee is solely accountable for his or her decision. Helpers need to remember that it is the helpee who has to carry out the plan, not them. A good rule of thumb is that helpees are the masters of their own fate, therefore, they should assume the major responsibility for their decisions (Stewart, 1978).

During this period of exploration it is not unusual for the helpee to experience a preliminary sensation that all is well, that his or her problem is resolved. Generally, this "flight into wellness" is premature. In some instances termination of the helping interview may be appropriate; however, more than likely this feeling of elation or success is only the result of initial discussions and does not represent true emotional or behavioral change. Aspects of the helpee's situation have been explored, but underlying alterations have yet to occur. One abusive parent wanted to end a helping relationship because he had not hit his child in over a month. His relief was evident, but he and the helper had not yet fully explored his feelings or their consequences in relation to his actions.

A final characteristic of this stage mentioned by Brammer (1979) is the possibility of helpee disillusionment and discouragement. It is not easy to explore inner feelings or have weaknesses exposed. For some, this can be an unpleasant encounter. Helpees may sense a loss of control or feel uncomfortable about the helping process and wish to terminate the relationship. This dilemma needs to be honestly discussed. If the relationship is too painful, termination may be a viable alternative. Yet if the helper provides support and encouragement and explains that many individuals experience anxiety at this time, the helpee may be able to overcome this critical hurdle (Brammer & Shostrom, 1977).

Phase III: action

As helpee and helper enter into the third phase and commence movement toward the helpee's goal, a transition occurs. The helper begins to take a more active role and increases the level of his or her supportive involvement. A change is also observed in the helpee's environment. In earlier dialogues, concerns and difficulties were often perceived as external; the helpee assumed little or no responsibility for their particular circumstance. In this third phase there is a shift from an external perspective to an internal posture. Rather than viewing difficulties as divorced from himself or herself, the helpee assumes an increased sense of personal responsibility for the situation and acknowledges ownership of the problem.

Tentative plans of action presently give way to more specific helping goals. In contrast to the exploratory behaviors of the preceding working stage, the action stage is distinguished by the helpee's commitment to performance. Talk is translated into action. Rather than discussing various alternatives or solutions, the helpee now puts into operation the content of previous interviews. This phase is similar to Brammer's (1979) concept of consolidation wherein the helpee explores alternatives, works through feelings, or practices new skills. Obviously, this task is easier if the helpee has personally decided on the course of action rather than responded to helper proposals. However, as the helpee embarks on his or her journey toward change, an element of risk is present. The helpee may, for example, experience setbacks, meet resistance from other people, or find that conditions will get worse before they get better. All of these factors could contribute to an early withdrawal from the helping relationship. The helper, therefore, must be supportive of the helpee's actions and point out that progress, although slow, is being made largely due to the helpee's efforts.

It is difficult to accurately indicate a time frame for this or any other stage. Yet the brevity of this discussion should in no way be interpreted as an indication of the importance of the action stage or how much time helpee and helper commit to it.

Phase IV: termination

Eventually all helping interviews and the relationship itself come to an end. But termination is not always easy. Beginning helpers as well as some experienced ones find closing to be a difficult task. This may partly be due to helper uncertainty about how to terminate. There is no preferred way of closing, nor are there prescribed formulas. Closing style is often determined by the participants and the content of the interview. Benjamin (1981) suggests that closing statements be short and to the point. Telling the helpee that his or her time is up is generally viewed as inadequate—yet the interview and ultimately the relationship must be terminated.

Terminating the interview   Helping interviews are generally circumscribed by time, either the helpee's or, more likely, the helper's. This time limitation provides an opportunity to end the interview on a natural note. Most helpees, however, are unaware of or insensitive to the amount of time available to them. A statement such as, "Our time together is almost over," communicates this temporal framework without giving the helpee the impression that he or she is being evicted. Even so, some helpees will still have to be escorted to the door.

Interviews are best ended on a positive chord. The helper can effectively close by reviewing with the helpee what has occurred during the interview or by asking the helpee to summarize and give his or her perceptions of the helping experience. The intent of having the helpee summarize accomplishments is to bring the discussion together and to ascertain what the next step might be. Furthermore, summarization helps decrease the helpee's feelings of ambiguity or unfinished business. Termination is generally a joint undertaking, with both helpee and helper actively participating. Helpers, for example, can put forth summary statements and ask for helpee clarification and verification—or if definite responsibilities were decided on or assignments given, then these can be jointly reviewed.

Principal:	Okay, let's see . . . as I understand it, you've been very concerned about Christina's excessive homework due to her being in the program for gifted children. You think better communication is needed between all the teachers. Christina is being penalized for being fortunate enough to be involved in the program.
Parent:	True. Her fourth grade teachers expect her to finish all their work even though she is out of the classroom two hours a day.
Principal:	Fine, let me talk with the teachers and I'll be back in touch with you before the end of the week.
Parent:	Thank you. I feel better. This has been bothering me since the beginning of the school year.

Helpers will invariably encounter helpees who defer new and possibly important material until the final moments of the interview. Thus the helper is hesitant to terminate without discussing "just one more thing" with the helpee. Yet Benjamin (1981) strongly believes that no new information should be discussed—closing should focus on what has already taken place. Moreover, this delay tactic could be a manipulative ploy employed by some helpees to control the interview and/or the helper. If new information is presented, it should be deferred and put on the agenda for future meetings. Frequently the helper will be torn between the desire to pursue this new line of thinking with the helpee and personal or professional commitments that preclude further action. Although interviews function best within prescribed time frames, helpers should also maintain a degree of flexibility. Effective helping cannot take place when the helper always has one eye on his or her watch. Under most circumstances, clear communication of the amount of time available for the helping interview minimizes the occurrence of this bothersome last-minute conduct.

It is important that termination occur smoothly. The helpee should depart with positive feelings about the helping contact. Often what transpires in the final minutes of the interview influences the helpee's opinion of the entire experience and sets the tone for future interviews.

Terminating the relationship   Finally the helpee and helper realize that it is time to terminate their relationship. Ideally, this should be a joint decision. The helpee has reached his or her helping goal or else believes that he or she no longer requires the helper's assistance. As Brammer (1979) notes, there is a natural awareness that "this is the end." Generally the helpee is eager to leave and continue alone. Feelings of gratitude are often communicated, or the helpee may even express resentment that he or she needed the helper's assistance in the first place.

In some instances termination occurs before the helpee obtains his or her objective. This may happen for a variety of reasons. Although it is not the desired outcome, helpers can never guarantee that a relationship will always be successful, nor can a helpee be forced to continue in a relationship. If appropriate, a referral to another helper should be considered.

The process of closing a relationship parallels in some ways that of terminating an interview. A summary occurs and the helpee is encouraged to review his or her accomplishments. The helper may also wish to leave the door open for future contacts, should they be needed. It is hoped, however, that the attainments of the preceding interviews will continue beyond the final termination period. "The outcome of counseling should lead to a general improvement not only in the client's ability to cope with himself, but also in his ability to meet the situational demands of daily functioning" (Stewart, 1978, p. 44).

Referrals

It is a wise helper who knows when to refer a helpee. A referral, the act of transferring a helpee to another helper or agency for specialized assistance (Stewart, 1978), can occur at any point in the relationship prior to termination. Referrals are generally for the benefit of the helpee and arise due to a variety of reasons. For instance, a cardinal rule of helping states that the helper must be honest about his or her abilities and limitations. Thus, if the helper is confronted with a situation beyond his or her level of competency, he or she is ethically bound to initiate a referral. A helper cannot be expected to meet the needs of everyone. Referrals may also be initiated because the helper believes that he or she will be ineffective due to the nature of the helpee's difficulty—for example, working with a sexually abusive parent. Although the helper's judgment in each of these two illustrations is subjective, it is important that the helper strike a balance between confidence and knowing when to refer (Hansen, Stevic, & Warner, 1982). Other referrals develop because the helper is unable to provide the needed time to the relationship, or the helpee may simply require a fresh start with another helper.

A successful referral should be clearly explained, without conveying the appearance of a crisis. Helpers must also guard against giving the helpee the false impression that his or her concern is more serious than originally imagined. Rather, it should be made clear that the helper's genuine concern for the helpee was what motivated the helper to seek a referral. Even when the reasons for a referral are shared with the helpee, the helper may still encounter helpee resistance. Some individuals, for example, may be hesitant to accept a referral because of a dependency relationship they have established with the helper. Others may be fearful of commencing a new relationship. In still other instances, helpees may perceive a referral as an indication of helper rejection. In addition to these internal inhibitors (Hansen et al., 1982), external variables such as difficulty with transportation, service fees, and time conflicts can also contribute to the helpee's reluctance to readily accept a referral. Yet, if the reasons for the referral are made known to the helpee and he or she shares in the referral process, then it will generally proceed smoothly.

A meaningful referral requires careful preparation. Helpers must be knowledgeable about the available community and professional resources and services; they must also be aware of the functions and limitations of these agencies or individuals. Although the helper will ordinarily make the initial contact, and might arrange transportation, the helpee has the responsibility for further contact and follow-up. During the referral process the helper must be extremely careful not to violate the helpee's confidentiality. Information should be shared ethically and only on a need-to-know basis. Helpers should remain involved until the referral is completed and the new relationship begun. In certain situations, a follow-up inquiry regarding the progress of the referral would also be appropriate.

Helper ethics

Ethics are generally considered to be standardized norms of conduct or behavior that have been formulated on the basis of an already existing set of values. Contrary to popular opinion, ethics are involved more with issues of professional judgment than legal entanglements (Seligman, 1979). Although common sense serves as the foundation of most professional judgments, conflicts do occasionally arise. For example, a helper may be confronted with a dilemma due to a conflict between institutional values or demands and his or her allegiance to the helpee. In one situation, for instance, a student confided to a first-year high school teacher that she was being sexually abused by her father. The teacher felt compelled to help the girl, yet could not get help without identifying the teen-ager involved. The teacher's dilemma was further compounded by the school's position that such instances are family matters and teachers should not be involved. The teacher, after talking to the girl on several occasions, was able to convince her to call the local abuse hotline and talk to a trained counselor.

Professional organizations such as the American Psychological Association, the National Education Association, and the American Personnel and Guidance Association have developed ethical principles for their members. These standards serve as guidelines governing the members' professional behavior. But one need not be a professional helper in order to behave in a professional fashion. Nonprofessional helpers should always conduct themselves in a professional manner.

Although most of the dilemmas that helpers encounter can be resolved by using good sense, one area in particular—confidentiality—deserves special mention. When one person agrees to help another, a certain degree of responsibility is assumed. The helper has a moral obligation to maintain the confidentiality of the relationship, especially of information shared within it. A breach of confidentiality can quickly destroy a helping relationship. Trust is a difficult goal to achieve. Once violated, it is extremely difficult if not impossible to reestablish. If the helper cannot guarantee confidentiality, the helpee should be informed. It is suggested that helpers never share information about a helpee without his or her informed written consent. Even then, unless there is a clear and imminent danger to the helpee or others, only involved individuals should be privy to confidential information. As a rule of thumb, Benjamin (1981) proposes that helpers reveal everything that is absolutely necessary and absolutely nothing that is not.

Ethical issues are not easily resolved. They generally require much soul-searching on the part of the helper. Therefore, as Brammer (1979) suggests, helpers need to be committed to ethical behaviors that reflect not only their own moral standards but also those of society and the helping professions.

A final word

As the journey through the various dimensions of the helping relationship is concluded, it is hoped that an appreciation of the intricacies of the helping experience has been developed. Not everyone will agree with the approach put forth, and certainly helping encounters do not always progress as described herein. What is important, however, is that a foundation has been established from which one can perfect ideas and methods about helping. The final measure of competency is the ability to successfully effect a helping relationship.

> *Men are disturbed not by things that happen, but by their opinion of the things that happen.*
>
> —Epictetus

References

Baxter, D. (1977). An open letter to those who counsel parents of the handicapped. *Journal of Rehabilitation of the Deaf, 10,* 1–8.

Benjamin, A. (1981). *The helping interview* (3rd ed.). Boston: Houghton Mifflin.

Bennett, J. (1974). Proof of the pudding. *Exceptional Parent, 4,* 7–12.

Brammer, L. (1979). *The helping relationship: Process and skills* (2nd ed.). Englewood Cliffs, NJ: Prentice-Hall.

Brammer, L., & Shostrom, E. (1977). *Therapeutic psychology: Fundamentals of counseling and psychotherapy* (3rd ed.). Englewood Cliffs, NJ: Prentice-Hall.

Combs, A., Avila, D., & Purkey, W. (1971). *Helping relationships: Basic concepts for the helping professions.* Boston: Allyn & Bacon.

Hansen, J., Stevic, R., & Warner, R. (1982). *Counseling: Theory and process* (3rd ed.). Boston: Allyn & Bacon.

Murray, M. (1959). Needs of parents of mentally retarded children. *American Journal of Mental Deficiency, 63,* 1078–1088.

Rogers, C. (1961). *On becoming a person.* Boston: Houghton Mifflin.

Roos, P. (1963). Psychological counseling with parents of retarded children. *Mental Retardation, 1,* 345–350.

Seligman, M. (1979). *Strategies for helping parents of exceptional children.* New York: Free Press.

Smith, R., & Neisworth, J. (1975). *The exceptional child: A functional approach.* New York: McGraw-Hill.

Stewart, J. (1978). *Counseling parents of exceptional children.* Columbus, OH: Charles Merrill.

Telford, C., & Sawrey, J. (1981). *The exceptional individual* (4th ed.). Englewood Cliffs, NJ: Prentice-Hall.

Tyler, L. (1969). *The work of the counselor* (3rd ed.). Englewood Cliffs, NJ: Prentice-Hall.

Chapter 8:
Helping approaches

> *Everybody thinks of changing humanity and no-body thinks of changing himself.*
>
> —Leo Tolstoy

Helpers in all fields of human service are exposed to a wide variety of helping theories. All of these approaches to behavior change claim to be effective. Hence helpers are often confronted with the questions, "What approach shall I use? Which one is really best?" As with many issues in helping, there is no clear-cut answer, nor is there one preferred strategy for aiding people. Little exists in the way of research evidence to indicate that one helping theory is superior to another (Shoben, 1962; Glass, 1976). Nonetheless, selecting a helping approach is an important task. Helpers who operate without some theoretical framework may be guilty of using "cookbook techniques" with their helpees (Brammer & Shostrom, 1977). Selection of a helping style is governed by both helpee need and helper beliefs. For instance, some people need help to stop a specific inappropriate behavior, whereas others may need to improve interpersonal skills. More important than the character of the helpee's concern or problem is what the helper believes regarding the fundamental nature of people, the manner in which human behavior develops and changes. Preference for a particular helping theory is also a reflection of the helper's personal needs and the beliefs he or she has about himself or herself and the individuals to be encountered (Combs, Avila, & Purkey, 1971).

Basically, helping theories are a sophisticated form of common sense (Brammer, 1979). They provide a practical means for making systematic observations and explaining or describing human behavior (Shertzer & Stone, 1980). The specific helping viewpoint that a helper subscribes to also determines how he or she functions in the helping relationship—for example, how much credence is given to interpretation or the importance of reflective and clarifying statements. In essence, theory provides a structure from which the helper operates in the helping relationship. According to Stefflre and Burks (1979a), theory not only guides the helper's behavior in the helping process, but also assists in making sense of and providing meaning to the helpee's actions.

From another perspective, theory functions as a useful way of summarizing facts and information while promoting understanding and explaining complex phenomena. Additionally, theory acts as a predictor of events, which in turn stimulate further research and even more theory (Shertzer & Stone, 1980). A theory not only predicts new facts and relationships but also integrates and organizes in a meaningful fashion those things that are already known. Hence theories are constructed rather than discovered (Patterson, 1980).

Beginning helpers, especially those interested in finding a theoretical home, often wonder how one knows if a theory is good. The answer may be found in the degree to which the theory meets certain requirements. Stefflre and Burks (1979a) cite five formal attributes that should be encompassed within a theory. The novice helper can judge how well his or her theory satisfies the following criteria:

1. *A good theory is clear,* in that there is agreement among its general principles (philosophy), and agreement of its consequences with observation (science).

2. *A good theory is comprehensive,* in that it has scope and accounts for much behavior. It will explain what happens to many people in many situations.

3. *A good theory is explicit;* that is, it has precision.

4. *A good theory is parsimonious* and does not overexplain phenomena. A theory that explains a given event in five different ways is not apt to explain at all.

5. Finally, *a good theory generates useful research.* (p. 9)

Patterson (1980) provides a second vantage point for evaluating various helping theories. His eight criteria parallel and extend those mentioned by Stefflre and Burks. Specifically, Patterson proposes the following evaluative yardsticks:

1. *Importance.* A good theory should not be concerned with trivial issues but should have wide applicability and relevance to real-life situations.

2. *Preciseness and clarity.* A theory must be understandable, free of ambiguities, and internally consistent.

3. *Parsimony or simplicity.* Although this concept is not synonymous with simplification, a theory should be minimally complex and contain few assumptions. Patterson believes that this criterion is the most widely violated in theory construction.

4. *Comprehensiveness.* A further criterion dictates that a theory should be complete, addressing the area of interest including all known data pertaining to the subject.

5. *Operationality.* Concepts incorporated within a theory must be precise enough to allow for measurement. That is, the theory should be capable of being reduced to procedures appropriate for assessing its predictions. Some concepts may indicate relationships and, therefore, need not be operationalized.

6. *Empirical validity or verifiability.* A theory must be supported by verifiable documentation and account for new knowledge.

7. *Fruitfulness.* Theories should lead to predictions that can be assessed, as well as provoke thinking and generate new ideas.

8. *Practicality.* Although seldom acknowledged, this final criterion requires that a theory assist practitioners in organizing their thinking by providing a conceptual model for practice. It allows the individual to move from being a technician to being a professional. As Lewin reportedly stated, "There is nothing as practical as a good theory."

Evaluated against these standards, most helping theories fall short of the mark and thus fail to qualify as good theories. Patterson (1980) and Stefflre and Burks (1979b) both suggest that perhaps it would be more accurate to describe such theories as counseling approaches or counseling viewpoints. Yet a final point needs to be made. A good theory does not simply *exist,* but rather is a tool to be *used.* Hence a good theory is one that proves to be the most helpful to the person using it (Hansen, Stevic, & Warner, 1972).

The purpose of this chapter is twofold. First, it will succinctly review the major tenets of five theories representative of various helping approaches. Second, it will guide the reader in developing his or her own theory of helping.

Dimensions of helping theories

For ease in discussion and understanding, helping theories are often formulated according to various schemes or formats. One example is Patterson's (1980) grouping based upon a cognitive versus affective dichotomy. Patterson's design classifies various theories in the following manner:

Cognitive   *Affective*

Rational   Learning   Psychoanalytic   Perceptual   Existential

A merit of this proposal is that it moves from the simple to the complex (Shertzer & Stone, 1980). However, using the same ordering, two additional contrasts are possible. The first considers these theories as directive versus nondirective; the second is based on a helper-centered versus helpee-centered classification. In actuality, the dichotomies are not as clear-cut as indicated and are best viewed as a convenience for comparison.

Although helping theories evidence great diversity, basic issues still cut across all appproaches. Differences among the theories are largely a matter of emphasis and conviction (Shertzer & Stone, 1980). For example, behavior change is a major goal of helping, yet theories differ as to how change comes about and the role of the helper as a change agent (Stefflre & Burks, 1979b). As an illustration, some believe that helpers should play a direct role in the helping process and that change is induced by altering specific features in the helpee's environment. Others would argue that the emotional climate established by the helper is crucial and that the helpee possesses the ability to change, given the right conditions. Although a difference in emphasis is noted, both viewpoints can account for helpee change within their theoretical configurations.

Representative helping viewpoints

The preceding discussion provides a point of departure for examining representative viewpoints. The following orientations are included for examination: rational-emotive, behavioral, client-centered, and existential. An eclectic or middle-of-the-road approach, although not part of Patterson's scheme, is also included, due to the attractiveness of this position to many beginning helpers. The psychoanalytic contribution of Sigmund Freud to the helping professions, however, has been excluded even though it is the most widely known helping theory. Its elimination was largely due to the extremely complex set of assumptions inherent in the Freudian school of thought that were judged to be beyond the scope and purpose of this book. Furthermore, as Brammer (1979) points out, "the methods of helping used in this approach are long, arduous, and unpredictable. Long and demanding training is required of helpers who wish to use psychoanalytic methods" (p. 156).

Rational-emotive therapy

Rational-emotive therapy, also known as RET, was formulated by Albert Ellis during the 1950s. Originally trained as a psychoanalyst,

Ellis practiced classical psychoanalytic theory for several years before becoming disillusioned and eventually abandoning this viewpoint. His ideas regarding RET, which is a highly cognitive way of helping people and is indigenous to the American helping community, were first put forth in his 1962 book, *Reason and Emotion in Psychotherapy.* Two later books, *Humanistic Psychotherapy: The Rational-Emotive Approach* (1973) and *Handbook of Rational-Emotive Therapy* (Ellis & Grieger, 1977), further explain his ideas.

Simply viewed, RET can be seen as stressing rationality or applying logical analysis and rational argument to the helpee's concerns or problems. Ellis views humans as both rational and irrational creatures, beings whose emotions are caused and controlled by thinking. Yet emotion and thinking, according to Ellis, are not necessarily two discrete functions. Ellis further believes that although human events are largely caused by factors beyond an individual's control, people can control their reactions to these events and thus regulate much of their own behavior. Emotional difficulties—that is, neurotic behaviors—are the result of illogical and irrational thinking and have their roots in early learnings acquired from parents and society. Ellis, however, also visualizes humans as biologically inclined toward irrational thinking.

Ellis contends that people can signficantly affect their behavior by the kinds of things they tell themselves. Continued emotional difficulties result from "self-talk" or internalized verbalizations of irrational ideas and thoughts. Repetition of these illogical thoughts reindoctrinates the helpee and perpetuates his or her problem. "For all practical purposes," Ellis writes, "the phrases and sentences that we keep telling ourselves frequently *are* or *become* our thoughts and emotions" (1962, p. 50). Thus, if the helpee can be persuaded to tell himself or herself one set of statements rather than another, feelings and actions would subsequently change. In other words, altering the helpee's belief system promotes changes in behavior.

Ellis (1979) speculates that when an individual experiences an emotional reaction (point C) to some event, fact, or agent (point A), C is not a direct consequence or result of A. Rather, it is the helpee's irrational belief system (point B) about point A that causes point C. These irrational beliefs usually take the form of absolute commands and musts. Hence, if the helpee can be assisted to recognize the relationship between points A, B, and C, the possibility of changing his or her behavior emerges.

Eleven widespread, irrational beliefs or values were originally postulated by Ellis; however, these were later reduced to three basic irrational ("musturbatory") thoughts, each with several subheadings (Ellis, 1977). Ellis suggests that these "shoulds," "oughts," and "musts" contribute to self-defeating or neurotic behavior because the individual is unable to achieve or live up to the statements. Yet people continue to believe that they should act or behave in a certain fashion. The "musts" identified by Ellis are:

1. I must (or should or ought to) do well and/or be loved by significant others; it is awful if I do not; I can't stand it; and I am therefore a rotten person (RP)!

2. You must treat me kindly and fairly; it is horrible if you do not; I can't stand you and your behavior; and you are therefore a bad individual!

3. The world must deal with me nicely and fortunately and give me virtually everything I want immediately; and it is terrible if it doesn't! I can't stand living in such an awful world; and it is an utterly abominable place. (Ellis, 1979, p. 177)

The helping process incorporated within RET is cognitively oriented and is described by Ellis as the "curing of unreason by reason." Self-defeating and illogical thoughts need to be realigned so that thinking becomes logical and rational. The goal of the helper is to demonstrate to the helpee that illogical thinking, not some earlier event, is the cause of his or her unhappiness. Furthermore, the helpee is maintaining his or her disturbed behavior by continuing to think illogically and irrationally. Although characterized by incisive probing and questioning, RET does not give much credence to the importance of diagnosis. The task thus becomes one of restructuring, that is, of eliminating illogical and irrational thoughts and substituting logical and rational ideas and beliefs in their place. Consequently, RET emphasizes the redevelopment of the individual.

Ellis (1979) points out that RET therapists are often wrongly accused of claiming to know what rational behavior is and persuading helpees to adopt this demeanor. Rather, as Ellis asserts, helpers "start with the clients' own values, goals, and purposes and try to show them how they are pursuing such values ineffectually or irrationally and how they could pursue them more rationally.

But RET therapists do not *give* clients their basic values or goals" (p. 175).

RET supports the position that helpers should take an active, directive role in the helping process and teach helpees to change their behavior and assume a rational approach to their problems. This strategy has been described as a reeducation of the helpee, a type of teacher-student relationship. Ellis writes:

Rational-emotive psychotherapy makes a concerted attack on the disturbed person's illogical positions in two main ways: (1) The therapist serves as a frank counterpropagandist who directly contradicts and denies the self-defeating propaganda and superstitions which the patient has originally learned and which he is now self-instilling. (2) The therapist encourages, persuades, cajoles, and occasionally even insists that the patient engage in some activity (such as doing something he is afraid of doing) which will serve as a forceful counterpropaganda agency against the nonsense he believes. (1962, pp. 94–95)

Change within RET requires action and dealing with the helpee in the present rather than the past. An RET therapist may assign a helpee both written and experiential "homework" activities. For instance, a helpee will be asked to encounter a situation he or she is fearful of, such as seeking employment. Finally, RET goes beyond focusing on specific illogical thoughts and ideas and deals with the helpee's general irrational thought process, which underlies all types of fears. Ellis believes that this is necessary in order to prevent other illogical ideas and beliefs from evolving at some future date.

RET is inappropriate for some helpees—for example, the very young or very old, the severely disturbed, those of low intellectual ability, or those who are too impressionable. Moreover, Ellis's approach has been criticized as being too unemotional, overly intellectual, authoritarian, confrontational, and requiring high verbal ability. In spite of these criticisms and an obvious client selection factor, Ellis claims that 90 percent of the helpees who experience ten or more RET sessions demonstrate distinct or considerable improvement. He further cites (Ellis, 1979) numerous controlled investigations demonstrating the efficacy of RET. Additional information about RET can be obtained from the Institute for Rational Living, Inc., 45 East 65th Street, New York, New York 10021.

Behavioral approach

Behavioral approaches to helping can trace their roots to the writings of several prominent theorists. Among the early proponents of a behavioral viewpoint were Michael and Meyerson (1962), Krumboltz (1966), Krumboltz and Thoresen (1969), and Hosford (1969). The term *behavioral counseling* was reportedly first introduced by John Krumboltz in 1964 at the annual convention of the American Psychological Association (APA). In a later article, based on his APA presentation, Krumboltz explained that his choice of the adjective *behavioral* was to be a constant reminder to the helper that his or her activity should focus on changes in helpee behavior, that is, *what* the helpee is doing (LaFleur, 1979).

A major assumption of the behavioral approach to helping is that most human behavior is learned, a product of the individual's interaction with the environment. Helpee problems or difficulties, therefore, are conceived as problems in learning. And if something is learned it can be unlearned—that is, behavior is modifiable. However, as Patterson (1980) observes, it is impossible to talk about *a* learning theory or *a* behavioral viewpoint of helping; no single learning theory exists today. The behavioral perspective described herein is based on research and derived from the work of B. F. Skinner. It is formulated on laboratory investigations and direct observation. It is empirical and experimental in nature.

To a behaviorally attuned helper, a human is a reactive being who enters the world not as innately good or evil but neutral, characteristic of the Lockean idea of a *tabula rasa* or blank slate, capable only of reacting to stimuli in his or her environment (Hosford, 1969). Although heredity and the interaction of heredity and the environment generate behavior, the helpee's behavior is defined by the frequency and kinds of reinforcement he or she receives in various situations (Shertzer & Stone, 1980). Hence behavioral helpers do not have to resort to theories or inferred hypothetical states; the focus is on behavior which can be observed and quantified.

Basic to the behavioral model of helping is the principle of reinforcement, simply defined by Shertzer and Stone (1980) "as the creation of desirable consequences that will strengthen or facilitate certain behavior" (p. 189). An individual's actions are thus largely controlled by the type of environmental consequences he or she experiences. That is, some behaviors will be reinforced or strengthened, whereas other performances will be weakened or reduced. As a result, the helpee learns by experience that certain circumstances result in satisfaction and others will prove unsatisfactory. Unlike other helping viewpoints, the behavioral approach does not attribute the helpee's behavior to inner reasons or innate characteristics, but rather to those experiences he or she has learned will bring gratification (Hansen, Stevic, & Warner, 1982).

As mentioned earlier, behavior is learned. This includes both appropriate and inappropriate actions. Atypical behavior differs from normal behavior not in the way in which it is acquired, but in the degree to which it is perceived by others in the environment as maladaptive (Hosford, 1969). Hence the helper does not consider the helpee's behavior as good or bad, appropriate or inappropriate. Instead, this is a value judgment communicated by the helpee's reference group and societal or cultural forces.

Inherent in the behavioral position is a belief that the cause or underlying reason for the helpee's behavior (the why) does not need to be determined. Behaviors are not viewed as symptoms, nor are the helpee's actions seen as the result of underlying problems (La-Fleur, 1979). The emphasis is on present determinants of behavior, not historical variables (Patterson, 1980). Behavioral helpers, according to Ullman and Krasner (1965), need to focus on the following questions:

1. *What* behavior is maladaptive; that is *what* subject behaviors should be increased or decreased?

2. What environmental contingencies *currently* support the subject's behavior?

3. *What* environmental changes, usually reinforcing stimuli, may be manipulated to alter the subject's behavior? (p. 1, italics added)

The helper thus becomes an environmental or behavioral engineer, rearranging the contingencies in the helpee's environment.

"Behavioral counselors are impatient with the subjective world of the phenomenologists. They are not concerned with inner states but rather how the integrated organism behaves" (Ewing, 1977, p. 336). In comparison to other helping viewpoints, the behavioral approach devotes far less attention to prior experiences, mediational constructs, and helpee attitudes. The helping process is simply viewed as a learning situation. Yet LaFleur (1979), from a slightly different orientation, prefers to see helping as an educational process in which the helper assists the helpee in learning new ways to act in order to resolve specific concerns. Observable outcomes of helpee behavior are stressed instead of the process. From a behavioral point of view, Stewart (1978) writes that "the most important aspect of the counseling relationship is to structure the situation so as to optimize observable changes in client behavior once the desired behaviors have been specified" (p. 59).

One of the bench marks of a behavioral approach is the precision of the helping goals. Krumboltz (1966) urges that the goals be specific, concise, and objective. They must also be observable and capable of being translated into specific behavior, that is, stated in terms of behavioral performance. As an illustration, a helpee who constantly complains about a poor self-image would need to redefine this problem in terms of specific, overt behavior. Goals are thus dependent on the particular problem or concern voiced by the helpee. They are individually tailored to the helpee, as are the techniques employed.

Techniques utilized by helpers will vary from situation to situation, depending on the helpee and the nature of his or her difficulty. This thought is echoed by LaFleur (1979), who believes that there is no standard helping technique appropriate to all helpees. On the other hand, helping is not a potpourri of procedures that are indiscriminately applied; rather it is the systematic application of learning principles to a specific behavior at a given time. (For a concise accounting of various learning concepts appropriate to behavioral counseling see LaFleur [1979] and Patterson [1980].) Not only are techniques tailored to the needs of the helpee, but they are also constructed for implementation outside of the helper's office. In fact, some would even argue that the environment should be the helper's office (LaFleur, 1979).

Helpers play a major role in the helping process. Hansen and his co-workers (1982) have accurately characterized the helper's importance and involvement as follows:

The counselor has the major responsibility for deciding what techniques will be utilized in the counseling process. Once the client and the counselor have defined and agreed upon the concern, the counselor controls the process of counseling and accepts responsibility for its outcome. It is the counselor's responsibility to launch the client on a course of action that will eventually help the latter resolve his or her difficulty. To accomplish this, the counselor must control the counseling process. This is not an arbitrary manipulative control that goes against the client's wishes; it is specifically designed to meet the goals of the client and is done with her or his full consent. (pp. 142–143)

Eventually, the helper is required to evaluate the effectiveness of the helping process. Behavioral helpers consider evaluation an ongoing process that is conducted in terms of *what* the helpee is doing. The performances exhibited by the helpee provide feedback regarding the effectiveness of the helper and the specific techniques employed (LaFleur, 1979). Michael and Meyerson (1962) believe that "observable behavior is the only variable of importance in the counseling and guidance process, and it is the only criterion against which the outcome of the process can be evaluated" (pp. 395–396). Brammer (1979) stresses that the primary measure of success is the degree to which the helpee accomplishes his or her goal. Once again, one can observe the behavioral emphasis on helpee actions and measurable outcomes.

The objective and scientific outlook incorporated within behavioral viewpoints has generated some criticisms. Brammer (1979) feels that one of the difficulties with this approach is the inability to adequately deal with emotional issues through observable behavior. Furthermore, "the emphasis on specificity, precision, and objectivity tends to lead the helper to focus on minute pieces of behavior and to ignore larger complex patterns" (p. 157). Shertzer and Stone (1980) add two additional criticisms: (1) "behavioral counseling is cold, impersonal, and manipulative and relegates the relationship to a secondary function, and (2) client changes are but symptoms removed that emerge later in other forms of behavior" (p. 191). Assets of a behavioral philosophy are the focus on the individuality of the helpee, the preciseness of the procedures employed, and the objectiveness of evaluation.

Client-centered therapy

Perceptual or phenomenological approaches to helping emphasize the helpee's unique perception of reality. Phenomenologists believe that reality consists of internal and external dimensions, but that the external world is perceived solely through internal experience.

Hence the only thing humans can be certain of is that they are experiencing streams of thoughts and feelings (Ewing, 1977). Patterson (1980) has also articulated this philosophy:

Phenomenology assumes that although a real world may exist, its existence cannot be known or experienced directly. Its existence is inferred on the basis of perceptions of the world. These perceptions constitute the phenomenal field, or the phenomenal world of the individual. Human beings can only know their phenomenal world, never any real world. Therefore, they can only behave in terms of how they perceive things, or how things appear to them. (p. 513)

Perceptual viewpoints are based on the premise that since behavior is determined by the person's perceptions, those perceptions must be altered before behavior can be changed. Each helping approach, however, differs in the techniques used to accomplish this change. Some of the theories usually associated with this school of thought are George Kelly's psychology of personal constructs, Gestalt therapy advanced by Fritz Perls, the widely popular transactional analysis of Eric Berne, and the influential work of Carl Rogers and his client-centered therapy. Presented here for closer scrutiny and examination are the ideas of Carl Rogers, one of the most important psychologists of the twentieth century. His writings represent an American contribution to the helping profession.

Originally labeled by Rogers (1961) as client-centered therapy, and now known as person-centered therapy, Rogers's helping strategy conceives of humans as basically good, rational, trustworthy, cooperative, and forward moving—capable, to a large degree, of determining their own destiny. As Ewing (1977) notes, Rogers attests to his abiding faith in the helpee's ability to move forward and grow with the following analogy: "People are just as wonderful as sunsets if I can let them be. I do not try to control a sunset. I watch it with awe as it unfolds, and I like myself best when appreciating the unfolding of a life" (p. 332).

Equally basic to the Rogerian viewpoint is the concept of the individual's movement toward self-actualizing growth. Rogers (1961) attributes all of behavior to a single incentive—self-actualization. Simply stated, it is the organism's "urge to expand, extend, develop, and mature" (1961, p. 351). In other words, it is movement characterized by adjustment, self-realization, independence, and autonomy (Grummon, 1979). Rogers labels this disposition as *ac-*

tualizing tendency, which he defines as "the inherent tendency of the organism to develop all its capacities in ways which serve to maintain or enhance the organism" (1959, p. 194). It is the primary motivating force of the human organism. As Hansen et al. (1982) observe, this motive provides a person with a goal toward which he or she is constantly striving. "Human behavior is goal directed toward control of the environment and the individual's place in that environment" (p. 94).

Rogers (1951) is inclined to view each human being as existing in the center of a world of continually changing experiences. Related to this proposition is a fundamental belief that what is perceived or experienced by the helpee is reality. The helpee does not react to an absolute reality, but to his or her perceptions of that reality. In other words, it makes little difference what actually happened—what is crucial is the individual's interpretation or perception of the event. As Hansen et al. (1972) note, "man is not a reactive being but responds to situational events by an active thought process. He is not passive in this situation, but an active agent" (p. 79).

The best vantage point for understanding behavior, according to Rogers, is from the individual's own internal frame of reference "which is available to the awareness of the individual at a given moment. It includes the full range of sensations, perceptions, meanings, and memories, which are available to consciousness" (1959, p. 210). From this perspective, the helper needs to focus on the subjective reality of the helpee's experience which requires empathic understanding. In contrast, understanding the helpee from an external posture, without empathy, usually results in an emphasis on objective reality. Furthermore, when viewing a helpee objectively, the helper is using his or her own internal frame of reference, which ignores the helpee's subjective reality. Some helpers will therefore have to unlearn familiar ways of relating to people (Grummon, 1979). This is necessary because, as previously alluded to, Rogers's helping theory is based on an understanding of the helpee's internal point of view. Rogers comments:

It is the counselor's function to assume insofar as he is able, the internal frame of reference of the client, to perceive the world as the client sees it, to lay aside all perceptions from the external frame of reference while doing so, and to communicate something of this empathic understanding to the client. (1951, p. 29)

Person-centered theory has been characterized as an if-then approach to helping. Specifically, if certain conditions are evident, then a process is established that produces certain results or outcomes in helpee behavior. "The basic hypothesis therefore, is that, given the establishment of the proper conditions for growth, the client will be able to gain personal insight and take positive steps toward solving his or her difficulties" (Hansen et al., 1982, p. 100). Rogers firmly believes that the helper possesses the ability to help establish these conditions. Thus conditions that promote behavior change are of critical importance.

Rogers postulates the existence of six necessary and sufficient conditions for helping—that is, if these conditions are evident, then change will take place. Rogers (1967) later admitted to the difficulty of establishing these conditions; he did not, however, abandon his conviction that the attitudes of the helper are more important than his or her skill and training. Helper attitudes rather than techniques and procedures promote behavior change. The six conditions identified by Rogers are as follows:

1. Two persons are in psychological contact.

2. The first, whom we shall term the client, is in a state of incongruence, being vulnerable or anxious.

3. The second person, whom we shall term the therapist, is congruent or integrated in the relationship.

4. The therapist experiences unconditional positive regard for the client.

5. The therapist experiences an empathic understanding of the client's internal frame of reference and endeavors to communicate this experience to the client.

6. The communication to the client of the therapist's empathic understanding and unconditional positive regard is to a minimal degree achieved. (1957, p. 96)

Grummon (1979) believes that the third, fourth, and fifth conditions are the important ones, and maintains that the remaining conditions do not deal with the helper attitudes but merely provide for completeness and clarity.

The preceding principles require closer scrutiny as to their definition and meaning. First, both helper and helpee must be minimally involved in the relationship. In Rogers's terms, it is the least experience between two people that could be referred to as a relationship. The second concept, that of incongruence, refers to the inconsistency or variance between a helpee's self-concept and his or her experiences. The helpee becomes vulnerable and anxious when there is a discrepancy between self-concepts and actual experiences. Rogers believes that the more anxious the helpee, the greater the odds are for successful helping. Helpers must also be congruent or genuine in a helping relationship. They cannot play a role or present a false front or façade—helpers must be themselves. One of the more popular terms associated with Rogerian therapy, and also one of its cornerstones, is the idea of unconditional positive regard—in other words, a caring, nonevaluative, warm acceptance of the helpee as he or she presently is. The helper respects the helpee without conditions. The fifth essential condition concerns the helper's attempt to understand the internal world of the helpee as accurately as humanly possible. As described by Grummon (1979), it is an attempt by the helper to become at home in the helpee's perceptual world. Yet the helper does not lose sight of his or her own identity. Finally, the helper's genuineness, unconditional positive regard, and empathic understanding for the helpee are not enough—the helpee must perceive these attitudes. That is, these conditions must be communicated to the helpee. But the preceding conditions are not, as assumed by some, all-or-none phenomena—rather they exist along a continuum. Not only is it important that these conditions exist, but their degree of evidence may be of even greater significance.

Generated from these propositions is a helping environment characterized by a warm, permissive climate, an atmosphere in which the helpee is able to communicate with a helper who is genuinely concerned about his or her welfare. Feelings of understanding and acceptance are engendered within an environment that is free from threat and evaluation.

One of the important dimensions of person-centered therapy is the nature of the relationship between the helper and the helpee. As Patterson (1980) comments, the relationship is not a cognitive or intellectual one, but focuses rather on affective aspects, that is, the feelings that the helpee has about himself or herself, other individuals, and events within his or her perceptual world. Stewart (1978) observes that this approach is formulated "upon the humanistic belief that people's problems are primarily of an emotional etiology and that most clients already possess the objective information they need to make a decision about a problem" (p. 52). Hence the responsibility for the relationship falls on the shoulders of the helpee. The helper does not provide solutions; rather, it is the helpee who holds the key and has the answers. The helper stresses not only the helpee's ability to determine issues of importance, but also the person's capacity to resolve his or her own concerns. Consequently, feelings of dependency on the helper are minimized. It is also important to note that the emphasis is on the helpee rather than a particular problem. Moreover, the focal point of the relationship is the immediate, the here and now, the helpee's present experiences and adjustments instead of past difficulties.

Person-centered therapy is often misconstrued as a laissez-faire or passive approach to helping, sometimes to the extent of being jokingly referred to as "um-hmm" therapy. While it is true that the term *nondirective* accurately describes this viewpoint, a great deal of emphasis is placed on the helper as an individual. He or she is actively involved in the relationship, more as a person than a therapist. Put simply, "the counselor's role is to create the conditions that make it possible for the counseling process to take place; the counseling process, in turn, will result in changes in the client" (Hansen et al., 1982, p. 103). Change in behavior, according to Shertzer and Stone (1980), "comes through releasing the potentiality of individuals to evaluate their experiences, permitting them to clarify and gain insight into their feelings, which presumably leads to growth" (p. 215). As Rogers describes it, the individual becomes a fully functioning person. This helping process stresses the importance of the relationship between the helpee and the helper. Again, the important element is not the techniques employed but rather the manifestation of unconditional positive regard and empathic understanding by a genuine helper in an environment free from threat. Equally significant is the ability of the helper to successfully communicate these attitudes to the helpee. The helper's task can best be described as encouraging free expression or allowing for emotional ventilation and then reflecting these feelings to the helpee. In essence, the helpers serves as an alter ego for the helpee, a self out of the self. The focus is not on intellectual elements or specific concerns, but on the helpee and his or her current feelings (Hansen et al., 1982).

Helpers who subscribe to the Rogerian approach to helping believe that the helpee has the responsibility for determining the helping goals. These are usually characterized as growth-type goals that emphasize the reorganization of the self. The aim is to assist the helpee in becoming a more fully functioning person. Helpers are uninterested in resolving a particular problem or promoting specific behavior change; instead the emphasis is on providing a relationship that the helpee can utilize for personal growth (Grummon, 1979). The helper is thus concerned with assisting the helpee in becoming less defensive, more congruent, and more open to experience (Rogers, 1959). An attempt is made to establish the proper therapeutic conditions so as to remove obstacles that impede the helpee's innate tendency to strive toward self-actualization. Rogerians would suggest that the goal of helping should be the release of an already present force in a potentially adequate person (Hansen et al., 1982).

Person-centered therapy has proven to be a vastly popular approach to helping. It has generated a plethora of research and placed emphasis on the positive development of the helpee. Also, Rogers (1967) observes that those who are capable of creating an effective helping relationship are not necessarily professionally trained helpers. However, as with all helping approaches, criticism is inevitable. Grummon (1979), for one, notes that growth-type goals are not necessarily appropriate for all helpees. Furthermore, person-centered therapy says little about how preexisting conditions and external events influence self-actualization. Stewart (1978) comments that "the major disadvantage of client-centered counseling is that the basic assumption of affective, emotional causation has the effect of making all clients fit the mold of having emotional problems regardless of what their own perception of their problems may be" (p. 54). Yet Rogers perceives of his theory in the same light as he does the helpee, that is, as being in a process of becoming rather than a static entity.

Existential viewpoint

Existential viewpoints focus on the humanness of the helpee. This perspective is a marriage of theology, psychology, and even art and literature. Its objective is to understand the individual. Brammer (1979) considers existentialism to be a philosophical outlook that addresses the issues of time, meaning, purpose, feelings, and the human potential. Patterson (1980) also acknowledges this attitude. He describes existentialism as being "concerned with the nature of humanity, with its existence in the modern world, and with the meaning of this existence to the individual. Its focus is on the individual's most immediate experience, his or her own existence and the experiencing of this existence" (p. 524). Basically, therefore, existentialism is concerned with *ontology*, the science of being.

Rooted in the diverse philosophical writings of Søren Kierkegaard, Paul Tilich, Jean Paul Sartre, Rollo May, Ludwig Biswanger, and Viktor Frankl, among others, existentialism is extremely difficult to comprehend. Its evolution cannot be attributed to one person, nor is there a single existential approach to helping. Existentialism is best thought of as an attitude or philosophy rather than a particular strategy for aiding people. Existentialism also holds a unique position within the helping realm: it has not created a new leader nor does it allege to have established a new school of therapy (May, 1958b).

In general, existentialism opposes the idea of segmenting the person. Instead, a holistic approach is adopted in order to comprehend the essence of being human. The individual is seen as a dynamic entity, a complex organism, one in the process of becoming. Perhaps Patterson (1980) best describes the relationship of the person to his or her world:

The human being as the subject can never be separated from the object that the human being observes. The meaning of objective fact depends upon the subject's relationship to it. Human beings exist in the world of which they are a part—beings-in-the-world. Existentialism focuses on the individual's experiences—particularly the nonintellectual modes of experience—and upon existence in its total involvement in a situation within a world. It makes an individual's experience the center of things. (pp. 524–525)

Therefore, an existential position, according to May (1958b), endeavors to fully understand the individual as he or she functions in his or her unique world of experience. "Unless one focuses on the fundamental fact of a person's existence and being, one cannot understand drives and behavior. All lose meaning unless viewed from the dynamic point of being and becoming" (Shertzer & Stone, 1980, p. 221).

Patterson (1980) identifies the following major themes appropriate to the various existential philosophies:

1. The distinctive attribute of human existence is *dasein*, or the being who is there, aware of his or her existence in the here and the now, a person who is responsible, free, capable of making choices and decisions. "Man is the being," according to May, "who can be conscious of, and therefore responsible for, his existence" (1958a, p. 41). Hence people are what they make themselves.

2. Existentialists argue that the individual cannot be separated from his or her world. In fact, people share their existence in three worlds simultaneously: the biological world, or *Umwelt*, without self-awareness; the world of interrelationships including mutual awareness, *Metwelt*; and finally, the world of self-identity or being-in-the-self, the *Eignwelt*.

3. Human beings are in a continual state of flux—emerging, evolving, essentially *being*. The individual is an active participant in the world, oriented toward the future and constantly developing.

4. Being necessitates nonbeing. The meaning of existence requires the recognition of nonexistence. Death is a fact that is inescapable and must be faced. Those of an existential persuasion believe that death gives life reality.

5. The threat of nonbeing is the origin of normal existential anxiety, normal in the sense that it is always present in all people. Anxiety strikes at the heart of the individual's self-esteem; it is the threat of the loss of existence itself. It involves a conflict between being and nonbeing, that is, between the emerging potentiality of becoming versus the loss of present security. Guilt is a concomitant of the failure to realize one's potentiality.

6. People are not carbon copies or duplicates of one another; they are unique, singular individuals, irreplaceable and thus significant.

7. The concept of transcendence is important to the existentialist. Human beings are considered capable of exceeding or going beyond their immediate situation. Transcendence is typified by people's ability to think abstractly, to view "themselves as others see them, and perhaps most

characteristically," according to Patterson (1980), "in the capacity to be aware that they are the ones who are acting—to see themselves as both subject and object at the same time" (p. 527). Transcendence is also the foundation of freedom, since it provides for the possibility of choice.

8. The modern individual is characterized by alienation from his or her world; he or she is but a stranger in it. Loneliness, depersonalization, and isolation are the common complaints.

In an existential relationship, the helper endeavors to fully understand the helpee in the here and now, as a being-in-the-world. The emphasis is on the experience or reality of the helping relationship. This relationship is viewed as an encounter between the helper and the helpee, the goal of which, according to Dreyfus (1964), is the elucidation of the helpee's uniqueness. Control and manipulation of the helpee are unimportant to the existential helper. May (1958a) writes that "the aim of therapy is that the patient *experience his existence as real.* The purpose is that he become aware of his existence fully, which includes becoming aware of his potentialities and becoming able to act on the basis of them" (p. 85). If this is to be accomplished, then the helper must demonstrate genuineness and authenticity in the relationship. Participation of the helper as a person in the relationship is more important than the techniques employed. Variability and flexibility of technique are the trademarks of existentialism. Some theorists would even argue that existential helping is distinguished by the technique of no technique. Existential helpers believe, however, that technique follows understanding rather than understanding being a consequence of technique (May, 1958a).

Although succinct, this review illustrates the diverse background and inherent complexity of existential thought. Yet this approach, which accentuates the uniqueness and individuality of the helpee and considers self-awareness as the basic antecedent of behavior, has been criticized as unscientific and nonsystematic. Possibly, Hora's (1961) statement that "that which is understood needs no interpretation. That which is interpreted is seldom understood" (p. 64), best refutes the criticism and capsulizes the essence of existentialism.

Eclectic approach

Many helpers, both novice and veteran, lean toward an eclectic approach to helping (Brammer, 1979; Garfield & Kurtz, 1977). Derived from the Greek root meaning to pick out or select, *eclecticism* represents a middle-of-the-road approach to helping. Eclectic helpers borrow and utilize the concepts, methods, and techniques of other helping viewpoints. The eclectic helper, according to Shertzer and Stone (1980), "believes that a single orientation is limiting and that procedures, techniques, and concepts from many sources should be utilized to best serve the needs of the person seeking help" (p. 179). The selection process used by the eclectic helper is neither random nor casual, but represents a systematic integration of other approaches into a personalized style of helping. "The true eclectic must choose techniques based on evidence that they believe will work with a particular client with a particular problem" (Hansen et al., 1982, p. 178). Helping decisions are based on what is needed for working with the individual helpee. As a consequence, no two eclectic helpers are exactly alike.

An eclectic viewpoint must be both consistent and comprehensive (Brammer, 1979). However, this may be easier said than done. As Snygg and Combs (1949) wrote many years ago, "an eclectic system leads directly to inconsistency and contradiction, for techniques derived from conflicting frames of reference are bound to be conflicting" (p. 282). Likewise, Shertzer and Stone (1980) comment that when eclectics select bits and pieces from other helping approaches, the result is often contradictory assumptions and incompatible principles and techniques. Others see an eclectic approach as simply a trial-and-error method of helping, a medley of ideas and methods without firm theoretical foundation. Supposedly, only the best from the various approaches is chosen. Notably absent, however, are any guidelines for the selection process. Thus, as Patterson (1980) notes, it is difficult to accurately describe an eclectic position. Furthermore, eclectic helping is what individual helpers resistant to theory and consistency engage in.

This attack on an eclectic philosophy has not gone unchallenged. Brammer (1969) persuasively argues for an "emerging eclecticism" wherein each helper develops a comprehensive, personal view of behavior allowing for the integration of his or her helping experience. "The emerging eclectic is a skilled observer in the scientific behavioral tradition; he knows the history of counseling theory and contemporary views; he is aware of his unique style and counseling setting. From these he forges his own comprehensive evolving view of behavior change" (p. 192). Brammer conceives of this model as a viable alternative to the negative connotations of eclecticism. Frederick Thorne's (1950, 1961) extensive writing also supports an eclectic position. As the leading advocate of eclecticism, Thorne maintains that all helping approaches are inadequate or deficient in certain aspects. He has developed a scientific, integrated approach that retains the best features of each helping school.

Perhaps eclecticism is best described as "simply a more comprehensive, loosely organized theory than a formal theory and attempts to be all-inclusive" (Patterson, 1980, p. 571). On the positive side, it allows for helper diversity and flexibility, thus benefiting a wider helpee population. On the other hand, one must be realistic and appreciate the demands an eclectic stance requires. It is an extremely difficult strategy to master. Eclecticism requires hard work and proficiency in a number of diverse theoretical positions. Those helpers capable of accomplishing this task are worthy of developing their own personal theory of helping.

Toward a personal theory of helping

Every helper needs to develop his or her own helping viewpoint. A helper cannot just go out and adopt someone else's helping stance. Thus arises the question of how a beginning helper determines which one of the many helping positions is best for him or her. The answer requires a certain degree of self-reflection and examination. Probably the most crucial aspect of discovering one's own notion of helping is an understanding of oneself. Before helpers can effectively assist other individuals, they must fully understand themselves, have their own psychological houses in order, and honestly acknowledge their biases and prejudices. A second component is the helper's unique set of life experiences. These experiences greatly influence the helper's values, self-concept, and outlook toward life itself. These two factors, in conjunction with the helper's training, offer a tentative helping home. As the helper gains experience, he or she slowly develops a helping style with a unique fit. However, as previously cautioned, helpers cannot just use another individual's helping beliefs. This is similar to the difference between purchasing a garment and borrowing a friend's favorite coat. Simply because it wears well and is right for your friend does not mean it will fit or necessarily be comfortable for you.

Helping can be viewed as a matter of learning to use oneself effectively. Any helper who acts or attempts to be someone else risks personal failure and frustration. Helpers must learn simply to be themselves.

A final word

The preceding outlines of various helping approaches are succinct, necessarily oversimplified, and perhaps unintentionally biased. Yet they do point out the many ways of explaining the process of behavior change. In spite of their great diversity, each of these viewpoints has its particular strengths and weaknesses, vocal proponents, and firm niche in the helping world.

Often beginning helpers admire and feel a strong kinship with a single individual and his beliefs. It must be remembered, however, that Rogers was not a Rogerian nor was Freud a Freudian; each was himself (Brammer, 1979). Likewise, each helper must be his or her own person, not a duplicate of another.

We learn wisdom from failure much more than success; we often discover what will do, by finding out what will not do; and probably he who never made a mistake never made a discovery.

—Sir Humphry Davy

References

Brammer, L. (1969). Eclecticism revisited. *Personnel and Guidance Journal, 48*, 192–197.

Brammer, L. (1979). *The helping relationship: Process and skills* (2nd ed.). Englewood Cliffs, NJ: Prentice-Hall.

Brammer, L., & Shostrom, E. (1977). *Therapeutic psychology: fundamentals of counseling and psychotherapy* (3rd ed.). Englewood Cliffs, NJ: Prentice-Hall.

Combs, A., Avila, D., & Purkey, W. (1971). *Helping relationships: Basic concepts for the helping professions.* Boston: Allyn & Bacon.

Dreyfus, E. (1964). The counselor and existentialism. *Personnel and Guidance Journal, 43*, 114–117.

Ellis, A. (1962). *Reason and emotion in psychotherapy.* New York: Lyle Stuart.

Ellis, A. (1973). *Humanistic psychotherapy: The rational-emotive approach.* New York: Julian Press.

Ellis, A. (1977). The basic clinical theory of rational-emotive therapy. In A. Ellis and R. Grieger (Eds.), *Handbook of rational-emotive therapy* (pp. 3–34). New York: Springer.

Ellis, A. (1979). The rational-emotive approach to counseling. In H. Burks and B. Stefflre (Eds.), *Theories of counseling* (3rd ed., pp. 172–219). New York: McGraw-Hill.

Ellis, A., & Grieger, R. (1977). *Handbook of rational-emotive therapy.* New York: Springer.

Ewing, D. (1977). Twenty approaches to individual change. *Personnel and Guidance Journal, 55*, 331–338.

Garfield, S., & Kurtz, R. (1977). A study of eclectic views. *Journal of Consulting and Clinical Psychology, 45*, 78–83.

Glass, G. (1976). Primary, secondary, and meta-analysis of research. *Educational Researcher, 5*, 3–8.

Grummon, D. (1979). Client-centered theory. In H. Burks and B. Stefflre (Eds.), *Theories of counseling* (3rd ed., pp. 28–90). New York: McGraw-Hill.

Hansen, J., Stevic, R., & Warner, R. (1972). *Counseling: Theory and process.* Boston: Allyn & Bacon.

Hansen, J., Stevic, R., & Warner, R. (1982). *Counseling: Theory and process.* (3rd ed.). Boston: Allyn & Bacon.

Hora, T. (1961). Existential psychiatry and group psychotherapy. *American Journal of Psychoanalysis, 21*, 58–70.

Hosford, R. (1969). Behavioral counseling—A contemporary view. *Counseling Psychologist, 1,* 1–33.

Krumboltz, J. (1966). Behavioral goals for counseling. *Journal of Consulting Psychology, 13,* 153–159.

Krumboltz, J., & Thoresen, C. (1969). *Behavioral counseling: Cases and techniques.* New York: Holt, Rinehart and Winston.

LaFleur, N. (1979). Behavioral views of counseling. In H. Burks and B. Stefflre (Eds.), *Theories of counseling* (3rd ed., pp. 250–253). New York: McGraw-Hill.

May, R. (1958a). Contributions of existential psychotherapy. In R. May, E. Angel, and H. Ellenberger (Eds.), *Existence: A new dimension in psychiatry and psychology* (pp. 37–91). New York: Basic Books.

May, R. (1958b). The origins and significance of the existential movement in psychology. In R. May, E. Angel, and H. Ellenberger (Eds.), *Existence: A new dimension in psychiatry and psychology* (pp. 3–36). New York: Basic Books.

Michael, J., & Meyerson, L. (1962). A behavioral approach to counseling and guidance. *Harvard Educational Review, 32,* 382–402.

Patterson, C. (1980). *Theories of counseling and psychotherapy* (3rd ed.). New York: Harper & Row.

Rogers, C. (1951). *Client-centered therapy: Its current practice, implications, and theory.* Boston: Houghton Mifflin.

Rogers, C. (1957). The necessary and sufficient conditions of therapeutic personality change. *Journal of Consulting Psychology, 21,* 95–103.

Rogers, C. (1959). A theory of therapy, personality, and interpersonal relationships, as developed in the client-centered framework. In S. Koch (Ed.), *Psychology: A study of a science.* (Vol. III: *Formulations of the person and the social context.*) pp. 184–256. New York: McGraw-Hill.

Rogers, C. (1961). *On becoming a person.* Boston: Houghton Mifflin.

Rogers, C. (1967). Autobiography. In E. Boring and G. Lindzey (Eds.), *A history of psychology in autobiography* (Vol. 4, pp. 343–384). New York: Appleton-Century-Crofts.

Shertzer, B., & Stone, S. (1980). *Fundamentals of counseling* (3rd ed.). Boston: Houghton Mifflin.

Shoben, E. (1962). The counselor's theory as a personal trait. *Personnel and Guidance Journal, 40,* 617–621.

Snygg, D., & Combs, A. (1949). *Individual behavior: A new frame of reference for psychology.* New York: Harper & Row.

Stefflre, B., & Burks, H. (1979a). Function of theory in counseling. In H. Burks and B. Stefflre (Eds.), *Theories of counseling* (3rd ed., pp. 1–27). New York: McGraw-Hill.

Stefflre, B., & Burks, H. (1979b). A summing up. In H. Burks and B. Stefflre (Eds.), *Theories of counseling* (3rd ed., pp. 317–335). New York: McGraw-Hill.

Stewart, J. (1978). *Counseling parents of exceptional children.* Columbus, OH: Charles Merrill.

Thorne, F. (1950). *Principles of personality counseling.* Brandon, VT: Journal of Clinical Psychology.

Thorne, F. (1961). *Personality: A clinical eclectic viewpoint.* Brandon, VT: Journal of Clinical Psychology.

Ullman, L., & Krasner, L. (1965). *Case studies in behavior modification.* New York: Holt, Rinehart and Winston.

Appendix:
Resources for parents
and professionals

The following is a representative listing of agencies, associations, and organizations concerned with the exceptional person and/or his or her family.

Behavior disorders

National Society for Autistic Children
1234 Massachusetts Avenue N.W.
Suite 1017
Washington, DC 20005
(202) 783-0125

American Orthopsychiatric Association
1775 Broadway
New York, New York 10019
(212) 586-5690

Communication disorders

American Speech and Hearing Association
10901 Rockville Pike
Rockville, Maryland 20852
(301) 897-5700

Alexander Graham Bell Association for the Deaf
3417 Volta Place N.W.
Washington, DC 20007
(202) 337-5220

National Association of the Deaf
814 Thayer Avenue
Silver Springs, Maryland 20910
(301) 587-1788

International Association of Parents of the Deaf
814 Thayer Avenue
Silver Springs, Maryland 20910
(301) 585-5400

Gifted

American Association for Gifted Children
15 Gramercy Park
New York, New York 10003
(212) 473-4266

The National Association for Gifted Children
217 Gregory Drive
Hot Springs, Arkansas 71901
(501) 767-6933

National Association for Creative Children and Adults
8080 Springvalley Drive
Cincinnati, Ohio 45236
(513) 631-1777

Learning disabled

Association for Children with Learning Disabilities
4156 Library Road
Pittsburgh, Pennsylvania 15234
(412) 341-1515

The Orton Society
8415 Bellona Lane

Towson, Maryland 21204
(301) 296-0232

Mentally retarded

National Association for Retarded Citizens
P. O. Box 6109
Arlington, Texas 76011
(817) 640-0204

Joseph P. Kennedy Jr. Foundation
719 13th Street N.W.
Suite 510
Washington, DC 20005
(202) 331-1731

National Association for Down's Syndrome
290 West Fullerton
Oak Park, Illinois 60302
(312) 543-6060

American Association on Mental Deficiency
5101 Wisconsin Avenue
Washington, DC 20016
(202) 686-5400

President's Committee on Mental Retardation
Regional Office Building #3
7th and D Streets S.W.
Washington, DC 20201
(202) 245-7634

Orthopedically and other health impaired

The National Easter Seal Society for Crippled Children and Adults
2023 West Ogden Avenue
Chicago, Illinois 60612
(312) 243-8400

United Cerebral Palsy Foundation
66 East 34th Street

New York, New York 10016
(212) 481-6300

Epilepsy Foundation of America
4351 Garden City Drive
Landover, Maryland 20785
(301) 459-3700

Muscular Dystrophy Association
810 Seventh Avenue
New York, New York 10019
(212) 586-0808

Cystic Fibrosis Foundation
3379 Peachtree Road N.E.
Atlanta, Georgia 30326
(404) 233-2195

March of Dimes
1275 Mamaroneck Avenue
White Plains, New York 10605
(914) 428-7100

Spina Bifida Association of America
343 South Dearborn Street
Room 317
Chicago, Illinois 60604
(312) 663-1562

National Multiple Sclerosis Society
205 East 42nd Street
New York, New York 10017
(212) 986-3240

Severely handicapped

The Association for Persons with Severe Handicaps
7010 Roosevelt Way N.E.
Seattle, Washington 98115
(206) 523-8446

Visually Impaired

American Foundation for the Blind
15 West 16th Street
New York, New York 10011
(212) 629-2000

National Association for Visually Handicapped
305 East 24th Street
Room 17-C
New York, New York 10011
(212) 889-3141

American Printing House for the Blind
1839 Frankfort Avenue
Louisville, Kentucky 40206
(502) 895-2405

American Association of Workers for the Blind/Association for the
    Education of the Visually Impaired Alliance
206 North Washington Street
Suite 320
Alexandria, Virginia 22314
(703) 548-1884

National Society for the Prevention of Blindness
79 Madison Avenue
New York, New York 10016
(212) 684-3505

The National Library Service for the Blind and Physically Hand-
    icapped
1291 Taylor N.W.
Washington, DC 20542
(202) 287-5100

National Federation for the Blind
1629 K Street N.W.
Suite 701
Washington, DC 20006
(202) 785-2974

Professional organizations

The Council for Exceptional Children
1920 Association Drive
Reston, Virginia 22091
(703) 620-3660

American Physical Therapy Association
1156 15th Street N.W.
Washington, DC 20005
(202) 466-2070

American Occupational Therapy Association
1383 Piccard Drive
Rockville, Maryland 20580
(301) 948-9626

General

Closer Look
National Information Center for the Handicapped
1201 Sixteenth Street N.W.
Washington, DC 20037
(202) 822-7900

Author/source index

Abrams, J., 47, 64
Akerley, M., 110–111, 113
Anderson, K., 32–33, 38
Avila, D., 123, 125–126, 128–129, 136, 139, 167, 173–174, 191, 194, 217

Balogh, S., 148, 167
Barsch, R., 5, 7, 9, 16, 19, 38
Baskiewicz, A., 19, 38, 48, 64
Baum, M., 19, 38
Baxter, D., 175–176, 191
Beckman, P., 5, 7–8, 10
Beckman-Bell, P., 111, 113
Begab, M., 14, 19, 38, 42, 47, 50, 64
Behmer, M., 42, 64
Benjamin, A., 119, 120, 122, 127, 128, 130, 131, 132, 133, 136, 139, 141, 147, 148, 149, 155, 159, 164–165, 167, 177, 185, 187, 190, 191
Bennett, J., 175, 191
Berdine, W., 2, 3, 5, 9
Blackhurst, A., 2, 3, 5, 9

Blocher, D., 118, 136
Block, J., 47, 64
Blume, R., 127, 136
Boggs, E., 41, 64
Brammer, L., 119, 120, 121 (fig.), 124–125 (tab.), 126–127, 130, 132, 134–135, 136, 138, 139, 146, 147, 148, 161, 167, 170–173, 171 (fig.), 179, 180, 183, 184, 185, 187, 190, 191, 193, 194, 197, 204, 210, 214–215, 216, 217
Brown, G., 16, 38
Bryant, J., 35–37, 38
Buchheimer, A., 148, 167
Burks, H., 194–195, 197, 219
Byalick, R., 5, 9

Cansler, D., 55–56, 64
Carr, J., 53, 64
Chinn, P., 46, 49, 50–51, 63, 64
Cohen, P., 47, 64
Combs, A., 123, 125–126, 127, 128–129, 136, 139, 167,

Combs, A. (*cont.*), 173–174, 191, 194, 214, 217, 218
Creal, D., 48, 65
Cross, A., 5, 7–8, 10

de Boor, M., 70
Des Jardins, C., 17, 38
Dreyfus, E., 213, 217
Drotar, D., 19, 21, 29, 39, 48, 64
Duncan, L., 22
Dunlap, W., 42, 64

Eisenpreis, B., 20, 38
Ellis, A., 197–200, 217
English, A., 118, 136
English, H., 118, 136
Ewing, D., 202, 205, 217

Farber, B., 44, 46, 48, 65
Farran, D., 49, 65
Feeley, M., 56–57, 66
Feldman, M., 5, 9
Fiedler, F., 119, 130, 136
Fiscus, E., 7, 10
Fishler, K., 50, 53, 65
Fotheringham, J., 48, 65
Freeman, R., 49, 65

Gallagher, J., 3, 5, 7–8, 10, 34–35, 39, 49, 65
Garfield, S., 214, 217
Gargiulo, R., 22, 29–30, 38, 65
Gath, A., 53, 65
Glass, G., 193, 217
Gliedman, J., 1, 10
Goldie, L., 43, 65
Gordon, R., 42–43, 65
Gorham, K., 17, 39, 110, 113
Graliker, B., 50, 53, 65
Greer, B., 17–18, 21, 39
Gregory, S., 49, 53, 65
Grieger, R., 198, 217
Grossman, F., 49, 50, 53–55, 65

Grummon, D., 206, 207, 208, 210, 217

Hansen, J., 118, 121, 129, 136, 188–189, 191, 196, 202, 203–204, 206, 207, 209, 210, 214, 217
Haskins, R., 49, 65
Hayden, V., 42, 60–63, 65
Heisler, V., 8, 10
Hollingsworth, S., 42, 64
Hora, T., 213, 217
Hosey, C., 76
Hosford, R., 201, 202, 218

Irvin, N., 19, 38, 48, 64
Ivey, A., 138, 146, 154, 167

Jan, J., 49, 65

Kaslow, F., 47, 64
Kennell, J., 19, 38, 48, 64
Kew, S., 50, 65
Kirk, S., 3, 10
Klaus, M., 19, 38, 48, 64
Klein, S., 50, 57–60, 65
Koch, R., 50, 53, 65
Krasner, L., 202, 219
Kroth, R., 141–145, 142 (fig.), 167
Krumboltz, J., 201, 203, 218
Kübler-Ross, E., 22, 39
Kurtz, R., 214, 217

Laborde, P., 120, 136
LaFleur, N., 201, 202, 203, 204, 218
La Greca, A., 111, 113
Laurence, K., 53, 67
Lichter, P., 139–140, 141, 165, 167
Lillie, D., 43, 65
Love, H., 48, 50, 66

Mac Keith, R., 19, 39, 44, 66
Mandelbaum, A., 3, 10

Mandell, C., 7, 10
Martin, G., 48–49, 64
Martin, P., 55–56, 66
May, R., 211, 213, 218
McDowell, R., 8, 10
McWilliams, B., 8, 10
Mesibov, G., 111, 113
Meyerson, L., 201, 204, 218
Meyerson, R., 41, 66
Michael, J., 201, 204, 218
Michaelis, C., 13, 17, 39, 53, 66
Morton, K., 46–47, 66
Moses, K., 15, 22, 23, 26, 39
Murray, M., 191
Myrick, R., 126, 130, 136, 138, 139, 152, 155, 158, 168

Neisworth, J., 19, 40, 175, 192
Newman, A., 127, 136
Newman, M., 53, 66
Novak, A., 53, 67

Olshansky, S., 31, 32, 39

Page, R., 17, 39
Patterson, C., 118, 136, 195, 196, 201, 202, 203, 205, 211–213, 215, 218
Paul, J., 111, 113
Pettis, E., 17, 39
Pieper, E., 47, 66
Pigman, B., 102
Poznanski, E., 53, 66
Purkey, W., 123, 125–126, 128–129, 136, 139, 167, 173–174, 191, 194, 217

Quinn-Curran, N., 5, 10

Reale, G., 2, 10, 14, 40
Reik, T., 139, 167
Robinson, F., 147, 148, 167
Rogers, C., 128, 129–130, 131,

Rogers, C. (*cont.*), 132, 133, 134, 136, 137, 168, 170–171, 191, 205–210, 218
Roos, P., 15, 16, 19, 21, 23, 28, 39, 111, 113, 175, 192
Rosedale, M., 5, 9
Ross, A., 4, 10, 14, 15, 39, 42, 66
Roth, W., 1, 10
Rubin, S., 5, 10
Russell, I., 48, 67

San Martino, M., 53, 66
Sawrey, J.., 4, 10, 21, 24–25, 40, 43, 47, 67, 174–175, 192
Scheiber, B., 17, 39
Schild, S., 19, 39, 42, 53, 66
Schleifer, M., 17, 28, 39
Schreiber, M., 56–57, 66
Schult, M., 22, 40
Schulz, J., 111, 113
Schwirian, P., 53, 66
Scott, E., 49, 65
Searl, S., 20, 40
Seligman, M., 10, 22, 40, 42, 44, 49, 50, 66, 120, 136, 149, 189, 192
Seligman, P., 10
Shere, M., 53, 66
Shertzer, B., 118, 119, 131, 134, 136, 146, 149, 168, 194, 196–197, 201, 204, 209, 214, 218
Shoben, E., 193, 218
Shostrom, E., 170–173, 180, 184, 191, 193, 217
Simeonsson, N., 43–44, 45 (fig.), 66
Simeonsson, R., 43–44, 45 (fig.), 66
Smiches, R., 6, 10
Smith, R., 19, 40, 175, 192
Snygg, D., 214, 218
Solnit, A., 14, 31, 40

Stark, M., 14, 31, 40
Stefflre, B., 194–195, 197, 219
Stevic, R., 118, 121, 136, 188, 191, 196, 202, 217
Stewart, J., 19, 40, 121, 129, 130, 134, 136, 139, 146, 168, 175, 183–184, 188, 192, 203, 208–209, 219
Stone, S., 118, 119, 131, 134, 136, 146, 149, 168, 196–197, 201, 204, 209, 214, 218

Telford, C., 4, 10, 21, 24–25, 40, 43, 47, 67, 174–175, 192
Tew, B., 53, 67
Thomas, M., 48, 67
Thoresen, C., 201, 218
Thorne, F., 215, 219
Turnbull, A., 6–7, 10, 73
Tyler, L., 123, 127, 128, 129, 131, 133, 136, 181, 192

Ullman, L., 202, 219

van der Veen, F., 53, 67

Walker, J., 48, 67
Walters, R., 46, 64
Ward, S., 2, 10, 14, 40
Warner, R., 118, 121, 136, 188, 191, 196, 202, 217
Warniment, J., 22, 29–30, 39
Warren, F., 73
Wass, H., 127–128, 136
Webster, E., 5, 9, 10, 111, 113, 119, 127, 136, 138, 168
Wentworth, E., 14, 21, 24, 26, 28, 30, 40, 50–52, 67
West, E., 20, 21, 40
Wheeler, M., 3, 10
Winn, J., 46, 64
Wittmer, J., 126, 130, 136, 138, 139, 152, 155, 158, 168
Wolfensberger, W., 50, 67

Ziskin, L., 27, 29, 40
Zuk, G., 17, 40

Subject index

Acceptance
    of handicapped child, 30
    of helpee by helper, 131–132
    as leading strategy, 149
Action
    phase of, in helping, 184–185
    tentative plans of, 183
Actualizing tendency, 205–206
Adaptation, and reorganization, 29–30
Adjustment, stages of psychological,
    acceptance, 30–31
    adaptation and reorganization, 29–30
    ambivalence, 24–26
    anger, 27–28
    bargaining, 29
    composite model of, 21–22
    dangers in categorizing, 20
    denial, 22–23
    fluid nature of, 21
    grief and depression, 23–24
    guilt, 26–27

    rejection, 26
    shame and embarrassment, 28–29
Advice giving, 161, 167
    alternatives to, 162
    appropriate, 163
    dangers in, 162
Ambiguity, in helping relationship, 172
Ambivalence, 24–26
Anger
    depression as form of, 23
    two manifestations of, 27–28
Attending, 146
Attention, nonhandicapped siblings' need for, 50
Attitudes
    effect of, on child's prognosis, 19
    societal, changing, 2–3
Autistic child, case study of, 73–76

Bargaining, 29
Barriers to effective helping
    advice giving, 161–163

Barriers to effective helping (*cont.*)
  examples demonstrating, 165–166
  helper-centered strategies, 159–160
  interpretation, 160–161
  reassurance, 160
  ridicule, 165
  moralizing, 164–165
  scolding and threatening, 165
  urging, 164
Behavioral approach to helping, 201–204
  goals in helping, 174–175
Berne, Eric, 205
Binding questions, 157
Biswanger, Louis, 211
Buck, Pearl, 13

Case studies
  autistic child and mother's helplessness, 73–76
  cerebral-palsied child and martyred mother, 24–25
  Down's syndrome child, TV interview about, 82–102
  learning disabled child, 102–110
  multihandicapped boy, 76–81
  retarded girl and father with file, 70–73
  siblings of handicapped children, 57–63
Children
  parents' views of, 15–16
  "perfect," 14–15
Clarifying statements, 150–151, 182–183
Client-centered therapy, 204-210
Closed questions, 156
"Cocktail party" nonlistening, 143–144
College students, attitudes toward handicapped siblings, 54–55

Communication
  between parents and professionals, 111
  lack of, 138
Community, resources in, 88
Compensating parents, 35–37
Confidentiality, 190
Congruence, 133–134, 208
Coping mechanisms, strain placed on, 18–19
Counseling, definitions of, 118–119
Crises, periods of in family development, 44

Davy, Sir Humphrey, 216
Day-care center, for handicapped children, 97–100
Death, symbolic, of ideal child, 23, 31–32
Depression, 23–24
DeSoyza, Dallas, 82–102
DeSoyza, Teddie, 82–102
Development, milestones in, 16, 37
Developmental tasks, of families, 44
Disabilities
  effect of, on entire family, 42–43
  initial exposure to, 19–20
  secondary to needs, 2
Double-bind questions, 157–158
Down's syndrome
  characteristics of, 87–88
  child with, TV interview about, 82–102
Dyslexia, 106

Eclectic approach, to helping, 214–215
Education for all Handicapped Children Act (PL 94-142), 6
Embarrassment, 28–29, 52, 58
Emerson, Ralph Waldo, 135
Emotional reactions, of parents, 18
  chronic sorrow, 31–32

in process of adjustment, 22–30
shopping behavior, 32–34
universality of, 21
unpredictable nature of, 37
See also Adjustment, stages of
Emotional reactions, of siblings,
    50–52
Empathy, 8, 132, 206
Enthusiasm, 135
Epictetus, 191
Erikson, Erik, 41
Ethics, 189–190
Exceptionality
    definition of, 3–4
    differing effects of, on families,
        42–43
    historical perspective on, 2–3
    relative to social environment, 4
Existential approach, to helping,
    210–213
Expectations, child's failure to
    meet, 16–17
Exploration phase, of helping,
    181–184
    determining real problems dur-
        ing, 182
    prerequisites to, 181–182
Eye contact, 146

Families
    cycle of, 44–46
    developmental tasks of, 44
    as interdependent systems, 42
    social changes affecting, 43
Family with handicapped child
    all members of, helpers' concern
        for, 63
    complex difficulties in, 42
    crises periods in development of,
        44
    needs of, 43
    problems of, common to all
        families, 41

Fear, 52, 178
Feedback
    reflection as, 151–153
    verbal, 146–147
Feelings
    examining, in exploratory phase,
        183
    fear of confronting, 178
    focus on, in initial interview, 181
    identifying, through reflection,
        152
    intellect vs., 174
Forced choice questions, 157
Frankl, Victor, 211
Freud, Sigmund, 197

Genuineness, 133–134
Gibran, Kahlil, 69
Goals
    of helping, 174–176
    in person-centered therapy,
        209–210
    unrealistic, 34
Grief, 23, 52
Guilt
    felt by parents, 16–17, 26–27
    felt by siblings, 52
    obsessive, 27
    shopping behavior precipitated
        by, 33

Handicapped people
    attitudes toward, historical
        development of, 2–3
    emotional impact of bearing,
        15–16
    increased understanding of, 2
    individualized education for, 6–7
    labeling of, 1–2
Helpees
    hesitancy of, 178–179
    incongruence of, 208

Helpees (*cont.*)
  internal frame of reference of, 206
  questions asked by, 158–159
  responsibility of, for decisions, 183, 209
Helpers
  directing, 159–160
  ethics of, 189–190
  goals of, 174–176
  good, characteristics of, 123, 125–126, 129–133
  purpose of, 173–174
  role of, in behavioral approach, 203–204
  self-awareness of, 128–129
  support from, increased during action phase, 184-185
  tools of, 127
  See also Professionals; Qualities of effective helpers
Helping
  art and science of, 119–120, 121
  barriers to, 159–166
  as basic human quality, 17, 119
  definitions of, 118–119
  goals of, 174–176
  interview phases in, 177–187
  motivating for, 126–127
  necessary conditions for, 207
  process of, phases in, 120–122, 124–125 (fig.)
  representative viewpoints of, 197–215
  setting of, 176–177
  skills and affective traits required in, 166
  strategies for, continuum of, 169
  theories of, 193–197
  as viewed by participants, 122–123
  See also Theories of helping
Helping process, Brammer's formula for, 120, 121 (fig.)

Helping relationship
  definition of, 170–171
  dimensions of, 171–173
  helper's purpose in, 173–174
  nature of, in person-centered therapy, 208–209
  reasons for entering, 178
  structuring, 179–181
  termination of, 187–188
Helping skills
  attending, 146
  contrasted with natural traits, 137, 166
  leading, 147–154
  listening, 138–145
  professionals' need for, 8
  questioning, 154–159
Hostility, 51

"If only" pattern of thinking, 27
Incongruence, 208
Individualized education program (IEP), 6–7
Information, eliciting, 147
Interdependence, of family members, 42
Interpretation, negative effects of, 160–161
Interruptions, avoiding, during helping, 176
Interviews, helping
  action phase of, 184–185
  exploration phase of, 181–184
  initial, 177–181
  termination of, 185–187

Jealousy, 51
Judgment
  society's tendency toward, 17–18
  suspending, 175–176, 179

Keller, Helen, xii
Kelly, George, 205
Kierkegaard, Søren, 211

Labels, 1–2
LaShan, Eda, 82–102
Leading
  acceptance in, 149
  clarification in, 150–151
  definition of, 147
  negative possibilities of, 147–148
  objectives of, 147
  paraphrasing in, 150
  reflection in, 151–153
  silence in, 148–149
  summarization in, 153–154
Learning disabled child, case study of, 102–110
Legislation, for handicapped children, 6–7
Liking, genuine, 130–131
Limitations, conveying, to helpee, 180–181
Listening
  active, 139–141, 179, 182–183
  essential to helping, 138
  genuine, 138–139
  model of, Kroth's, 141–145, 142 (fig.)
  passive vs. active, 139–141
  skill involved in, 139
"A Look Back: Learning to Live with Learning Disabilities," case study, 102–110

Markham, Edwin, 9
Marriage, effect on, of handicapped child, 29–30, 47–49
Martyr syndrome, 24–25, 27
May, Rollo, 211
Milestones, of development, 16, 37
Moralizing, 164–165
Motivations, for helping, 126–127
Multihandicapped boy, case study of, 76–81

Nondirective therapy, 209
Nonlistening, 143–145

Nonverbal messages
  attending to, 146
  reflection and, 152
Normalcy
  deviations from, intolerance toward, 1–3, 14
  family's attempt to maintain, 46–47
  society's standards of, 1

Objectivity
  balancing, with emotional involvement, 172, 208
  of behavioral helping approach, 204
Ontology, science of being, 211
Open questions, 156
Overachievement, tendency toward, in nonhandicapped siblings, 53
Overcompensation, 27, 35–37

Paraphrasing, 150
Parent-professional relationships, 4–7, 110–112
Parents of handicapped children
  difficulties in working with, 5–6
  emotional responses of, 18–19, 22–36
  guilt felt by, 16–17
  legislation mandating involvement of, 6–7
  potential contributions of, 4–5
  reactions of, crucial to sibling adjustment, 49–50, 55
  role of, 13–14
  as untapped resource, 4
  viewpoints of, 70
Passive listening, 139, 142
Passive nonlistening, 143
Peer interaction, 57–58
Perls, Fritz, 205

Person-centered questions, 156–157
Person-centered therapy, 204–210
Personality traits, of good helpers, 123, 125–126. *See also* Qualities of effective helpers
Phenomenology, 204–205
Pope, Alexander, 169
Privacy, 176
Problems, surface vs. underlying, 182
Professionals
  anger directed toward, 28
  ethical guidelines for, 190
  parents' relationships with, 4–7, 110–112
  skills required of, 7–8
  traits and biases of, 120
  uncaring, case study of, 73–76
  See also Helpers
Public Law 94-142 (Education for All Handicapped Children Act), 6

Qualities of effective helpers, 127–130
  acceptance, 131–132
  empathy, 132
  genuine liking, 130–131
  genuineness, 134
  helping skills, contrasted with, 137
  rapport, 134
  unconditional positive regard, 134–135
  understanding, 133
Quarterback and receiver, leading compared to, 147
Questioning
  overuse of, 155
  strategies for, 155–158
Questions
  binding, 157

describing helping process, 170–171
  double-bind, 157–158
  forced choice, 157
  of helpee, 158–159
  of nonhandicapped siblings, 55–57
  open vs. closed, 156
  soliciting agreement, 157
  "why," 158

Rapport, 134
Rational-emotive therapy, 197–200
Reaction formation, 35
Reactions to handicapped children. *See* Emotional reactions of parents
Reality, absolute vs. perceived, 206
Reassurance, negative effects of, 160
Referrals, 188–189
Reflection, 151–153, 179
Reinforcement, 201
Rejection of handicapped child, 26, 34–35
  primary vs. secondary, 35
  by siblings, 52
Relaxation, 146
Research, on siblings of exceptional children, 52–55
Resentment, 51
Resources for parents and professionals, 221–226
Responsibility felt by nonhandicapped siblings, 60, 61–63
Ridicule, 165

Sarcasm, 165
Sartre, Jean Paul, 211
Scolding and threatening, 165
Seating arrangements, 176–177
Self-actualization, 205

Self-esteem, loss of, 28–29
Sensitivity, 111
Setting, physical, of helping, 176–177
Shaftesbury, Lord Anthony, 167
Shaw, George Bernard, 113
Shame, 28–29, 52
Shock phase, 22, 78
Shopping behavior, 32–34
Siblings of handicapped children
    attitudes of, related to parental reactions, 49–50, 55
    concerns and questions of, 55–57
    emotional responses of, 50–52
    mental health of, 53
    needs of, 50
    peer interaction of, 57–58
    problems encountered by, 53
    research findings concerning, 52–55
    responsibility felt by, 60, 61–63
    viewpoints shared by, 57–63
Silence
    as leading strategy, 148–149
    worth of, 137, 149
Sincerity, 133–134
Skills. See Helping skills
Skinner, B. F., 201
Society
    expectations of, 16–17
    historical attitudes of, toward handicapped people, 2–3
    judgmental stance of, 17–18
    myth of, against seeking help, 178
    role of family in, 43
"A Society That Is Going to Kill Your Children," case study, 73–76
Sociocultural status, effect of, on adjustment, 54–55
Soliciting agreement questions, 157
Sorrow, chronic, 31–32

Spouses, support between, 29–30, 48
Stages in helping process, 120–122, 124–125 (fig.)
Stages of psychological adjustment. See Adjustment, stages of psychological
Stevenson, Robert Louis, 117
Structuring the helping relationship, 179–181
Summarization, 153–154, 186

Termination
    of helping relationship, 187–188
    of interview, 185–187
Theories of helping
    behavioral approach, 201–204
    client-centered therapy, 204–210
    cognitive-affective continuum for, 196–197
    eclectic approach, 214–215
    evaluating, 194–196
    existential viewpoint, 210–213
    need for, 193–194
    personal, developing, 215–216
    rational-emotive therapy (RET), 197–200
Third ear, listening with, 139
Tillich, Paul, 211
Tolstoy, Leo, 193
Trust
    confidentiality and, 190
    in helping relationship, 172–173
    privacy and, 176
Twain, Mark, 1

Unconditional positive regard, 134–135, 208
Underlying problems, 182
Understanding
    as goal of helping, 175
    listening with, 139, 141
    three levels of, 133

Uniqueness, of helping relation-
    ship, 171–172
Urging, 164

Verbal feedback, 146–147

"What Is to Become of Katherine?,"
    case study, 70–73
"Who Cares What Happens to

Miriam?," case study, 82–102
Wilde, Oscar, 64
"Wipe-out artist" nonlistener, 145
Withdrawal, from social contact,
    24, 28
"Why" questions, 158
World of Nigel Hunt, 101–102

"Yes, Our Son Is Still with Us," case
    study, 76–81